The Origins of
Southern Sharecropping

In the series, Labor and Social Change,
edited by Paula Rayman and Carmen Sirianni

The Origins of Southern Sharecropping

Edward Royce

Temple University Press
Philadelphia

Temple University Press, Philadelphia 19122
Copyright © 1993 by Temple University. All rights reserved
Published 1993
Printed in the United States of America

∞ The paper used in this publication meets the minimum requirements
of American National Standard for Information Sciences—Permanence
of Paper for Printed Library Materials, ANSI Z39.48-1984

Library of Congress Cataloging-in-Publication Data
Royce, Edward.
 The origins of southern sharecropping / Edward Royce.
  p. cm.—(Labor and social change)
 Includes index.
 ISBN 1-56639-069-9 (alk. paper)
 1. Sharecropping—Southern States—History—19th century. 2. Re-
construction. I. Title. II. Series.
 HD1478.U62A13 1993
 333.33′5563—dc20   93-18076

· Contents

· *Acknowledgments*

I have accumulated many debts in the course of writing this book. I would like to thank especially Lewis Coser, Bill Miller, Naomi Rosenthal, Richard Williams, and the late Gene Weinstein for their advice, criticism, and direction during the early stages of this work. I am especially indebted to Michael Schwartz, who first got me interested in southern sharecropping and who has provided continuous encouragement and good counsel.

For their friendship and their moral support over the years and for their various contributions to this project, I would like to thank the following people: Debbora Battaglia, Wendy Berg, Dan Czitrom, Rick Eckstein, Michele Ethier, Meryl Fingrutd, Louisa McDonald, Scott McNall, Eva Paus, Susan Rosen, Tom Wartenberg, and Don Weber. Without the help of these friends and colleagues, I could never have completed this book.

I owe a special debt of gratitude to three people. Dave Harvey has provided both intellectual inspiration and practical assistance for almost two decades. His close reading and intelligent criticism of an early draft of this work played a crucial role in reshaping it into its present form. Doug Amy offered useful comments on the entire manuscript and nudged me along when I needed it. I am especially grateful for his invaluable help on the final chapter and for his constant encouragement and support. Lynn Morgan read the entire manuscript with great care, supplied detailed criticism of every chapter, and aided me immensely in the final revisions. Virtually every page of this book owes something to her thoughtful comments and editorial skills.

I would like to express my appreciation to Michael Ames at Temple University Press and series editor Carmen Sirianni for their patience and support for this project. I also benefited greatly from the comments of two anonymous reviewers.

Chapter 1 · Southern Sharecropping and the Constriction of Possibilities

The slave labor force on the large antebellum plantation was typically organized into work gangs subject to harsh discipline and continuous supervision. This mode of labor organization persisted into the years immediately following the Civil War. Throughout the period from roughly 1865 through 1867, despite the abolition of slavery, the plantation remained the basic unit of production, the landlord maintained strict control over the labor process and work schedule, and workers and their families continued to be housed in centralized slave quarters. There were, however, significant differences between the postwar plantation system and the mode of labor organization under slavery. Most important, employers were required to contract for the services of their labor force and were prohibited from using physical coercion as a means of labor control. Planters were not only expected to pay wages, but to refrain from beating their laborers as well. This modification of the plantation regimen—the substitution of "cash" for the "lash"—satisfied most northern proponents of free labor.

Southern planters and most northern officials favored the plantation system, but it soon gave way to sharecropping. By 1868, sharecropping was well on its way toward becoming the principal replacement for slavery and the dominant economic arrangement in postbellum southern agriculture. According to one report, by 1870 sharecropping was so prevalent that "any other form of contract is but the exception."[1] Precisely how and why sharecropping displaced the gang-labor system and ultimately came to fill the vacuum created by the abolition of slavery remains a puzzle, however. According to Harold Woodman, for example, the details of southern sharecropping's origins are "shrouded and obscure."[2]

Sharecropping, at first glance, appears to be a unique form of wage labor where the labor force, rather than receiving periodic money wages, was compensated by a share of the crop at the end of the season. It would be misleading, however, to regard this peculiar system of remuneration as the defining characteristic of sharecropping. In fact, because of the shortage of capital and credit, landlords typically paid black laborers with a share of the crop in the first years after the war, under the plantation system and prior to the emergence of sharecropping proper.[3] The share method of payment, therefore, does not distinguish sharecropping from the gang labor system that immediately preceded it. Rather, what uniquely characterized southern sharecropping was the mode of labor organization that it introduced into the postbellum South. With the rise of sharecropping, the large plantations—as units of production—were divided into small farms and allotted to individual families, who, at the end of the season, received a share of the crop for their labor. The adoption of sharecropping, therefore, signaled the demise of the plantation as the basic unit of agricultural production in the South.[4] This decentralization of plantation agriculture and the rise of the family-farm arrangement distinguished sharecropping from both the slave mode of labor organization and the postwar gang-labor system.

In the following two sections of this chapter, I critically evaluate two explanations for the rise of southern sharecropping: the "predisposing conditions" argument and the "good reasons" argument. Both of these exemplify explanatory strategies that are commonly employed in the study of social change. After considering the empirical and conceptual weaknesses of these two theories, I offer an alternative perspective, arguing that the rise of southern sharecropping is best conceived as occurring through a "constriction of possibilities."[5] This conception of social change draws upon and elaborates the class-conflict argument found in many historical studies of the origins of southern sharecropping.[6]

The Predisposing-Conditions Argument

From one perspective, based upon comparative studies on the origins of alternative labor arrangements, southern sharecropping arose as the result of the presence of certain favoring conditions. Daniel Chirot, for example, attributes the emergence of "servile labor systems," referring to southern sharecropping specifically, to the existence of three factors: a class of large landholders, a shortage of labor, and a level of technology not so advanced that it provides incentives to mechanization. Under these circumstances, to secure an adequate supply of workers, landowners will seek to establish a labor-repressive mode of agricultural production, such as that presumably represented by sharecropping. This requires, of course, that landholders possess sufficient political power to bring about the enactment of legal measures restricting labor mobility.[7]

Robert Evans, proposing a similar theory, contends

that "coerced labor" systems are likely to appear where the industry in question is socially or economically essential, where there is a shortage of labor that derives from "the non-pecuniary aspects of the employment," such that it cannot be adequately addressed by raising wages, and where other important sectors of the economy do not oppose the implementation of such a system. The lack of demand for black labor in the North, according to Evans, gave powerful interests there little incentive to enforce a genuinely free labor system in the South. As a result, Evans argues, southern planters were free to implement the coercive system of "debt-sharecropping." This enabled them to retain a sufficient labor force—despite the scarcity of labor—and to maintain their commitment to cotton cultivation.[8]

In another variation of this argument, Evsey Domar, emphasizing the importance of the land/labor ratio, proposes that in an agricultural setting, of the three elements—"free land, free peasants, and non-working landowners—any two . . . but *never all three can exist simultaneously.*"[9] Which combination arises in any particular historical setting depends upon the political power of landowners. Where a high land/labor ratio exists but the state does not support the landowning class, the labor force will be transformed into an independent peasantry. Where the state sides with the landowning class and cooperates with it to restrict access to land and the mobility of labor, a forced-labor system, like sharecropping, will result.[10]

Some historians of Reconstruction and economic development in the postwar South have also found this approach convincing. Enoch Banks, for example, though enumerating a different set of prior conditions, expresses great confidence in the explanatory power of the predisposing-conditions argument: "Rarely does it happen that an arrangement can be so easily and surely explained as the product of the existing economic situation. . . . These three circumstances, namely, the landlord's scarcity of capital, the negro's poverty, and the negro's uneconomic mobility, combine to explain the rise of the cropping arrangement."[11] Finally, according to Vernon Wharton, in a study of Reconstruction in Mississippi, sharecropping emerged "naturally" under the influence of these "predisposing conditions": "the existence of a large class of landless workers, a shortage of money or ready credit, and a general dependence upon a cash crop which requires a long growing season."[12]

The predisposing-conditions argument has three serious weaknesses. First, the conception of social change and the explanatory strategy implied by this approach neglect an important consideration noted by Sartre in his critique of orthodox Marxism. While "men make their history on the basis of real, prior conditions," Sartre emphasizes, "it is *the men* who make it and not the prior conditions."[13] The explanatory weight in comprehending the rise of southern sharecropping cannot be carried by antecedent conditions alone. The *process* through which prior conditions yielded sharecropping needs to be given more explicit consideration. Why in the presence of such prior conditions was sharecropping called forth, and through what agency or logic of events was this brought about? Although this issue is sometimes addressed, at least by implication, it is typically assumed that what links prior conditions to the adoption of sharecropping are the needs of landowners, facilitated by the political power of the state. But even if it were the case that sharecropping suited the interests of planters, this argument fails to explain how the labor force was led to agree to its adoption or how planters were able to prevail over their opposition.[14] By focusing on prior conditions and subsequent outcomes, the predisposing-conditions argument gives insufficient attention to the mediating mechanism of social change, to the conflictual process through which such prior conditions are translated into subsequent outcomes. As Barry Hindess observes, outcomes of social change "are produced in the course of struggle itself and are rarely the simple products of initial conditions."[15]

A second problem with this argument is that it regards the predisposing conditions of sharecropping as historically given. In fact, the conditions typically identified as explaining the emergence of sharecropping were themselves the contingent products of struggles and social forces. The existence of a labor shortage, the continued dependence of the South on cotton cultivation, the landlessness of freed blacks, the latitude enjoyed by planters in their effort to rebuild southern agriculture— conflict surrounded all of these "prior conditions." The postwar labor shortage, for example, was not a fact of nature, but rather a joint product of the successful resistance by blacks to the plantation system and the inability of planters to increase the supply of labor through immigration or coercion. Regarding this shortage of labor as a prior condition ignores the historical circumstances responsible for its appearance. Rather than constituting the bedrock of an explanation, therefore, the "predisposing conditions" of southern sharecropping must themselves be subject to historical investigation.

A final problem with the predisposing-conditions argument is that its explanatory strategy can easily produce misleading conclusions about the causal significance of selected antecedent conditions.[16] The extent to which sharecropping derived from specific prior conditions as a unique outcome can be adequately assessed only by comparing it to alternative possibilities. The predisposing-conditions argument, however, fixes on sharecropping as the end product of the process of social change. It then traces backward in search of relevant antecedent conditions. But in so doing, it fails to consider how outcomes other than sharecropping might have been equally favored by the same set of prior conditions. For example, a labor shortage, a lack of capital, a large class of landless laborers, and a long growing season—factors usually associated with the rise of sharecropping—were no less consistent with the postwar plantation system that preceded sharecropping, where laborers were organized into gangs and paid collectively a share of the crop. In fact, none of the predisposing-conditions arguments cited above include within their explanatory purview the central characteristic of southern sharecropping—the decentralized, family-farm system of labor organization.

In general, the predisposing-conditions argument does not leave enough room for historical agency and conflict and for the contingencies these introduce into the process of social change. Nevertheless, research that follows this particular strategy of explanation does have the virtue of identifying some of the key variables that need to be taken into account in any attempt to explain the rise of southern sharecropping.

The Good-Reasons Argument

A more influential and well-developed theory of sharecropping draws upon neoclassical economics.[17] From this perspective, sharecropping arose as "an understandable market response," as the mutually advantageous product of welfare-maximizing behavior on the part of both white landowners and black laborers.[18] Ralph Shlomowitz, for example, suggests that "the adoption of the sharecropping system represented a convergence of the interests of most planters and freedmen."[19] Similarly, Joseph Reid argues that sharecropping was "chosen because of its efficiency"; the "essential cause of sharecropping," Reid contends, was "the joining of the tenant's and the landlord's interests."[20] The secret to the origins of sharecropping, accordingly, is to be found in the characteristics and functions of sharecropping itself. These special advantages and efficiencies constitute the "good reasons" that presumably account for the adoption of sharecropping.

Proponents of the neoclassical approach typically cite one or more of the following "good reasons" in explaining the rise of southern sharecropping: (1) By giving the tenant an interest in the crop and an incentive to work diligently, sharecropping reduced the landlord's supervision costs, while also allowing greater independence for the labor force.[21] (2) Sharecropping permitted the laborer easy access to the managerial expertise and assistance of the landowner and provided the latter with an incentive to supply such expertise and assistance.[22] (3) Since gains and losses were apportioned automatically, sharecropping gave landlords and laborers an inducement to alter contract terms in midseason to take advantage of changed conditions, and it permitted them to do this without costly renegotiation and without conflict over how to distribute the unexpected gain (or loss). Thus, sharecropping minimized transaction costs, promoted flexibility over the course of the season, and facilitated aggregate risk reduction.[23] (4) Sharecropping served as a means for the relatively more risk-averse tenant to shift some of the income uncertainty onto the landlord.[24]

From the good-reasons perspective, in sum, planters and freedpeople were led to the adoption of sharecropping because of its mutual benefits and because it best served their interests.[25] Very little direct empirical evidence is presented in support of this argument, however. The good reasons that are said to account for the adoption of sharecropping are not discovered by examining the actual considerations and decisions of historical actors themselves. Rather, they are deduced from assumptions about rational economic behavior, derived from theoretical models, or inferred from aggregate econometric findings. The point made by the critics of Fogel and Engerman's *Time on the Cross* applies equally well to the neoclassical theory of southern sharecropping:

> We have been obliged to draw attention to the point that underlying motivations and modes of individual behavior cannot be uniquely inferred from an analysis of the outcomes of a social process, or of a market process for that matter. The tools of behavioral science, and particularly of modern economics . . . cannot be readily turned to answer to the needs of the historian who seeks to . . . understand human events within the objective and subjective contexts in which they transpired.[26]

Contrary to the good-reasons argument, the historical evidence shows that sharecropping lacked an eager constituency. Neither planters nor freedpeople supported its adoption; both applied their energies to the promotion of alternative arrangements. Freedpeople wanted to become independent farmers, and planters hoped to preserve the gang-labor system.

The preeminent aim of freedpeople in the immediate postwar years, fueled by the widespread expectation that they were to be the recipients of grants from the government of "forty acres and a mule," was to acquire land of their own. For most black people, the meaning of freedom was inseparably tied to the possession of land and to the independence and autonomy that landownership promised. Whitelaw Reid, during his tour of the South in 1865 and 1866, found that "again and again" freedpeople declared that "unless they were to own the land on which they had been working," it would do them little good to be free.[27] Freed blacks intended to work under conditions of their own choosing and to reap the rewards of their own labor. They sought to secure their newly won freedom by acquiring means of subsistence independent of the plantation system. At best, sharecropping was their third choice—preferable to gang labor certainly, because of the greater autonomy it permitted—but inferior to landownership or renting. It was less the advantages of sharecropping that led blacks to agree to its adoption than their inability to achieve more desirable alternatives, particularly that of obtaining land of their own.

Planters expressed even more hostility toward sharecropping than did freedpeople. Their periodicals are filled with warnings against its adoption and, where already in practice, complaints about its operation. Planters preferred and fought to preserve the gang-labor system, which they had depended upon and grown used to under slavery. Sharecropping, by contrast, threatened to diminish their control over the labor force and over the process of agricultural production. In particular, planters feared that sharecropping would lead to the neglect of all work except that directly related to the crop; that, in contrast to wage labor, it would make it more difficult to dismiss workers and find replacements during the course of the season; that the deferred-payment system associated with sharecropping would fail to induce hard work in the present; that sharecropping would encourage laborers to assume the rights and privileges of partnership; and that, unlike gang labor, sharecropping would make it impossible to manage the labor force effectively and procure obedient service. Planters ultimately agreed to the adoption of sharecropping—"that most pernicious of all systems under which the labor of a country has ever been employed"—not because of its advantages but despite what they perceived to be its numerous disadvantages.[28] Because of their inability to maintain the gang-labor system against the opposition of blacks or to realize other preferred alternatives, planters too were drawn unwillingly into sharecropping.[29]

A second problem with the good-reasons argument is that it exhibits a restricted historical perspective. By tracing sharecropping back only as far as the decisions and choices directly preceding its adoption, this perspective neglects the larger historical context within which those choices were made.[30] Even if the final transactions leading to sharecropping agreements consisted of voluntary choices made in a free-market setting, this would not provide unqualified support for the good-reasons argument. It would still be necessary to assess the extent to which the terms under which planters and freedpeople bargained with one another at this final point (e.g., relative market power, access to resources, availability of alternatives) were themselves set by market forces. What sense does it make to argue that sharecropping was "an understandable market response" if the presumably free negotiations between planters and laborers ratifying its adoption occurred within a context whose parameters were established through the prior exercise of domination, prior episodes of struggle, and the prior impact of nonmarket forces? Why should we assume that proximate negotiations were more important than prior conflicts in determining the rise of southern sharecropping? Harold Woodman, though not specifically referring to the issue of sharecropping, makes a similar point. He argues that the neoclassical theorists

> narrowly and exclusively define the market strictly in terms of the final economic transactions. . . . This creates

an artificial distinction between the final economic transactions and the social and political context within which those final transactions take place. . . . It blinks the fact that the market itself is a product of the society in which it exists. In other words, the market is a political and social as well as an economic institution, and final transactions are already sharply circumscribed before they take place.[31]

Sharecropping was not simply a product of bargaining and negotiation. In fact, freedpeople and planters each hoped to avoid having to deal with the other, the former aiming to become independent proprietors and the latter intending to dictate, not deal. Rather, sharecropping originated from the circumstances that *compelled* freedpeople and planters to bargain with one another and that determined the conditions of their negotiations. Sharecropping originated only as a result of prior struggles that closed off to each more desirable alternatives.

Finally, the conception of social change found in the good-reasons argument does not give enough consideration to the conflicting interests of planters and freedpeople. According to Shlomowitz, social change from the neoclassical perspective "is viewed as the consequence of rational decisions made by individuals on the basis of weighing up the expected gains and costs of alternative ways of meeting various ends, where these include both pecuniary and nonpecuniary considerations."[32] This idea that social change results from individuals rationally weighing the costs and benefits of competing alternatives, with its implicit recognition that people make their own history, has a certain plausibility. But while the rational decisions of individuals certainly enter into any process of social change, it does not follow that the outcome can be simply derived by aggregating these decisions. From the neoclassical perspective, it would seem, people make their own history, but, contrary to Marx, they make it just as they please. This approach does not necessarily neglect the objective circumstances in which people, not of their own choosing, find themselves, for these can be taken as entering into the rational decisions of individuals. Rather, it fails to recognize how the rational decisions of individuals less often produce unanimity than a multitude of conflicting goals. Individuals may rationally pursue incompatible objectives that they are loathe to bargain away, as did freedpeople and planters in the immediate postwar years. Social-change outcomes, therefore, cannot be simply derived from the rational decisions of individuals. We also need to consider the clashes of wills and the struggles between contending groups to which rational decisions give rise. The outcome of social change, since it originates from conflicts of interest and not simply the implementation of rational decisions, may therefore appear "irrational" from any particular standpoint. The resulting outcome, although intended and deliberate, may be something that no one in particular especially desired. This characteristic of social change—that new social arrangements often arise by default—is what the idea of constriction of possibilities is intended to illuminate.

Class Conflict and the Rise of Southern Sharecropping

In contrast to both the predisposing-conditions argument and the good-reasons argument, many historical studies, whether implicitly or explicitly, adopt a class-conflict model. Southern sharecropping, from this perspective, emerged from the conflict between planters and freedpeople in the postwar South as they confronted one another with mutually antagonistic visions of a new economic order. Though these studies all emphasize how class struggle and contests of power characterized the process through which sharecropping arose, they disagree about whose interests finally prevailed in this conflict or why precisely it culminated in sharecropping. Three different versions of the class-conflict argument can be identified, distinguished according to who is perceived to have emerged victorious.[33]

First, some historians maintain that freedpeople managed to impose sharecropping on resistant planters. According to Ronald Davis, for example, planters "were dragged kicking and screaming into the [sharecropping] system"; they "accepted sharecropping because they had no choice in the matter."[34] Jonathan Wiener, similarly, contends that sharecropping was a "major concession" forced upon planters by the effective resistance of freed blacks to the gang-labor system.[35] For Charles Flynn, too, "because of the relative latitude it allowed," blacks preferred sharecropping to the gang-labor system, and they "had sufficient economic leverage to enforce their choice" upon landowners.[36] The adoption of sharecropping in these interpretations represented a victory for freedpeople.

Other historians argue that sharecropping was more of a victory for planters. According to Jay Mandle, for example, landowners, "in the coercive circumstances of the South," forced freedpeople to agree to sharecropping by successfully closing off "more desirable options" and taking advantage of the latter's weak bargaining position.[37] This evaluation of southern sharecropping emphasizes the historic setback experienced by blacks with the defeat of the possibility of "forty acres and a mule"; the rise of sharecropping, Mandle argues, occurred at the expense of southern land reform. Thus, Mandle purports to offer a corrective to "the tendency to overstate the extent of progress which the transition from slave to tenant plantations represented."[38] James Oakes also presents a less sanguine interpretation of southern share-cropping. Since "planters still owned the land," Oakes explains, the majority of black people "had no choice but to continue working" for them; and even under sharecrop-ping, planters "retained substantial control" over the black labor force.[39] While Mandle and Oakes acknowl-edge that sharecropping was preferable to gang labor, both also emphasize that as a result of the limited alternatives available to them, and their inability to gain land in particular, freedpeople were ultimately unable to free themselves from planter domination.

How one evaluates the rise of sharecropping—with respect to its impact on the conflicting interests of planters and freedpeople—depends on the baseline alter-native from which one starts. If looked at from the vantage point of what planters most desired—the restora-tion of the gang-labor system—sharecropping appears to be a victory for blacks. And if looked at from the vantage point of what freedpeople most desired—the opportunity to become independent landowners—sharecropping ap-pears to be a victory for planters. From either of these perspectives, the appearance of victory conceals the fact that, in agreeing to sharecropping, both planters and freedpeople suffered a defeat (though not necessarily a defeat of equal magnitude). To achieve a more compre-hensive perspective on southern sharecropping, therefore, and to avoid the one-sidedness of either of these interpre-tations, systematic consideration needs to be given to the broad range of alternative possibilities promoted by *both* planters and freedpeople.

The third version of the class-conflict model recog-nizes that neither planters nor freedpeople emerged with a clear victory; proponents of this perspective propose a compromise conception of sharecropping. Ransom and Sutch, for example, maintain that "the adoption of sharecropping was the result of a compromise between the laborers' pursuit of independence and higher incomes and the landlords' desire to retain control and minimize risk."[40] James Roark also argues that sharecropping was a "compromise." "It offered blacks more freedom than the labor gangs, but less than owning land or renting it; it offered planters a means of resuming production and of exercising some supervision, but less leverage over labor than they desired or believed necessary."[41] Similarly, Gavin Wright suggests that sharecropping was "a balance between the freedmen's desire for autonomy and the employer's interest in extracting work effort and having labor when it was needed."[42]

The compromise conception of sharecropping has the virtue of placing the conflicting interests of planters and freedpeople at the center of its analysis. It also appears to offer a viable alternative to explanations that give too much emphasis to the initiatives and interests of either planters or freedpeople. Yet, the term *compromise* is more accurately a *characterization* of sharecropping than an *explanation* of how it came to be; it serves better as a description of the *outcome* of the transition from slavery than as an interpretation of the *process*. Furthermore, with its connotation of peaceful negotiation across a bargaining table, the term *compromise* does not adequately describe the conflict-ridden course of economic reorganization in the postwar South. In using the term *compromise* to describe the rise of southern sharecropping, these historians often fail to do justice to the findings of their own research, which document in such rich detail the bitter and often violent antagonism between planters and freedpeople in the years after the war.

The compromise conception of sharecropping, furthermore, is not fully grounded in the experiences and perceptions of the historical actors themselves. In other words, it is doubtful that either planters or freedpeople would have accepted this characterization of sharecropping. A convincing explanation, however, needs to concern itself with how planters and freedpeople themselves saw the process of social change and with the considerations that finally led them to settle on sharecropping. The idea of constriction of possibilities addresses this issue by restating the class-conflict argument to give more emphasis to the perspective of planters and freedpeople and how they perceived the process of economic reconstruction.

Social Change and the Constriction of Possibilities

The premise of the alternative perspective offered here is that social change is best conceived as occurring through a "constriction of possibilities." This notion elaborates the class-conflict argument, by suggesting that it is through the effect of constricting possibilities that class conflict operates to produce historical outcomes.[43] The idea of constriction of possibilities emphasizes the empirical relationship between what occurs in history and what fails to occur; it recognizes that the defeat of some possibilities is implicated in the process through which the realization of other possibilities results.

The idea of constriction of possibilities draws attention to the existence of alternative, though unrealized, historical possibilities. It emphasizes how social change invariably involves conflict between such alternative possibilities. And it leads to the inference that historical outcomes cannot be fully understood except in relation to the failed possibilities upon whose defeat the "successes" of history arise. "Victorious events come about as the result of many possibilities," Fernand Braudel observes, and "for one possibility which actually is realized, innumerable others have drowned"; yet "it is necessary to give them their place because the losing movements are forces which have at every moment affected the final outcome."[44] The struggles of people to achieve their objectives, even when they suffer defeat, inevitably shape the course of social change.[45]

The idea of constriction of possibilities implies that historical outcomes originate from conflict between contending groups through which proposed alternatives are discredited, barred from implementation, rendered unworkable, forcibly eliminated, or otherwise suppressed. What finally arises from this process is usually not what any particular group is fighting for. Because the logic of conflict, as Theda Skocpol notes, is never fully "controlled by any one class or group," it invariably gives rise "to outcomes neither fully foreseen nor intended—nor perfectly serving the interests of—any of the particular groups involved."[46] The actions of one class or group are always constrained, to a greater or lesser extent, by the actions of other classes or groups. The power of a contending group is usually able to exert itself at least—if only—to the extent of obstructing those alternatives of its adversaries most disadvantageous to its interests. Class struggle and social conflict shape the course of history especially through the effect of preventing certain outcomes from arising; conflict operates to preclude possibilities and to narrow channels of action.

My perspective differs somewhat from that of Barrington Moore, who also makes a case for studying the "suppression of historical alternatives."[47] Moore's premise is that "historical events need not have turned out the way they did: that history may often contain suppressed possibilities and alternatives obscured or obliterated by the deceptive wisdom of hindsight."[48] Moore seeks to disclose historical alternatives that, in some objective sense, could have come to pass. In contrast, I use the term "possibility," somewhat contrary to normal usage, not to refer to what actually could have occurred necessarily, but rather to the historical objectives that people struggled to realize, whatever their reality quotient. It is the aspirations of contending groups, however much shaped and constrained by objective circumstances, that constitute the dynamic of history and give movement to social change. The historical importance of a "possibility," from this perspective, depends not upon its practical feasibility or the likelihood of its having been achieved, but on the significance of the actions taken on its behalf, on the ramifications of the failed struggles to realize it, and on the empirical repercussions of its ultimate defeat.

Conceiving the process of social change in this way, as consisting of conflict between competing alternatives and as occurring through a constriction of possibilities, helps us to avoid falling victim to certain pitfalls in historical explanation. We are less likely, for example, to commit what Alan Dawley calls the "ontological fallacy": the error of regarding "what *was* as what *had to be.*" Instead, according to Dawley, "it is essential to keep . . . historical alternatives in mind, to interpret events as causes of other events, and to avoid the fallacy of regarding whatever happened as the sole and inevitable conclusion to the logic of events."[49] The recognition that something other than what did happen could have happened, even if acknowledged for heuristic reasons only, highlights alternative historical possibilities and encourages us to adhere to an explanatory strategy that takes such possibilities into account. Similarly, this conception of social change also avoids what Reinhard Bendix refers to as "the fallacy of retrospective determinism." "Looking backward," Bendix points out, "always presents an overdetermined depiction of fate; by this perspective we leave out of focus the possibilities of action which existed at the time."[50] The explanatory strategy implied by the idea of constriction of possibilities, however, does not look backward for causes, but rather begins with the various possibilities pursued by people at the time. Such an approach is less likely to evade the demands of an explanation by attributing inevitability to the process of social change.

The idea of constriction of possibilities implies an explanatory strategy that employs a broad historical perspective. The predisposing-conditions approach seeks the origins of sharecropping by tracing backward in search of sharecropping-type causes. The good-reasons approach tries to solve the puzzle of sharecropping's origins by scrutinizing the characteristics of sharecropping itself. The idea of constriction of possibilities, on the other hand, shifts the focus from the phenomenon of sharecropping itself to the actual historical point of departure: the alternatives promoted by planters and freedpeople, the struggles surrounding those alternatives, and the consequences of their defeat. The explanatory problem, therefore, is formulated differently: instead of conceiving the adoption of sharecropping as a product of either its own characteristics or its prior conditions, I set the rise of southern sharecropping against the wider backdrop of the alternative possibilities pursued by planters and freedpeople. I reconstruct the rise of southern sharecropping by following the conflictual course of the historical process itself—that is, from the past forward rather than from sharecropping backward. By focusing on these alternative possibilities, this strategy explicitly raises the question of why sharecropping arose rather than some other system.

The idea of constriction of possibilities, in sum, suggests that new social arrangements arise not necessarily because of their especially advantageous qualities (as implied by the good-reasons approach) or because of the particular strength of the social forces or objective conditions favoring their development (as implied by the predisposing-conditions approach). Rather, it suggests that new social arrangements arise as a by-product of the defeat of alternative possibilities. Instead of conceptualizing southern sharecropping as a "positive" product, of either its own special qualities or of antecedent forces pushing inexorably toward culmination, I maintain that sharecropping was something of a "negative" product, emerging from the failure of both planters and freedpeople to realize the possibilities they each most highly valued and actively promoted. Planters and freedpeople, in effect, backed into sharecropping. They were not "pulled" into this arrangement in anticipation of its advantages, they were "pushed" into it as a consequence of the inability of each to achieve more favorable outcomes. In explaining the adoption of sharecropping, therefore, it is at least as important to highlight those factors that limited the availability of alternatives as it is to focus on the features of sharecropping that finally rendered it acceptable.

Research Strategy

The research strategy implied by the idea of constriction of possibilities privileges the considerations of historical actors themselves. Such a strategy is especially called for in this case. Despite the fact that sharecropping suited the interests of neither planters nor freedpeople, contracts were drawn, agreements signed, crops planted, and a living, however meager, was made. In other words, planters and freedpeople consciously adopted sharecropping; it did not arise behind their backs. The explanatory task, accordingly, is to identify the considerations that led them to agree to this particular labor arrangement. It is especially important, therefore, to show the subjective side of the process of economic reconstruction: how planters and freedpeople themselves experienced and

construed the course of events that finally culminated in
the signing of sharecropping contracts. As far as possible,
then, I examine the origins of southern sharecropping
from the perspective of former masters and former
slaves—as they considered their options, as they pursued
their interests, and as they struggled with one another
over the fate of competing possibilities. My argument,
therefore, relies heavily on the presentation of historical
testimony and anecdotal evidence.

Much of the controversy about the origins of southern sharecropping has to do with the question of whose
interests finally prevailed. Was sharecropping adopted
because it suited the interests of planters, because it
suited the interests of freedpeople, or because it brought
their interests together? Or, as I argue, did planters and
freedpeople agree to sharecropping despite the fact that it
suited the interests of neither? To evaluate sharecropping
in this way requires that we identify and understand the
attitudes, perceptions, and deliberations of planters and
freedpeople. To assess the impact of southern sharecropping on their respective interests, we must first understand what planters and freedpeople wanted in the
context of the postwar South. For only then can we
measure the gap between what they hoped to achieve and
what they finally settled for. The purpose of presenting
such an evaluation of sharecropping also dictates an
emphasis on the subjective side of the process of social
change.

Chapter Summary

My analysis of the origins of southern sharecropping
is organized around an exploration of the diverse possibilities for economic reconstruction in the postwar South. I
examine how each possibility related to the objectives
and worldview of its proponents, what considerations led

them to pursue it, how they saw it serving their needs and interests, how they envisioned it in relation to what they hoped for the future, how it conflicted with the interests of other groups, what they did practically to advance its cause, how it fared, and why it failed. The specific possibilities I examine in the following chapters were arrived at by identifying the alternatives that planters and freedpeople most frequently advocated and seriously pursued. Subsequent chapters each focus on a specific possibility or set of related possibilities. Together these chapters constitute a series of partially overlapping chronologies, like a map of superimposed overlays. The story of economic reconstruction is retold in each chapter from the vantage point of a different possibility.

The possibility represented by the preservation of the plantation system and gang labor is the subject of Chapter 2. I discuss the planters' commitment to gang labor, their efforts to preserve the plantation system, and their struggle to regain control over the black labor force. I also emphasize the sources of black resistance to plantation labor and show how freedpeople managed to prevent planters from effectively operating the gang-labor system in the context of the postwar South.

Chapter 3 concerns the possibility of the former slaves' freeing themselves from the plantation system, either by acquiring homesteads of their own or by renting land. This chapter focuses on the issues of black independence and planter opposition. Together, Chapters 2 and 3 establish the fundamental conflict of interest between planters and freedpeople.

The possibilities examined in Chapters 4 and 5 reflect the difficulties planters experienced in their efforts to preserve the plantation system. In Chapter 4, I discuss the planters' campaign to attract Chinese and European immigrants to the South. Planters hoped to flood the plantation labor market, so they could regain control over the labor force and thereby maintain the plantation system.

Chapter 5 is primarily devoted to the possibility of black colonization. Many southern whites were prepared to tolerate the presence of black people in the South only if they could be kept as slaves or bound under some other system of forced labor. Thus, one response to the abolition of slavery was to call for the colonization of the black race. In this chapter I also briefly discuss the possibility of white emigration. Faced with the loss of their antebellum world, some southern whites seriously considered leaving the South altogether and taking up residence in Latin America.

In Chapter 6, I analyze specifically the transition from the gang-labor system to sharecropping. I focus on planters' perceptions of the relative merit of alternative labor arrangements, emphasizing especially their criticisms of the share-wage system and sharecropping. I also examine the fit between sharecropping and the interests of freedpeople. My objective in this chapter is to demonstrate that both planters and freedpeople were forced to accede to the adoption of sharecropping, despite the fact that neither preferred it or fought for it.

Chapter 2 · Gang Labor and the Plantation System

In the years immediately following the Civil War the black labor force in the South found itself in familiar economic circumstances: employed by their former masters, organized into work gangs, placed under the strict supervision of white overseers, subjected to a slavelike work regimen, set to work cultivating cotton, rice, or sugar, housed in the antebellum slave quarters, and bound by a variety of rules and regulations governing everything from work schedule to deportment. The antebellum plantation system and gang labor had evidently survived the abolition of slavery.[1]

The postwar plantation system, which prevailed throughout the cotton South from 1865 through 1867, was an inherently precarious arrangement, however. Planters no longer had recourse to the rights and prerogatives they possessed as slaveholders; abolition deprived planters of the legalized coercive power that made it possible for them to exercise effective control over the labor force. Under the nascent free-labor system, planters were expected to procure a labor force through contracts, bargain with their former slaves over wages and work conditions, and refrain from the use of corporal punishment. Few planters believed that plantation agriculture under such a "free-labor system" would work; most thought that the "experiment of free negro labor is bound to be a failure."[2] And through various means—physical intimidation and coercion, vigilante terror, legislative restrictions, employer cartels, and long-term, detailed labor contracts—even those planters who favored giving the free-labor experiment a try sought to restrict severely the new elements of freedom to which black laborers now laid claim. Even when planters gave grudging acceptance to emancipation, they aimed to maintain as far as possible the degree of labor control that they had enjoyed under slavery.

Planters' determination to restore a forced-labor system in southern agriculture collided with blacks' demands for autonomy, land, and the right to control their own labor. There was no mutually satisfactory way to reconcile these diametrically opposed objectives. Planters and freedpeople confronted one another with contradictory concepts of the meaning of free labor and radically different hopes for the future of a reconstructed South.[3] What ensued, reported R. K. Scott, an assistant commissioner of the Freedmen's Bureau, was a battle "between the land-owner and the laborer, the former struggling to retain absolute control, and the latter determined to maintain his newly acquired freedom to its full extent."[4] Sidney Andrews, writing from the South in 1865, described the situation similarly: "The whole struggle between the whites on the one hand and the blacks on the other hand is a struggle for and against compulsion."[5] Upon the outcome of this struggle hinged the future of gang labor and the plantation system.

The postwar period thus witnessed an archetypical instance of class conflict, not just in the sense of established classes confronting one another with antagonistic economic interests, but in the more profound sense that class formation was the very object of the conflict. Planters and freedpeople struggled to determine the basic structure of economic relations governing postbellum southern agriculture. At stake in this conflict, furthermore, was a new racial order as well as a new mode of production. Were freedpeople to remain a subordinate race and a subservient agricultural labor force, a possibility necessitating the preservation of the plantation system? Or were they to achieve racial equality and become independent producers, a possibility requiring that blacks have the opportunity to obtain land of their own?

In the first section of this chapter, I briefly discuss how black initiatives during the war contributed to the destruction of slavery and influenced the agenda of northern policymakers. The topic of slave resistance is important here partly because the rebellious behavior of slaves during the war carried over into black resistance to the plantation system in the postwar years. Following this, I provide an overview of northern policy toward black labor during the war and assess its impact on the development of postwar labor relations. Federal intervention, I argue, played a critical role in the perpetuation of the plantation system. Turning then to the immediate postwar period, I examine the conflicting interests of planters and freedpeople in the aftermath of slavery. I describe southern planters' attitudes toward free black labor and their commitment to the preservation of the plantation system, and I analyze the sources of black resistance to gang labor and the problem of labor scarcity. The second half of this chapter considers how planters perceived and responded to the problem of labor control. On this issue, I devote a separate section each to the Black Codes, the Ku Klux Klan, postwar labor contracts, and the

Freedmen's Bureau. My objective in analyzing these four instruments of labor control is to understand how, despite the imbalance of power, blacks managed to compel planters to abandon gang labor and the plantation system. I return to this issue again in the final chapter, where I present a more detailed analysis of the transition from the gang-labor system to sharecropping.

The Self-Emancipation of the Slaves

"When Edwin Ruffin, white-haired and mad, fired the first gun at Fort Sumter, he freed the slaves. It was the last thing he meant to do. . . . When northern armies entered the South they became armies of emancipation. It was the last thing they planned to be."[6] The onset of the Civil War roused among slaves an anticipation of freedom impossible to restrain. Ultimately, the demise of slavery resulted as much from the "pull" of freedom as it did from the "push" of the Union army. Slavery was undermined from within as the Confederacy was being overridden from without. Acting on the belief that the war was a war of emancipation, slaves made an originally false assessment come true.[7] With a nod to E. P. Thompson then, it might be said that slaves emancipated themselves as much as they were emancipated.[8] Rather than waiting for their liberators to come to them, thousands of black people seized the opportunity to flee to their ostensible liberators. With this act rebellious slaves transformed the nature of the war. The thousands of slaves who sought refuge behind Union lines or who otherwise came under federal custody during the war forced the issue of their fate onto reluctant northern policymakers and made the question of their future central to the war effort of the North.

The "contraband" policy developed by General Benjamin F. Butler illustrates the reciprocal influence of slave initiatives and government mandates. In May of 1861, Butler, commanding occupying forces at Fortress Monroe, Virginia, faced the politically sensitive problem of devising a policy to deal with several runaway slaves. He suspected they had been used in a military capacity, building fortifications in support of the Confederate army. So instead of returning them to their owners as required by the fugitive slave law, Butler declared them "contraband of war" and retained them under military custody. This inventive contraband policy permitted Butler to justify an apparent abrogation of the law, while not formally freeing any slaves or disavowing the legality of slavery per se. By granting runaway slaves sanctuary under the contraband policy, Butler also avoided antagonizing northern interests opposed to emancipation and worried about private property rights. As military authorities increasingly adopted this plan and as news of the contraband policy spread along the "grapevine telegraph," thousands more slaves fled from the plantations. Everywhere the Union army subsequently appeared in the South, black people seeking freedom followed.[9]

Slaves, therefore, were by no means just the passive recipients of the beneficence of northern liberators; they contributed in a variety of ways to Union victory and to the downfall of slavery.[10] First, by seeking refuge behind Union lines, they deprived the Confederacy of its primary source of labor, forced the South to reallocate resources to fill the resulting shortage, and made it necessary for southern whites to mobilize on a second front, to ward off further defections by the slave population. Second, the defiance and "disloyalty" of slaves during the war shook the ideological foundations of slavery and undermined irrevocably the worldview of the slaveholder. "We went to sleep one night with a plantation full of negroes," wrote the astonished wife of a Georgia planter, "and woke to find not one on the place. . . . We had thought there was a strong bond of affection on their side as well as ours!"[11] The pervasive fear of slave revolts in the antebellum South suggests, however, that planters were never truly convinced of the faithfulness of their slaves.[12] Third, many southern blacks took more direct action against the regime of slavery, engaging in everything from spying to sabotage, and from insubordination to outright insurrection. Finally, as the war continued, more than 180,000 blacks eventually enlisted as soldiers in the invading Union army and fought in many of the pivotal battles that destroyed the Confederacy and put an end to slavery.

Southern planters too did not fail to notice the role their own slaves were playing in the conduct of the war against them. A Georgia slaveholder painted a vivid picture of this "monstrous evil":

> Our Negroes our property—the agracultural class of the Confederacy, upon whose order & continuance so much depends, may go off, (inflicting a great pecuniary loss both private & public) to the enemy—convey any amount of valuable information—and aid him by building fortifications: by raising supplies for his armies—by enlisting as Soldiers—by acting as Spies & as guides & pilots on his expeditions on land & water & bringing in the foe upon us to kill & devastate.[13]

Through their wartime acts of resistance to slavery—which "took on revolutionary significance"—blacks put the question of their status onto the political agenda, decisively shaped the evolution of federal policy during the war, and fundamentally "redefined the sectional crisis."[14] Nevertheless, the course of action undertaken by the government in the North, while partly a response to black initiatives, was also constrained by competing interests and circumstances. Despite the efforts of certain Radical Republicans to inaugurate a revolutionary transformation of the southern economy, federal policy during the war ended up contributing to the perpetuation of the antebellum plantation system.

Federal Policy Toward Black Labor During the War

On March 16, 1863, the War Department, at the urging of Charles Sumner, a leading Radical Republican, authorized the establishment of the American Freedmen's Inquiry Commission (AFIC).[15] Consisting of three supporters of the antislavery cause, the commission was ordered to report on how best to prepare blacks to defend and support themselves and how they might be used to assist in the suppression of the rebellion. Although founded under Radical auspices, the AFIC proposed a surprisingly modest approach to southern economic reconstruction. The proper objective of northern policy, the commissioners advised, was to protect blacks from the restoration of slavery "and then let them take care of themselves." There was just as much danger, they warned, "in doing too much as in doing too little." The AFIC, committed to the ideology of free labor, gave the following recommendation:

> The freedman should be treated at once as any other free man. He should be subjected to no compulsory contracts as to labor. There should not be, directly or indirectly, any statutory rates of wages. There should be no interference between the hirers and the hired. Nor should any regulations be imposed in regard to the local movements of these people, except such regulations, incident to war, relative to vagrancy or otherwise, as apply equally to whites. The natural laws of supply and demand should be left to regulate rates of compensation and places of residence.[16]

The report of the AFIC—later described as the "Blueprint for Radical Reconstruction"—did not specifically prescribe the reinstatement of the plantation system. Nevertheless, it contributed to that end by refusing to sanction official efforts to promote alternatives that might have enhanced the possibilities for black independence. The ideological commitment of most northern officials (many Radicals included, as the AFIC report attests) extended only so far as to ensure the replacement of slave labor by wage labor. In this respect, the free-labor ideology and the economic reforms promoted under its authority represented no necessary threat to the maintenance of the antebellum plantation system.

As the war progressed and slavery continued to disintegrate, thousands of blacks—more than a million by the end of the war—came under the jurisdiction of federal authorities.[17] Although confronted by enormous problems of management and social control, made even more complicated by diverse political and military considerations, federal officials during the war assumed the task of initiating the transition from slave labor to free labor. Free labor, for northern authorities, meant that blacks would sign contracts, work for wages, and continue to labor diligently on the plantations.[18]

Federal authorities introduced many refugee slaves to the system of free labor by employing them on abandoned plantations, under the supervision of northern lessees, military officers, or agents of the Treasury Department. Those in charge believed that the experience of hard work as "free laborers" on abandoned plantations would prepare blacks to assume their proper economic role after the war. This program had the further advantage of handing over to blacks themselves the burden of responsibility for their care and protection, thus making them less of a nuisance to the military and less of a drain on scarce northern resources. Federal authorities also hoped that placing black people under the control of employers on abandoned plantations might alleviate fears in the North that the abolition of slavery would unleash a wave of black emigration from the South. Furthermore, especially given the height to which cotton prices had climbed during the war, the Treasury Department and northern economic interests expected to reap generous profits from putting blacks back to work on the plantations. Finally, if it demonstrated that blacks could successfully fend for themselves and perform efficiently under a free-labor system, the policy of settling refugee slaves on abandoned plantations might also placate northern critics and ease the process of emancipation.

Inauspiciously, however, black workers on abandoned plantations labored under conditions closely resembling those of slavery, even while authorities responsible for the implementation of this policy proclaimed its value as a way of introducing slaves to the world of free labor. General Grant's policy for the Mississippi Valley area, which came under the occupation of the Union army early in the war, embodied this contradiction. As historian Ronald Davis shows, Grant's plan, though intended to instill in blacks the meaning of free labor, was "curiously one-sided." Besides prescribing only a subsistence wage, unrelated to individual effort, Grant's policy greatly curtailed the freedom that was the alleged hallmark of the new labor system: blacks were organized into work gangs, given no voice in setting contract terms, and subjected to strict measures of discipline and control. "But Grant thought the slaves would now be selling their labor for wages and would therefore benefit by learning the meaning of a contract."[19]

In 1864, General Lorenzo Thomas assumed administrative authority over the refugee slaves and abandoned plantations under federal custody in Mississippi. The labor regulations set forth by Thomas in his "Orders No. 9," which were if anything even more repressive than those implemented by Grant, illustrate the prevailing concept of black labor held by northern officials:

> These regulations are based upon the assumption that labor is a public duty and idleness and vagrancy a crime. ... That portion of the people identified with the cultivation of the soil, however changed in condition by the revolution through which we are passing, is not relieved from the necessity of toil, which is the condition of existence with all the children of God. The revolution has altered its tenure, but not its law.[20]

Northern policy assumed that, even with the new free-labor system, black people—"that portion of the people identified with the cultivation of the soil"—would remain a subordinate agricultural labor force. Southern blacks, while no longer slaves, were not expected to be relieved of their "class responsibilities," foremost among which was to provide "good and faithful labor."[21]

The well-known "rehearsal for Reconstruction" on the Sea Islands of South Carolina—the "Port Royal experiment"—provides another illustration of how northern policy toward black labor during the war, guided by the ideology of free labor, contributed to the maintenance of the plantation system.[22] When the Sea Islands came under Union occupation, the North found itself in possession of ten thousand slaves and sixty thousand acres of arable land vacated by southern whites. The proponents of free labor got a promising opportunity to put their principles into practice. Many of the Sea Island plantations were eventually acquired by Edward Philbrick, an engineer with ties to northern textile interests. Philbrick proposed to demonstrate that cotton could be produced more cheaply with free labor than with slave labor. This would prove the relative merits of the free-labor system and render the abolition of slavery acceptable even to northern manufacturing interests concerned about the effects of emancipation on the cotton supply from the South.

The goal of demonstrating the relative efficiency of free labor over slave labor presupposed the continued existence of plantation agriculture and put a premium on the maximization of production. This led Philbrick to preserve many of the most objectionable features of the slave-labor system, including the use of armed overseers, a strict system of discipline and control, and regulations prohibiting the movement of blacks. Furthermore, black employees received only minimal compensation under this new free-labor system, for it was believed that high wages or grants of land would undermine the salutary effect of hard work and would encourage idleness and dependency. Philbrick and other free-labor advocates also maintained a commitment to the continued cultivation of cotton. Blacks, on the other hand, because it provided opportunities for greater independence, preferred subsistence farming.[23] The Port Royal blacks, however, did manage to successfully resist the restoration of one of the essential elements of the slave mode of labor organization. In a foreshadowing of what was to occur on a much larger scale in the first few years after the war, black laborers on Philbrick's plantations forced him to abandon the gang-labor system.[24] But more generally, as one historian points out, few among the Yankee missionaries and plantation superintendents on the Sea Islands "hoped to liberate the blacks from the traditional plantation labor."[25]

In the occupied territory of southern Louisiana,

under the jurisdiction of the Department of the Gulf, the preservation of the plantation system and the continued subordination of the black labor force were even more explicitly the objectives of federal policy.[26] Rather than being atypical, moreover, programs implemented in the Gulf Department influenced federal wartime policy toward blacks elsewhere in the South. Thomas's "Orders No. 9" for the Mississippi Valley area, for example, were derived from labor regulations originally developed by authorities in the Louisiana area. Furthermore, federal policy in the Gulf Department constituted a model for the North's approach to southern economic reconstruction in the postwar period, as evidenced by the continuity between the labor program of the military in Louisiana and the labor policy adopted by the Freedmen's Bureau after the war.[27] In addition, the specific "rehearsal for Reconstruction" in the Gulf Department more accurately anticipated the actual performance as it was played after the war. In contrast to the Port Royal experiment, for example, in which southern planters did not participate, the situation in Louisiana included all of the principals that were to be involved in the postwar process of economic reconstruction. Since this area came under occupation and was effectively pacified early in the war, the evolution of federal policy there was also less encumbered by considerations of military necessity.

When southern Louisiana came under Union occupation in April 1862, responsibility for federal policy in the region fell to General Butler, the same man who had originated the contraband policy while at Fortress Monroe. Once again Butler was called upon to deal with the problem of runaway slaves. Unlike the situation in Virginia, however, the runaway slaves in Louisiana were owned by planters still loyal to the Union, whose allegiance federal authorities did not wish to alienate.

The threat of black insurrection and violence also caused Butler to proceed cautiously. In a letter written in July 1862, Butler warned of the possibility of another "San Domingo":

> Be sure that I shall treat the negro with as much tenderness as possible but I assure you it is quite impossible to free him here and now without a San Domingo. A single whistle from me would cause every white man's throat to be cut in this city. Accumulated hate has been piled up here between master and servant, until it is fearful. . . . There is no doubt that an insurrection is only prevented by our *Bayonets*.[28]

The fear of violent rebellion among blacks, combined with the politically motivated desire to appease loyal whites, convinced Butler of the need to reassert control and discipline over the black labor force and restore the viability of the plantation economy. Butler proceeded to reassure the white population that property rights would be respected, that no assault on slavery was intended by the military, and that the existing labor system would be maintained.[29]

Butler's first priority was to stop the migration of slaves from the plantations. Since by this time the military was prohibited from enforcing the fugitive slave law, Butler adopted a policy of excluding from Union lines all slaves of loyal planters, except for those who could be usefully employed by the military; thus most blacks were returned to the authority of the local white community. Butler further ordered that all blacks find employment; those who refused to remain with their masters were required to work on plantations under the control of the military or to accept some form of public employment. Military and local authorities enforced strict vagrancy

regulations, and the army patrolled plantations to discourage runaways and to help planters maintain order and
discipline.[30]

Butler's efforts proved futile however. Some of his
own officers and troops, either from sympathy to blacks or
hostility to planters, refused to enforce the labor policies
that Butler set forth.[31] Even more significantly, many of
the slaves under Butler's jurisdiction began taking emancipation into their own hands. They continued to flee
from their owners; some settled by themselves on abandoned estates, and others forcibly appropriated their
masters' land. Those who remained on the plantations
refused to obey orders, cultivated their own garden plots,
and, when willing to work for planters at all, insisted
upon compensation and refused the supervision of white
overseers. Slavery and the plantation order in southern
Louisiana were on the verge of breaking down, and many
southern whites feared a slave insurrection.[32]

In late 1862, Butler, hoping to negotiate a truce
between loyal planters and rebellious slaves, began introducing a new labor program—the "contract system"—
which became the standard policy of northern authorities
both during and after the war. Butler's contract system
explicitly repudiated any permanent interference with
slavery. It required blacks to commit themselves to an
employer for ten hours a day, twenty-six days a month,
and prohibited them from leaving the plantations without
a pass. It required planters to compensate black laborers
with wages and rations and prohibited them from using
corporal punishment. In response to planters' objections
to this curtailment of their authority, however, Butler
gave district provost marshals the right to punish blacks
for insubordination and for refusal to work.[33]

Butler's contract system was not intended to make
inroads against slavery, which was disintegrating any-

way. Indeed, many blacks—by refusing to obey their masters and by demanding compensation for their labor— had already, in effect, quit being slaves. Rather, the contract system was an attempt to stem the tide of black rebellion and to restore some semblance of stability and order to the southern Louisiana economy. Northern authorities introduced the contract system, not to initiate the transition from slavery to freedom, but to reestablish a system of social control and a mechanism of labor exploitation.

In December 1862, General Nathaniel F. Banks replaced Butler as commander of the Gulf Department. This change in command did not significantly alter the military's labor program; if anything, planters found Banks even more accommodating than Butler.[34] In early 1863, Banks appointed a Sequestration Commission, consisting of several military officers, which was charged with the task of working out the details of the contract system. Banks also authorized a committee of planters to confer with the commission and to suggest recommendations for contract regulations; black laborers were given no such offer of participation. Ripley gives the following description of the commission's guidelines:

> Under the auspices of the Sequestration Commission the government agreed to "induce the slaves to return to the plantations where they belong," requiring them "to work diligently and faithfully . . . for one year, [and] to maintain respectful deportment to their employers, and perfect subordination to their duties." For their part planters agreed to "feed, clothe, and treat properly" the laborers. At the end of the year compensation was promised in the form of three dollars a month for semi-skilled workers. . . . As was usual, all unemployed blacks were required to labor on public works without pay. . . . A provision added to the final contract forms stated that "acceptance of the

> contract does not imply the surrender of any right
> of property in the slave or other right of the
> owners."[35]

Like Butler before him, Banks's objective was to maintain the plantation system and ensure the continued subordination of black laborers. Radical critics of federal labor policy in Louisiana accused Banks of intending to substitute serfdom for slavery.[36] In an even harsher attack on Banks, a black newspaper, the New Orleans *Tribune,* in one of its many sarcastic articles on the "Free Labor" system in Louisiana, charged that Banks's policy preserved slavery "under a different form. . . . The name only has been changed; not much has been touched of the principle. The dynasty of slavery is still existing."[37]

As these examples of wartime reconstruction illustrate, federal policy toward black labor during the war, while intended to effect a transition from slave labor to free labor, did not seek to alter the status of blacks as a dependent plantation labor force; and when the smoke finally cleared, gang labor and the plantation system remained intact. Political, economic, and military concerns, assumptions about the appropriate status of blacks as a free people, the ideology of free labor, and the fear of black insurrection—these considerations combined during the war to produce an outcome that most blacks found little different than slavery. Indeed, the alternative vision of free labor held by blacks—which presupposed that they would maintain control over their own labor—differed from the northern version of the free labor system more than the latter differed from slavery. Where, after all, was the freedom in a "free-labor system" that forced them to work, bound them to their former masters, instructed them to be obedient, restricted their mobility, and compelled them to labor on cotton plantations under the supervision of white overseers? If blacks were to achieve the autonomy and independence called for by their vision of free labor, then, given the direction of federal policy during the war, it seemed clear that they would have to supply the initiative themselves.

Southern Planters and Free Black Labor

Most planters greeted with incredulity the prospect of profitable cotton cultivation with free black labor. If the free-labor experiment were to have any chance of success at all though, planters regarded it as imperative that the gang-labor system be maintained and a strict system of labor control established. This issue of labor control remained at the heart of the battle between planters and freedpeople throughout the postbellum years.

Not all planters were left convinced by the outcome of the Civil War that the fate of slavery was thereby sealed or that they would have to surrender proprietary control over the black labor force. Particularly in the remote interior regions of the South, relatively untouched by the war or far from the authority of the Union army and the Freedmen's Bureau, planters sometimes refrained from informing blacks of their freedom and refused to accept the abolition of slavery. Where they faced little threat of northern interference, planters, through a combination of deceit and coercion, tried to preserve slavery for as long as possible. Some blacks in Chester County, South Carolina, for example, did not learn of their freedom until two years after the end of the war.[38]

Many planters also held lingering hopes that slavery, with modest changes perhaps, might be restored. "The belief is by no means general here that slavery is dead," wrote a Union army officer from Danville, North Carolina, in 1865, "and a hope that, in some undefined way, they will yet control the slaves, is in many minds, amounting with some to a conviction."[39] Planters in Mississippi, similarly, according to the report of a Freedmen's Bureau agent, could not yet bring themselves to believe that slavery was really gone: "There is a disposition on the part of planters to continue their control over their former slaves, with the hope that some change will be made, by which they will be allowed the work of these people free of charge, or that some new form of slavery will be substituted for the old."[40] Convinced that slavery would soon be revived, planters in South Carolina agreed to contract with their former slaves with the ulterior motive of keeping them on the plantations so they would be nearby when emancipation was rescinded.[41] Some southern whites, furthermore, doubted that the North could effectively secure the abolition of slavery. "These niggers," boasted one planter, "will be all slaves again in twelve months. You have nothing but Lincoln's proclamation to make them free."[42] Numerous witnesses before the Joint Committee on Reconstruction also testified to the fragility of black freedom, predicting that, without the protective presence of federal troops and the Freedmen's Bureau, blacks would soon be reenslaved, exterminated, or forced into some other form of bondage.[43] Among freedpeople, too, fears persisted that they might yet be returned to slavery.[44]

Probably only a minority of planters truly expected that slavery would be restored just as before. Most reluctantly consented to emancipation. But that blacks were no longer slaves did not necessarily mean that they were to enjoy the same kind or degree of freedom as that possessed by whites. "It is," reported one witness before the Joint Committee on Reconstruction, "very difficult for the people of the South to look upon the negro as a free man—as having rights such as white men have."[45] The difficulty of looking "upon the negro as a free man" was no less a problem for many people of the North. Sent in September 1865 to report from the South for President Johnson, Benjamin Truman gave an assessment of the future of freedpeople that "the people of the South" could have accepted with no great difficulty: "The South always has been, and always must be to a great extent the guardian of the negro, for the time will never come, so long as he remains a part of our society, then, from the very nature of his inferiority, he will not require a certain guardianship."[46] The commitment of northern policymakers to the abolition of slavery did not necessarily imply a commitment to racial equality or to the end of black subordination. Plenty of undefined territory existed *between* slavery and freedom, and it was within this "contested terrain" that the battle over the meaning of emancipation took place.[47]

For southern whites, the need to preserve racial domination and the existing class structure set the parameters for their interpretation of emancipation. In particular, planters refused to accept that with the abolition of slavery they would cease to maintain control over the black population. Colonel Samuel Thomas, an assistant commissioner of the Freedmen's Bureau, found that southern whites, despite emancipation, still regarded blacks as their property:

> The whites esteem the blacks their property by natural right, and however much they admit that the individual relations of masters and slaves have been destroyed by the war and by the president's emancipation proclamation, they still have an ingrained feeling that the blacks at large belong to the whites at large, and whenever the opportunity serves they treat colored people just as their profit, caprice or passing may dictate.[48]

That blacks were to remain a dependent agricultural labor force, under the control of the "whites at large," was not, presumed many southern planters, a condition proscribed by the abolition of slavery. "Although it is admitted that he has ceased to be the property of a master, it is not admitted that he has a right to become his own master."[49] Though no longer slaves, planters still expected blacks to carry out the duties of a subordinate race and a dependent laboring class. Planters, therefore, did not interpret the abolition of slavery as precluding the possibility—indeed, the necessity—of the continued subordination of blacks under some alternative system of forced labor; they "think that some species of serfdom, peonage, or some other form of compulsory labor is not slavery, and may be introduced without a violation of their pledge."[50] Planters regarded it as inevitable, a Union general testified, that blacks "shall be under some compulsory system of labor."[51] Planters wanted blacks to enjoy only the limited freedom of a permanently subordinate laboring class. A white Virginian, sounding a more optimistic note than most, predicted, revealingly, that free black laborers would make "the best peasantry in the world."[52]

The planters' commitment to reestablishing a system of forced labor to take the place of slavery derived in part from their conviction that blacks would not work unless compelled to do so. "Two hundred years of experience" prove "that the only way to make the negro work," a correspondent to the *Southern Cultivator* concluded, "is to keep the fear of corporeal punishment continually before him."[53] Hardly any opinion was more widely held among southern whites than this.

> In at least nineteen cases of twenty the reply I received to my inquiry about their views on the new system was uniformly this: "You cannot make the negro work

without physical compulsion." I heard this hundreds of times, heard it wherever I went, heard it in nearly the same words from so many different persons, that at last I came to the conclusion that this is the prevailing sentiment among the southern people.[54]

Reports from other travelers in the South confirmed the prevalence of this conception of free black labor. "Three fourths of the people," declared Sidney Andrews, "assume that the negro will not labor except on compulsion."[55] Whitelaw Reid found, similarly, that "nothing could overcome this rooted idea that the negro was worthless except under the lash."[56] Planters repeatedly complained that the new free-labor system, which barred corporal punishment, provided them with insufficient control over the black labor force.[57] Indeed, many planters took it for granted that the new labor system would include compulsory measures. How else after all would black laborers be made to work? Accustomed to a forced-labor system and convinced that blacks would not work except under compulsion, planters had great difficulty grasping the possibility that they might exercise something less than total control over the black labor force.[58]

This analysis gave rise to frequent predictions of failure for the free-labor experiment. According to one report, barely one in twelve of the "intelligent thinking men" of South Carolina thought that free black labor would prove successful.[59] Likewise, a correspondent for the *Nation* estimated that only one in a hundred southern whites believed that the free-labor system would be anything but a failure.[60] With the new free-labor system, planters complained, "the negroes would not work," they refused to remain on the plantations, they "preferred a life of idleness and vagrancy to that of honest and industrious labor," they would not agree to or abide by labor contracts, they were "insubordinate" and "insolent," and they had no conception "of the obligations freedom imposed upon them."[61]

A brief visit to the Sea Islands shortly after the war left a South Carolina planter with the impression that free blacks would not make "a useful and efficient peasantry." The "negro labor upon the plantations could not be controlled," this planter reported in a letter to the local Union military commander; they "would not stand to any engagement whatever" and they "will not work regularly or systematically"; moreover, they "work when they please and do just as much as they please, they visit the neighboring cities or plantations as they please, do not work on Saturdays at all, get paid for just what they do."[62] Many northern observers shared this negative assessment of free black labor. Freedpeople, reported the commissioner of agriculture in 1867, were "inclined to use too freely their newly-found liberty"; as a result, "idleness became contagious . . . crops were neglected . . . and the cotton fields were in many cases left in the lurch at the critical season of picking."[63] Both southern planters and northern authorities were distressed to discover that with emancipation black people refused to labor as they had under slavery.

Because it required the commitment of a labor force throughout the duration of the season, planters were particularly pessimistic about the feasibility of relying on free black labor for cotton cultivation. Even if they could hire a sufficient number of workers at the beginning of the year, planters had no assurance that the labor force would still be around when the crop was ready to harvest. "The system of wages was a precarious and arbitrary innovation," wrote an assistant commissioner of the Freedmen's Bureau, recording the views of planters in Alabama; "it could not be that a crop requiring twelve months unremitting care was safe with labor altogether free. Without security in some form, no one would give employment requiring any outlay."[64] A South Carolina planter also doubted the possibility of cotton cultivation with free black labor: "Labor must be commanded completely or the production of the cotton crop must be abandoned. Many experienced long cotton planters will tell you that at certain Seasons *three* days in working it will make such a difference as almost to make or ruin a crop."[65] Many planters despaired of ever raising cotton again.[66] Evidently, though, some hoped their prophecies of failure would prove true, for then Congress might recognize the need to restore their power to compel black labor.[67]

Planters also believed that a compulsory labor system was required because black people, governed by the dictates of "immediate gratification," lacked the motivation necessary to the operation of a free-labor system. The promise of fair wages, planters frequently asserted, afforded an insufficient incentive to free black labor. "Money is no inducement that will incite him to work," complained a Savannah resident. "He works for comfort, that is, he wants to gain something and then enjoy it immediately afterwards."[68] Whitelaw Reid attested to the prevalence of this view:

> I have conversed with dozens of planters, before and since, whose talk all runs in the same channel. . . . "Why not depend on the power of wages, if they work, or of want, if they don't, to settle the labor question?" I asked one. "They'll work just enough to get a dollar, and then they'll desert you in the midst of the picking season, till they've spent it all, and have become hungry again. . . . Southern laborers are nothing but niggers, and you can't make anything else out of them. They're not controlled by the same motives as white men, and unless you have the power to compel them, they'll only work when they can't beg or steal enough to keep from starving."[69]

Many of the respondents to Loring and Atkinson's 1868 survey of labor conditions in the South registered similar complaints about the motivation of black laborers. Typical was the remark of a Texas planter: "Negroes are good-natured and lazy, and ninety-nine out of a hundred are satisfied with their daily bread, and are willing for the morrow literally to take care of itself."[70] A Mississippi planter, responding to the same survey, argued that the black population "retains the innate vice or defect of all tropical people; indisposition to provide for the future by sustained industry and preserving efforts. The immediate wants of life provided for, they seem in the main to be satisfied; and are careless, or rather thoughtless of anything beyond."[71]

There was some truth to planters' assessment of free black labor. But this was a matter of conflicting conceptions of the meaning of emancipation rather than the "innate vice or defect" of black people.[72] Indeed, with the abolition of slavery, blacks were more oriented toward "immediate gratification"—or at least more so than was possible when they were slaves. One way for freedpeople to express their new independence was to enjoy the fruits of their labor. "What's the use of living if a man can't have the good of his labor," responded a black man to a reproach from a northern reporter for spending his earnings "carelessly."[73] Freedom gave blacks the opportunity to enjoy themselves more than they had under slavery. Yet precisely to the extent the former slave gained the right to "have the good of his labor," it threatened the ability of planters to control the black labor force for their own economic benefit. This loss of control is what explains planters' complaints about the work habits of free black laborers.

The crux of the labor problem experienced by planters after the war was that blacks, as free laborers, refused to offer on the market for hire the number of labor hours that they had been forced to work as slaves. Judging by the amount of labor that had been available through coercion under slavery, planters arrived at the conclusion that with emancipation the natural indolence of blacks had resurfaced. "Whence comes the assertion that the 'nigger won't work'?" one former slave asked. "It comes from this fact: . . . The freedman refuses to be driven out into the field two hours before day, and work until 9 or 10 o'clock in the night, as was the case in the days of slavery."[74] Moreover, as historian Eric Foner explains, planters regarded as "indolent" "not simply blacks unwilling to work at all, but those who preferred to work for themselves."[75] Frances Leigh, the daughter of a Georgia planter, while on the one hand complaining that freed blacks proved "worthless as laborers," also observed that, when given the chance to work for themselves on their own piece of land, freedpeople did not exhibit their usual "laziness."[76] Significantly, however, from the perspective of planters, the fact that blacks were willing to work hard on land of their own made them no less "worthless as laborers." The crucial issue for planters, of course, was never the work habits of blacks considered as an abstract moral issue, but rather the availability of black labor for plantation agriculture.

Planters' complaints about the "indolence" of blacks were yet another expression of their inability to regain control over the labor force. Planters did indeed wish to eradicate black "indolence," but the achievement of this objective was subordinate to the goal of preserving class relations and maintaining the status of their former slaves as a subservient race. Planters wanted blacks to work, to be sure; but more to the point, planters wanted blacks to work *for them*, they wanted exploitable labor. Thus, what was indolence from the perspective of planters, accustomed to making prodigious demands on the labor force, was for blacks a determination to escape plantation labor and to live an independent existence on their own land. The supposed "indolence" of blacks was not a manifestation of their aversion to labor—witness, for example, the eagerness of freedpeople to work on land of their own—but rather reflected their resistance to the plantation system and their desire to put as much distance between themselves and slavery as possible.

Black Resistance and Labor Scarcity

Because of the scarcity of labor in the immediate postwar years, planters found it nearly impossible to procure obedient and reliable laborers.[77] This scarcity of labor was not simply the product of "natural" forces—market, demographic, or otherwise—but rather resulted from blacks' opposition to plantation labor, from their determination to gain independence from their former masters, and from their relative preference for leisure and family life. By expressing the preferences and exercising the options now at least partially open to them with emancipation, freed blacks created a scarcity of labor. This, in turn, gave them considerable leverage in their dealings with planters.

The first breach in planters' control over the labor force came during the war, when thousands of blacks fled the plantations in order to escape slavery and hurry the process of emancipation. The labor situation remained unsettled during the early Reconstruction period, as many blacks greeted their freedom by leaving the plantations: migrating to towns and cities, tracking down relatives, seeking alternative economic opportunities, trying to discover what the government had in store for them, enjoying their freedom, and testing the limits of their new independence.[78] Though slighting the practical interests motivating their migration, a former slave from North Carolina, when asked about the behavior of blacks after the war, said that they "were like a bird let out of a cage."[79] This "wanderlust," as southern whites sometimes disparagingly referred to it, added greatly to the labor problems experienced by planters.

The desire of blacks to acquire their own land caused the most serious strain on the plantation labor market after the war.[80] Even if they could gain only a "meagre support" on "old worn out lands," freedpeople much preferred the uncertainty of subsistence farming to working for their former masters:

> Those who have watched the movements of the negro, must have seen that the laborers are retiring from plantation service to any and all other vocations, whereby they can gain even a meagre support. Very many of them . . . are retiring from the more fertile fields and advantages offered by the owners of good lands, to work upon old worn out lands, where they can enjoy and assert the innate love of independence.[81]

Blacks further expressed this "innate love of independence," while at the same time exacerbating planters' labor problems by migrating to towns and supporting themselves by working odd jobs and urban occupations, which also afforded more autonomy than plantation labor.[82]

The widespread belief among blacks that they were soon to receive grants of land from the government also contributed to the problems of labor scarcity and labor control. Blacks' expectations of land redistribution were especially pronounced around Christmas for several years after the war. According to one report, freedpeople all "had the idea that in January [of 1866] the lands of their former masters were to be divided among them"; as a result, planters were unable to persuade enough laborers to contract for the ensuing year.[83] Blacks, after all, did not want to be bound by a contract when the anticipated redistribution of land took place. Landowners, therefore, found themselves without a sufficient supply of laborers that could be counted on for the entire season. The plantation system could not survive such labor-force instability. The successful operation of the agricultural system in the South, advised the commissioner of agriculture in 1867, required "disabusing the minds of freedmen (at present unsettled and disturbed) of anticipation of dividends of confiscated estates."[84] Though they ultimately met with little success, agents of the Freedmen's Bureau tried to convince freedpeople that there would be no land redistribution program and to persuade them to agree to yearly contracts with planters.

The attraction of landownership and independence drew blacks away from plantation labor. So too did the similarity between the plantation system and slavery. Blacks were particularly opposed to working under overseers, one of the most unpalatable reminders of slavery.[85] They also objected to the cultivation of cotton—the "slave crop." "If ole massa want to grow cotton, let him plant it himself. I'se work for him dese twenty year, and done got nothin' but food and clothes, and dem might mean; now I'se freedman, and I tell you I ain't going to work cotton nohow."[86]

As free laborers, moreover, many blacks refused to bind themselves to an employer through a labor contract and claimed instead the right to unrestricted mobility in the labor market. The New Orleans *Tribune*, writing on behalf of free blacks, went so far as to declare labor contracts incompatible with a free-labor system; "no contract, but on the contrary, freedom to both parties"—

this, argued the *Tribune*, "is the motto of free labor."[87] The contract system and plantation labor smacked too much of slavery, and freedpeople were "fearful of forfeiting their newly acquired liberty in some manner."[88] Anxious to ensure their independence, blacks rejected contracts and pursued alternatives outside of the plantation system. "If a man got to go crost de riber and he can't git a boat, he take a log," explained one former slave. "If I can't own de land, I'll hire or lease land, but I won't contract."[89] Most freedpeople shared this man's conviction. "I find very few negroes who seem willing to make contracts for the coming year," reported Sidney Andrews in 1865. "Many appear to have a notion that they can live more easily and comfortably by job work. A considerable number are anxious to become landholders, by lease or by time purchases."[90] A black soldier, in a letter to the South Carolina *Leader* in 1866, also voiced opposition to the contract system: "I hope soon to be called a citizen of the U.S. and have the rights of a citizen. I am opposed myself to working under a contract. . . . I expect to stay in the South after I am mustered out of service but not to hire myself to a planter."[91]

Most freedpeople, if they had to hire out, preferred short-term arrangements. They "are unwilling to make contracts for farming labor, to be paid at the end of the year in kind or in money, their food being provided," stated the 1866 Report of the Commissioner of Agriculture, discussing labor conditions in Georgia. But they "are more willing to work when they can be paid by the week or month, as they thus obtain ready money. . . . [In some cases] they are unwilling to contract to labor for more than two days in the week."[92] Short-term arrangements made it possible for blacks to be continually on the lookout for better employment elsewhere and to take advantage of any opportunities for acquiring land. Year-long contracts, on the other hand, prevented freedpeople from entering the labor market and discovering their highest price except for the one time at the beginning of the season. For the same reason, blacks in the immediate postwar years expressed some preference for periodic money wages over a share of the crop. Under a share system of payment employees were necessarily bound for the entire year if they hoped to receive full compensation.[93] The records of the Freedmen's Bureau show, however, that throughout the South, especially in 1865 and 1866, freedpeople were regularly cheated out of their wages and driven off the plantations without compensation after the crops had been harvested.[94] In response, some blacks—evidently believing that by having an interest in the crop they could better protect themselves from being defrauded—increasingly opted for the share-payment system.

Blacks' resistance to the plantation system and their reluctance to sign labor contracts resulted in a substantial decline in the availability of labor for hire in the years after the war. Ransom and Sutch estimate that the number of per capita labor hours supplied by black workers fell by between 28 and 37 percent as a consequence of emancipation, with a considerable proportion of this decline attributable to the withdrawal of women and children from the labor market.[95] At least two problems arose for planters from this decline in the supply of labor. First, approximately one-third of the labor-force hours utilized under slavery was no longer available for plantation labor. Second, those blacks who remained in the labor market found themselves in a relatively strong bargaining position. Planters would now have to compete in the market or find alternative means for securing a labor force.

The scarcity of labor, therefore, had ramifications

even for those planters fortunate enough to procure a labor force. The existence of alternative economic opportunities gave blacks the power to make demands—for higher wages and greater autonomy—and presented landowners with severe management problems. The contrast between blacks' desire for independence and their current situation as dependent field hands fueled their discontent. Blacks' preference for independence affected not only their availability in the plantation labor market, but also, once under contract, their willingness to serve as obedient workers. The difficulty for planters was not only in getting laborers under contract, but in wresting labor from them once hired and ensuring their continued service throughout the duration of the planting season. The most serious problem, an Arkansas planter explained, was that of labor "uncertainty":

> The greatest difficulty we now labor under in the cultivation of cotton is the uncertainty and unreliableness of the labor of the blacks, as few of them have any idea of the obligations of a contract, and most of them will leave you in the midst of your crop if they thought it to their interest. They will not in three-quarters of cases carry out their agreement if they thought it to their interest to break it. It is not the price of the labor, but the uncertainty of it that makes it so objectionable.[96]

This labor "uncertainty" that planters complained so much about—the disturbing proclivity of freedpeople to act on their own interests—was precisely what blacks understood to be free labor.

Planters' complaints about labor "uncertainty" reveal an interesting contradiction in their assessment of free black labor. The problem with the free-labor system, as portrayed by planters, was twofold. On the one hand,

planters believed that the free-labor system would not
work because blacks, naturally inclined toward leisure
and independence, were not responsive to market incentives and could not be induced to labor with the promise
of fair wages. Blacks lacked the proper motivation requisite to the effective operation of the free-labor system. But
on the other hand, planters believed that the free-labor
system was unworkable, particularly where sustained
cotton cultivation was concerned, because blacks were so
easily lured to other employment opportunities by the
prospect of higher wages or better working conditions—
because in effect blacks played the free-market game too
well. "Grant them one thing, and they demand something
more," complained a disgruntled Georgia planter. "There
is no feeling of gratitude in their nature. Let any man offer
them some little thing of no real benefit to them, but
which looks like a little more freedom, and they catch at
it with avidity."[97] Planters discovered that freedpeople
were all too eager to assert their new market freedom;
they demanded pay for everything they did: they "want 10
cents—for each time they water a horse."[98] By exercising
their market rights, blacks deprived planters of the
assurance of a secure and stable labor force or compelled
them to pay "exorbitant" wages.

In short, when freedpeople opted for leisure and
independence over plantation labor, planters accused
them of lacking the requisite pecuniary motivation; and
when freedpeople bargained over wages and work conditions or were enticed by the prospect of a better offer,
planters accused them of ingratitude. In addition, planters
also found repugnant the very idea of their former slaves'
demanding the right to negotiate and bargain as equals.
Planters "did not feel kindly that their old slaves should
take time to consider the question of hiring with them,
and should presume to haggle about wages." Much

"sullen bitterness," accordingly, "was displayed against the negro."[99]

The contradictory attitudes of planters toward free black labor reflected the contradictory character of the free-labor system in the postwar South. The emerging free-labor system, in important respects, did not conform to the interests of either freedpeople or planters. Insofar as it assigned to blacks the role of plantation wage laborers, the free-labor system was incompatible with their desire to obtain land of their own. But insofar as it sanctioned competition and labor mobility, the free-labor system conflicted with the labor-force requirements of plantation agriculture. The emerging free-labor system, while allowing blacks a certain amount of mobility in the labor market, failed to satisfy their demand for independence; and while promising planters laborers for hire, the free-labor system failed to adequately meet their need for a secure and stable labor force. Free labor combined with plantation agriculture produced an unstable mixture that met the needs of neither freedpeople nor planters.

In the immediate postwar period, as an expression of their desire to obtain land and as a sign of their opposition to the wages and work conditions offered by planters, freedpeople, in effect, went on a labor strike.[100] By choosing not to work as many hours or under the same conditions as they had under slavery, blacks not only gained an increase in leisure time and the opportunity to enhance their independence, they gained a significant amount of power as well. Of course, blacks did not thereby acquire sufficient power to achieve what they most desired—landownership. But they were able to obstruct planters' efforts to reestablish the plantation system. Planters, however, refused to accede to the abandonment of gang labor and plantation agriculture without putting up a fight.

The Problem of Labor Control

Planters regarded the problem of labor control as the most pressing issue of the day. The reports of visiting journalists and the records of both the Freedmen's Bureau and the Union army show that planters constantly worried about this issue. The numerous recommendations and proposals on the "labor question" that appeared in southern newspapers and planter periodicals after the war also attest to planters' preoccupation with the problem of labor control. The evidence on black resistance to the plantation system indicates, furthermore, that planters did indeed face a genuine problem.

One cause of the "demoralization" of free blacks, southern whites agreed, was the continued occupancy in the southern states of the Union army, especially black soldiers.[101] Planters were particularly alarmed about the disruptive effect of the presence of black soldiers on the plantation labor force. In a letter to three state legislators calling for the removal of the "Negro Soldiery," a Mississippi landowner voiced the concerns of planters throughout the South:

> The Negro Soldiery here are constantly telling our
> negroes, that for the next year, The Government will give
> them lands, provisions, Stock & things necessary to carry
> on business for themselves,—& are constantly advising
> them not to make contracts with white persons, for the
> next year. . . . The consequence is they are becoming
> careless, & impudent more & more, for they are told by
> the soldiers that they are as good as the whites. . . .
> Furthermore I have good cause to believe that our negroes
> are told that when the soldiers are withdrawn, that the
> whites will endeavor to enslave them again—& that
> they are urged to begin at an early day, perhaps about
> Christmas, a massacre of the whites, in order to ensure

> their freedom. . . . Let the Soldiery remain—& our negroes
> will refuse to hire will grow more & more insolent & will
> without a doubt—(relying upon the help of the Soldiery
> which they will be sure to get) will endeavor by universal
> Massacre to turn this fair land into another Hayti.[102]

The accusation that black soldiers were inciting insurrection and "universal Massacre" may have been nothing more than a calculated attempt to elicit a quick and favorable response from the state legislature. A black soldier from Mississippi, suspecting an even more devious plot, believed that planters were spreading lies about a possible insurrection "in order that they might get arms to carrie out their wicked designs . . . and reestablish a kind of secondary slavery."[103] But even if fears of insurrection were groundless, the presence of black soldiers in the South undoubtedly created a real problem for planters. Black soldiers gave armed support in protection of the freedom of newly emancipated slaves, they encouraged freedpeople to assert their rights, and they helped spread the gospel of "forty acres and a mule." By pressing the demand for freedom and land, the "Negro Soldiery" did indeed foster discontent and insubordination among the black labor force. Through their very example, black soldiers promulgated a vision of freedom and equality that threatened the authority of the planter class.

Many planters believed that the resolution of their labor problems required the cessation of all northern interference in the economic affairs of the South. Where black soldiers were not held responsible, southern whites often attributed the discontent among the labor force to the instigation of northern politicians and "carpetbaggers," as though black hostility to plantation labor could result only from the corrupting influence of outsiders. The chief obstacle to freed blacks readily adapting to the new labor system, wrote a contributor to the *Southern Cultivator*, was the "unfriendly and unnatural legislation of Congress," which—by turning blacks away from their true friend, "the Southern white man"—prevented planters from managing the labor force effectively.[104] "Observation has taught me," recounted one planter, "that there is an incalculable loss by careless plowing, hoeing, thinning & c; and this will continue to be the case as long as radical promises and political harangues keep the negroes irresponsible and discontented."[105] If only relations between the races were rid of disturbance by northern agitators and political demagogues, free black labor might yet prove useful. "I think, if left alone," a white resident of Alabama predicted, "we would have no difficulty between laborers and employers in our country."[106]

To maintain control over the labor force, planters recognized that more direct action was also needed to undermine labor mobility and keep blacks on the plantations. An agent of the Freedmen's Bureau found that in Georgia, "every possible expedient was resorted to for frightening and keeping them at home, to enable employers to hire them at shamefully inadequate wages."[107] An ex-slave from Louisiana reported that he and several others, upon trying to leave the plantation, were confronted by a group of white men who threatened "to kill every nigger they found leaving their masters."[108] In order to prevent blacks from deserting the plantations, planters also sometimes enlisted the assistance of "Regulators"— descendants of the wartime "citizen patrols" and predecessors of the Ku Klux Klan.[109] In South Carolina, according to a report from the Freedmen's Bureau, "regulators offered to kill any freedmen who refused to contract with the planters for a fixed sum per head."[110]

Planters also adopted less violent measures to diminish the market power of blacks. They formed associations, held meetings, passed resolutions, and made pledges; instead of haggling with their former slaves over wages and work conditions, planters sought to control the labor market by organizing combinations and cartels.[111] Through collective agreements among themselves— establishing a set wage and restricting hiring practices— planters hoped to eliminate the costly competition for the labor of freedpeople, undermine their ability to play employers off against one another, and thereby regain control over the labor force. After several years of unsuccessful experience with free black labor, one planter, in 1868, offered this advice:

> Don't go out to look up hands, by any means. Let them hunt homes and they will not be so arrogant and self inflated. Dictate your own terms to them and they will not be so apt to waiver and doubt—thinking they might have done better. Let a certain price rule the land throughout, and they will not be telling of what one and another has offered. Let those who are not known bring written recommendations from former employers.[112]

An Alabama planter explained the underlying strategy to a visiting journalist: "Planters will have an understanding among themselves: 'You won't hire my niggers, and I won't hire yours;' then what's left for them? They're attached to the soil, and we're as much their masters as ever."[113] Collusion among employers may have had some short-term impact on local labor markets, but it did not result in planters becoming "as much their masters as ever." Because of the continuing shortage of labor throughout the South and the determined refusal of blacks to accept the unfavorable terms that employers tried to dictate, planters' efforts to control black labor through cooperative agreements were largely unsuccessful.[114]

Planters also pursued a political solution to their labor problems. They lobbied for the enactment of governmental measures that would legally bind black labor to the plantations and that would make "the relation between master and man . . . the subject of wise legislation."[115] A white resident of Georgia, for example, proposed "the passage of such laws as will *compel* the faithful and steady discharge of all labor contracts and obligations on the part of the laborer."[116] A South Carolina planter advocated a "system of 'permits' or passports," by which, he hoped, "the freed negro will be prevented from running all over the country vagabondizing from city to city and idling from one place in the country to another."[117] The *Carolina Times*, in a mixture of arrogant paternalism and economic self-interest that was common to such proposals, also recommended a legislative solution to the "Negro problem":

> To ameliorate their condition, and to make them useful and self-supporting, should be the care of the approaching Legislature. That much may be done by that body by the enactment of a compulsory code of enforced labor we do not doubt. Experience in the emancipated colonies proves that that is the only course to keep the Negro from dying out or relapsing into barbarism.[118]

Many southern whites suggested, more specifically, that the legislature establish an apprenticeship system under which blacks, or perhaps just minors lacking adequate parental care, would be put under the control of employers. A North Carolina planter advocated the passage of apprenticeship laws applicable to all black people under the age of twenty-one, requiring them "to be bound out to their former masters." Though he added that "enactments with reference to the older Negroes would also be necessary."[119]

The Black Codes and Labor Control

The fear of violent insurrection, the assumption that blacks would not work except under the lash, the problem of labor scarcity and "uncertainty," and the skepticism about the free-labor experiment—these considerations convinced planters that freed blacks needed to be placed under the strict control of white employers. From the perspective of planters, both economic prosperity and social stability required that the void left by the abolition of slavery be filled by an alternative compulsory labor system. Planters' clamor to legislate restrictions governing free black labor did not go unheeded. During the early years of Reconstruction, state governments in the South, though obliged to ratify the Thirteenth Amendment, otherwise operated relatively free of northern interference and remained very much under the control of the landed elite. In 1865 and 1866, beginning in Mississippi and South Carolina, legislatures throughout the southern states enacted the notorious Black Codes.[120]

The aim of the Black Codes, according to legislation passed in Louisiana, where the state assembly did not mince words, was to make the labor of freed blacks "available to the agricultural interests of the State."[121] The Black Codes were intended as the legal centerpiece of the system of labor control that planters sought to establish as a substitute for slavery. Specifically, the Black Codes were designed to limit the mobility of labor, drive blacks out of towns and back onto the plantations, reduce competition among planters, restrict the employment opportunities of freedpeople, enforce contractual obligations, and ensure the continued subordination of black people in the South. The Black Codes, as Du Bois observed, "looked backward toward slavery" rather than forward toward freedom.[122]

The specific language and stipulations comprising the Black Codes varied from state to state, but typically they included statutes relating to vagrancy, enticement, breach of contract, and apprenticeship. Vagrancy laws were a common fixture in the aftermath of emancipation throughout the new world.[123] And nearly every southern state passed some kind of law against "vagrancy" (an offense encompassing a potentially wide range of behavior). Although the northern press and many federal and military authorities castigated the Black Codes, vagrancy laws specifically were not a new departure, as both the Union army and the Freedmen's Bureau had already established similar restrictions on the black population.[124]

Typically, vagrancy laws required freed blacks to carry proof of employment and to be under contract by some set date at the beginning of the year, and they provided that blacks convicted as "vagrants" work off their fines in lieu of payment. Vagrancy laws restricted the labor-market mobility of blacks and prevented them from negotiating for better employment conditions. As Du Bois explains, "To make the best labor contracts, Negroes must leave the old plantations and seek better terms; but if caught in search of work, and thus unemployed and without a home, this was vagrancy, and the victim could be whipped and sold into slavery."[125] Black artisans and the like, whose occupations did not guarantee regular employment, could also be arrested as vagrants and indentured to an employer under the Black Codes. Vagrancy laws functioned to restrict access to alternative occupations and to funnel blacks back into the plantation labor market.

The objective of vagrancy laws was to bind blacks to the plantation system and to ensure that emancipation did not alter their status as a dependent agricultural labor force. Vagrancy laws gave legislative expression to the widely held belief among southern whites that "the negro exists for the special object of raising cotton, rice and sugar *for the whites.*"[126] In principle, with the abolition of slavery, black laborers were free to contract with whomever they wanted; but the enactment of vagrancy laws challenged their freedom to opt out of the plantation system altogether. Vagrancy laws presupposed that, while not the possession of any particular planter, black laborers did belong to the planter class as a whole. By denying freedpeople the right to *refuse* to contract, vagrancy laws threatened to undermine the power blacks possessed by virtue of their capacity to withhold their labor from the plantation market.

Southern legislatures also enacted enticement statutes and laws curbing the practices of emigrant agents. Though widely condemned as "an offense against neighborhood courtesy,"[127] the enticement of the employees of fellow planters was common enough to be regarded as the principle cause of contract breaches on the part of the black labor force.[128] Enticement laws and emigrant agent laws addressed this problem by restricting the rights of employers and their agents to lure or "entice" employees already under contract to other planters. By reducing competition among employers and limiting the bargaining power of black laborers, these measures gave planters some assurance that the labor force would remain on the plantation throughout the season. Enticement laws were one among several means through which planters sought to reestablish their proprietary control over the black labor force.[129]

The Black Codes also included breach-of-contract

laws. By making it a criminal offense to violate the terms of a contract, such laws gave planters legal recourse to enforce diligence and obedience from their labor force. The Florida law, for example, sanctioned the punishment of black laborers for "willful disobedience of orders, wanton impudence, or disrespect to his employer or his authorized agent, failure to perform the work assigned to him, idleness, or abandonment of the premises."[130] The Louisiana code contained similar stipulations:

> Bad work shall not be allowed. Failing to obey reasonable orders, neglect of duty, and leaving home without permission will be deemed disobedience; impudence, swearing, or indecent language to, or in the presence of the employer, his family, or agent, or quarreling and fighting with one another shall be deemed disobedience.[131]

The language of breach-of-contract laws makes it clear that their intent was not just to enforce adherence to contractual obligations, but also to ensure the continued obedience and subordination of the black labor force.

Most southern states also enacted apprenticeship laws, described by an agent of the Freedmen's Bureau as "an attempt to reestablish slavery under the mild name of apprenticeship."[132] These laws allowed for the children of parents unable to provide for them to be bound to an employer, with their previous master having first claim. Precisely such a provision was included in a bill brought before the Alabama legislature in 1865, entitled "An act to regulate the relation of master and apprentice as relates to freedmen, free Negroes, and mulattoes." This particular act was not initially approved by the governor, though he subsequently signed a similar version.[133] The objective of some planters in apprenticing children, it appears, was less to possess the children than to coerce their parents into returning to the plantation.[134] In any case, to many blacks, particularly parents with children abducted under this law, the apprenticeship system seemed little more than legalized kidnapping.[135]

Some provisions enacted by southern legislatures were more specific to individual states. The Mississippi Black Codes, for example, prohibited blacks from renting or leasing land outside of the town limits, thus hindering their efforts to become independent farmers. The South Carolina legislature deliberately restricted blacks' access to alternative occupations by establishing prohibitively expensive licensing fees and other discriminatory certification requirements. In other areas of the South, blacks had to gain written permission from their employers in order to leave the plantations.[136]

The Black Codes were relatively short-lived. In Mississippi and South Carolina, where especially harsh and blatantly discriminatory laws were passed, military commanders almost immediately declared the Black Codes void. And in 1866, the Freedmen's Bureau nullified at least some of the provisions contained in the Black Codes. Nevertheless, the historical significance of the Black Codes and their impact on labor relations in the postwar South should not be underestimated. First, legislation similar to that of the Black Codes—rewritten minus explicit references to race—remained in effect throughout the South, shifting the locus of discrimination from written law to its enforcement and prosecution. Second, authorities responsible for defending freedpeople from discriminatory legislation, most importantly Freedmen's Bureau officials, were too few in number to provide adequate protection and were not always themselves fully committed to ensuring justice for freed blacks. Thus, local enforcement of the Black Codes persisted even after they were enjoined by federal authorities.[137] Third, though Radical Reconstruction brought about the abrogation of the Black Codes as originally enacted, the new laws passed in state legislatures in 1867 and 1868, at least with respect to labor relations, represented only modifications of the sorts of laws making up the Black Codes.[138] Indeed, according to one study, the Black Codes contained "in embryo . . . the system of involuntary servitude" that persisted in the South throughout the nineteenth century.[139] Finally, as John Hope Franklin points out, the Black Codes "reflect, better than dozens of statements of sentiment or feeling, the actual attitude of the Southern leaders toward Negroes at the end of the war."[140] The Black Codes offer ample evidence of planters' designs and their determination to recreate a system of forced labor in southern agriculture.

Yet the Black Codes were by no means the effective instrument of labor control planters hoped they would be. By reinstating some of the harshest features of slavery and by revealing so clearly the intentions of planters, the Black Codes may have actually hardened the resistance of freedpeople to plantation labor, thereby contributing to the very problem they were designed to alleviate.[141] Moreover, that planters were forced to seek a political solution to their labor problems gives striking evidence of the precariousness of their economic position and the effectiveness of black opposition to the reestablishment of the plantation system. The failure of planters to create a substitute for slavery through legislative measures, however, did not stop them from trying to realize the same objective through alternative means.

The Ku Klux Klan and Labor Control

Black people in the South were the frequent targets of violence in the years after the war. The willingness of southern whites to resort to terror as a means of enforcing the continued subordination of blacks is one measure of how high the stakes were in the postwar economic reconstruction. With the rise of the Ku Klux Klan, the use of violence and intimidation assumed a more organized and systematic form. While groups similar to the Klan had already appeared during and immediately after the war—"Regulators," for example—the Ku Klux Klan proper, though perhaps founded as early as 1865, became active only after 1867, coinciding with the repeal of the Black Codes, the advent of Radical Reconstruction, and the breakdown of the gang-labor system.

Most studies have found that the Ku Klux Klan arose from primarily political motives and that its principal objective was to restore "white supremacy." The targets of Klan violence in the postwar years were, for the most part, Republicans and black people determined to exercise their rights as citizens.[142] Yet the extent to which the terror of the Klan was also used as a means of enforcing the economic subordination of blacks and maintaining the plantation system should not be overlooked.[143] Two studies—by Jonathan Wiener and J.C.A. Stagg—provide convincing evidence that, at least on some occasions and in some parts of the South, the Klan served the interests of the planter class and functioned as an instrument of labor control.[144]

Wiener's study of Reconstruction in Alabama shows that the social composition and objectives of the Klan in the postwar South varied by region. In the hill country, confirming the more traditional interpretation, the Klan consisted largely of poor whites banding together in order to drive blacks out of the area. In the black belt, on the other hand, Wiener argues that the Klan "was an instrument of the planter class," which played a significant role "in creating and perpetuating the South's repressive plantation labor system."[145] The Klan in the black belt resorted to terror in order to prevent blacks from leaving the area, to restrict their movements off the plantations, to keep them at work and under the control of planters, and to limit their access to economic alternatives outside of the plantation system, especially renting or purchasing land. According to a local lawyer cited by Wiener, the Klan in this region of Alabama was "intended principally for the negroes who failed to work."[146] Klan violence, insofar as it functioned as a means of labor control, operated as an extralegal alternative to the Black Codes. A judge in Alabama reported that the rise of the Klan in that state was a response to the inability of planters to "control the labor . . . through the courts"; planters intended to "compel them [freedpeople] to do by fear what they were unable to make them do by law."[147]

Stagg also emphasizes the relationship between Klan violence and labor control. Like Wiener, Stagg argues that well-to-do whites, including planters, were active organizers and participants in the vigilante activities of the Klan.[148] Furthermore, Stagg denies that the Klan had exclusively political motives or targets. Rather, Stagg maintains that the pattern of violence in South Carolina supports the interpretation that the Klan arose in response to the severe labor problems experienced by planters. Planters resorted to violence and intimidation because they were unhappy with existing land-tenure arrangements, which gave them insufficient control over the labor force. Stagg reports that in one mass arrest for "white-capping" (vigilante violence) many Klansmen confessed that they joined to try to keep blacks working on the plantations.[149] Even the apparently political objectives pursued by the Klan, Stagg contends, were rooted in economic concerns. Planters, he argues, came to believe that they could not resolve their agricultural problems without gaining control over political institutions; thus, the manifest political motives of the Klan often had an economic basis. "In this situation violence could become an 'easy' solution for the planters' dilemma. It could intimidate the negro both as a voter and as a worker and would leave the planter in undisputed control on the farm and in the county court-house."[150]

The threat of Klan violence represented one more obstacle to freedpeople's efforts to overturn the plantation system and to achieve independence from the planter class. Yet Klan violence was by no means altogether successful and could even be counterproductive. Though intended to keep blacks on the plantation and ensure their subordination, Klan violence sometimes had the opposite effect, encouraging freedpeople to flee their employers and seek out a less hostile environment. Thus the Klan, like the Black Codes, did not function as an altogether effective means of labor control. Fearing they might drive off an already scarce labor supply, planters had to be circumspect in their reliance on violence.[151] Furthermore, the interests of planters, after all, required that their one and only labor force not be unduly harmed. Given the need to transform freedpeople into useful laborers, cruelty to them, admonished the Richmond *Times* in 1865, "would be just as absurd a piece of inhumanity as cruelty to a horse or an ox."[152]

Labor Contracts and Labor Control

Postbellum labor contracts were more than just a means for matching employees to employers and defining their respective rights and obligations. Plantation contracts typically included numerous provisions explicitly designed to reestablish the absolute authority of the planter.[153] John De Forest, a Union officer and agent of the Freedmen's Bureau, found that planters seemed incapable of understanding that work "could be accomplished without some prodigious binding and obligating of the hireling to the employer. Contracts which were brought to me for approval contained all sorts of ludicrous provisions."[154] Through detailed contract stipulations and various "ludicrous provisions," planters sought to ensure the continued subservience of the black labor force.

Some planters tried to ease the burden of emancipation and avoid the trouble of negotiating annual agreements by persuading or coercing freedpeople into signing lifetime contracts.[155] A South Carolina planter, at the end of the 1865 season, demanded that his former slaves, who had worked for him during the previous year, agree to lifetime contracts. When four refused, the planter drove them off without pay; two of the four were killed by armed guards sent out to retrieve them, another escaped, and the fourth, a woman, was recaptured and tortured.[156] Even when resorting to force, though, planters were generally unsuccessful in getting freedpeople to sign lifetime contracts, and the Freedmen's Bureau refused to approve such agreements.

Planters also sought to augment their control over the labor force through the payment schedule written into the typical contract. In an effort to decrease the "uncertainty" of labor, planters dispensed only partial payment during the year; this compelled laborers to remain at work until the end of the season to receive their full wages. Where share rather than cash wages were used, such contractual stipulations were, of course, unnecessary. Freedpeople, naturally, opposed deferred-payment systems, partly because they wanted their earnings as they were due them, but also to be free to seek better employment at any time during the course of the year. Moreover, numerous freedpeople at the end of the 1865 and 1866 seasons had been cheated out of their wages and were understandably skeptical about promises of payment at some later date.

The detailed provisions included in postwar labor contracts show how planters intended to use labor agreements to regain control over the labor force.[157] The contract entered in to by Alonzo Mial and twenty-seven freedpeople in January 1866 was fairly typical. This agreement required the labor force to "rise at day brake" and begin working "by Sun rise, and work till Sun set," and longer when necessary. Employees were obligated to "work faithfully" and be respectful in their deportment. Laborers were also held responsible for loss or damage of tools and were subject to fines for absence without permission. The Mial contract also stipulated that half the employees' wages be withheld until the end of the season.[158] The 1866 contract between the South Carolina planter Peter Bascott and forty-one freedpeople for the year 1866 included similar provisions. This contract obligated laborers "to conduct themselves faithfully, honestly, civilly: & diligently to perform all labor." Bascott specified daily tasks, and, like Mial, levied fines for missed work and included provisions relating to the care of tools and residences.[159] A contract written by a Georgia planter in 1866 likewise directed workers "to labor faithfully . . . and to obey all orders."[160] The employees on the plantation of a South Carolina planter were contractually bound to behave "in such a manner as to gain the good will of those to whom we must always look for protection."[161] Other postbellum contracts stipulated that employees be "prompt and faithful," exhibit "perfect obedience," refrain from consuming alcohol, and obey the orders of all overseers. Laborers were also sometimes prohibited from owning firearms, bringing guests to their quarters, and engaging in conversation in the fields.[162] Postwar labor contracts, these examples

illustrate, commonly included diverse provisions having
to do with the deportment of laborers. One economic
historian suggests, accordingly, that planters seemed "as
concerned about the 'impudence' of the freedmen as they
were about the wage rate."[163]

In a study of the agreements administered and
sanctioned by the Freedmen's Bureau for three counties in
South Carolina between 1865 and 1868, Lewis Chartock
provides an extensive analysis of postwar labor contracts.
Chartock's study is significant, not only for what it reveals
about the intentions of planters, but also for what it shows
was permitted by officials of the Freedmen's Bureau.
Generally, according to Chartock, most labor contracts
during this period were collective agreements, as was
typically the case under the gang-labor system, and contract stipulations consisted primarily of the obligations of
freedpeople rather than the responsibilities of planters.
Chartock found that contract provisions pertaining to the
behavior of employees could be sorted into three rather
indistinct groups: (1) clauses concerning work-related behavior, including provisions stipulating obedience, diligence, a respectful attitude and demeanor, hours to be
worked, the proper treatment of tools and animals, and
prohibitions against idleness, stealing, and unauthorized
absences; (2) clauses regulating the personal behavior of
employees, including stipulations prescribing politeness,
orderliness, sobriety, and "good behavior" in general; and
(3) clauses governing the behavior of laborers toward their
employers, including stipulations requiring faithfulness,
honesty, industriousness, respect, subservience, humility,
courteousness, dutifulness, and so on.[164] Indeed, Chartock
found, unexpectedly, that contracts "were used more in an
attempt to regulate freedmen's behavior than to specify
explicitly tasks that were to be performed."[165] According to
Chartock, in sum, southern planters used the labor con-

tract in order "to define a social role for freedmen which was not far removed from the status which they had occupied when they were slaves."[166] Though they afforded freedpeople some protection of their rights, labor contracts ultimately were less a symbol of blacks' entrance into the world of free labor than they were another mechanism of labor control. Planters used labor contracts to reassert the multifaceted authority they had possessed under slavery. Indeed, one contract stipulated that freedpeople were to refer to their employer as "master."[167]

The Freedmen's Bureau and Labor Control

On March 3, 1865, Congress enacted a bill creating the Bureau of Refugees, Freedmen, and Abandoned Lands (the Freedmen's Bureau).[168] The original mandate of the Freedmen's Bureau instructed it to supply food, clothing, and other provisions to needy victims of wartime dislocation, both black and white. More importantly, the bureau was granted the authority to provide forty-acre plots of land to freed blacks. In May of 1865, however, President Andrew Johnson issued an amnesty proclamation, which restored the property rights of former rebels and returned to its original owners most of the captured and abandoned property under the jurisdiction of the Freedmen's Bureau. Johnson's restoration policy deprived the bureau of the land necessary to provide homesteads for newly emancipated slaves.[169] In the absence of any immediate prospect of freedpeople's becoming independent landholders, and concerned about economic and social disorder, the Freedmen's Bureau turned to the contract system, which had already been adopted in occupied regions of the South during the war. By deciding to encourage planters and freedpeople to agree to annual written contracts, the Freedmen's Bureau tacitly acquiesced to the continuation of the plantation system.

The most important obstacle to the implementation
of the annual contract system was the expectation among
freedpeople that they were to receive grants of land from
the government. Bureau agents tried to persuade blacks to
forget about the dream of "forty acres and a mule" and to
return to the plantations. Through coercion and inducement—the precise combination of which varied with the
sympathies of the local agent—the bureau prevailed upon
freedpeople to agree to year-long labor contracts. Bureau
agents sometimes used their prerogative to withhold
rations as leverage for compelling blacks to return to the
plantations.[170]

The bureau also assumed responsibility for supervising negotiations between planters and laborers, approving
contracts, and enforcing the obligations agreed to. The
bureau set forth only the most general guidelines for
contractual agreements. The most conscientious agents,
however, tried to ensure that contracts contained no
blatantly inequitable provisions, that employees received
a reasonably fair market rate of compensation (though no
minimum wage was set), and that both parties lived up to
the terms of the agreement. The Freedmen's Bureau
served as a job-information and employment agency as
well. In response to shifting patterns of supply and
demand, the bureau facilitated the relocation of labor and
sometimes provided transportation. By thus encouraging
labor mobility (though not always with the voluntary
cooperation of those being relocated), the bureau sought
to establish a prevailing wage throughout the South.[171]
Though there was considerable local discretion on how
this might be handled, bureau agents also assisted planters in maintaining stability and order on the plantations
and in dealing with problems of insubordination and
disobedience among the labor force.[172] The Freedmen's
Bureau did not give free reign to the employer however;

many bureau agents genuinely tried to ensure that freedpeople were treated fairly. But insofar as it served to maintain the plantation system and enforce annual contracts, the Freedmen's Bureau facilitated labor control and buttressed the authority of the planter.

However much the contract system made possible the continuation of plantation agriculture, most planters still regarded this arrangement as an objectionable departure from slavery. And however much the Freedmen's Bureau served as an instrument of labor control, most planters still deeply resented its presence in the South. By trying to impose an altogether unworkable free-labor system in southern agriculture, planters argued, the Freedmen's Bureau infringed upon their ability to discipline and manage the labor force effectively. The Freedmen's Bureau, planters protested, interfered "with the regular operations of labor."[173] To the extent that "the regular operations of labor" implied the absolute authority of planters, this was no doubt true. Although they expected blacks to work diligently and obediently, bureau agents sought to protect them from violence, physical intimidation, corporal punishment, and reenslavement.

The presence of the Freedmen's Bureau, therefore, confronted planters with a competing source of authority, and threatened their singular command over the labor force; if they felt they were treated unjustly, black laborers could, in principle, appeal to bureau agents, who might shield them from the arbitrary authority of the planter. Because it sometimes acted on the complaints of freedpeople, southern whites regarded the Freedmen's Bureau as a pernicious influence on relations between blacks and whites, and they attributed much of the conflict between planters and freedpeople to its unwarranted interference. A South Carolina judge, in 1866, articulated this criticism of the bureau:

> We are greatly embarrassed in the management of our
> domestic affairs by the presence and interference of the
> Freedmen's Bureau. I believe if the difficult and delicate
> problem of organizing the labor of our former slaves was
> entirely left to us, who once owned the freedmen,
> understanding their character and feel for their condition,
> things would be so managed as to enable us, very soon, to
> regain their confidence and to infuse into their minds a
> feeling of security and protection. . . . But, as matters now
> stand, distrust is engendered, the freedmen are taught to be
> suspicious of their old masters—to believe that their
> interests are antagonistic—and encouraged to distrust their
> counsel, advice and aid; all of which would soon cease, if
> this interested and prejudiced Bureau was removed.[174]

This illustrates a common theme. Southern whites liked
to believe that were it not for the incitement of northern
intruders like the Freedmen's Bureau, freedpeople would
willingly submit to the "counsel, advice and aid" of their
old masters.

Not all planters, however, objected to the presence
of the Freedmen's Bureau; a few freely admitted the role
played by the bureau in controlling the labor force, and
many more were happy to accept the assistance provided
by the bureau, even if unwilling to acknowledged it
openly.[175] Charles Stearns, a northern planter, conceded
that the Freedmen's Bureau was an invaluable resource in
managing the plantation labor force:

> For my part I can safely say, that I relied upon the
> Freedmen's Bureau, fully as much to enable me to govern
> my hands, as they did to enable them to protect
> themselves against my rapacity. I do not know as I could
> have successfully managed my own plantation if it had not
> been for this power in reserve; to whom I could appeal if
> my hands failed to comply with my orders.[176]

Occasionally, at least in the case of especially accommodating agents, the bureau received praise even from native planters. In Georgia, for example, one planter acknowledged that the local bureau agent "lets you do pretty much as you liked. They had a mighty good man there—let you whip a nigger if you liked."[177]

The Freedmen's Bureau never set forth a clear and unambiguous policy with respect to the regulation of labor relations in southern agriculture. Thus, whether the bureau in practice sided with the interests of freedpeople or the interests of planters depended partly on the predilections of local agents. This worked to the disadvantage of blacks. Bureau agents were likely to be more sympathetic to the interests of planters than to those of freedpeople. Even bureau agents from the North, after all, still had much more in common with their defeated enemies than with black people just released from bondage; and many shared the opinion held by most southern whites that blacks were an inferior race destined to remain a subordinate agricultural labor force. Furthermore, social pressures led many local bureau agents to accommodate to the interests of planters. A decent existence in a southern community was not easily attained by the local agent who antagonized its leading citizens. The rewards to agents for diligently advancing the interests of freedpeople were few indeed, and even the most responsible agents found it difficult not to follow the path of least resistance.[178] And by no means were all bureau agents responsible; some accepted their positions simply for the money, some were no less hostile to blacks than the most prejudiced of southern whites, and some were actively engaged in planting themselves. According to the reckoning of one observer, about half of the local bureau agents were "wholly unfit for the work entrusted to them."[179]

Political constraints and practical difficulties also limited the ability of the Freedmen's Bureau to advance the interests and protect the rights of freedpeople. Bureau agents sympathetic to the desires of the former slaves found themselves frustrated in their efforts by the president's commitment to rapid reconstruction and, especially, by his restoration of southern lands. Condemned to carry out the program of the federal government, sympathetic agents simply lacked the means to serve the best interests of freedpeople. Those who resisted the direction of federal policy found themselves dismissed, transferred, reprimanded, and, in at least one case, court-martialed.[180] The failure of the Freedmen's Bureau also resulted from the practical difficulties faced by a relatively small group of officials with few resources trying to assist millions of black people spread throughout the southern states.[181] The bureau suffered not only from an inadequate supply of manpower, but also from the hostility and opposition of local enforcement agencies, which remained largely under the control of unsympathetic southern whites.[182]

The bureau did not originally consider the contract system as a permanent labor arrangement for southern agriculture.[183] But bureau officials were also hesitant to pursue alternatives that might have enhanced black independence. Planters, for example, could have been pressed to rent land to freedpeople; or annual contracts could have been dispensed with altogether, allowing blacks freedom of labor mobility throughout the entire year.[184] Bureau officials, however, were worried about planter opposition and were apprehensive about the disruption that might result from pursuing such alternatives. Historian Donald Nieman describes the dilemma faced by the Freedmen's Bureau: "The contract system offered stability and order at the expense of blacks' independence and self-reliance; abandonment of the contract system offered blacks greater independence at the expense of stability and order."[185] The bureau opted for stability and order. The decision to implement the contract system, however, did not suggest simply a bias toward order, but a bias toward a particular order where the status of blacks as a subordinate plantation labor force remained unchanged.

By the end of 1865, then, the Freedmen's Bureau was promoting the labor contract as the means through which former slaves would be introduced into the world of free labor. The contractual relationship of employer to employee would replace the property relationship of master to slave. Once committed to the contract system, the primary task of the Freedmen's Bureau was to induce freedpeople to return to the plantations and labor diligently under the supervision of their former masters. Bureau officials throughout the South propagated a new message to replace that of "forty acres and a mule": in the words of commissioner Howard, "freedom means work."[186] A circular written toward the end of 1865, by Orlando Brown, an assistant commissioner, illustrates how far the terms of freedom for blacks were set by the requirements of the contract system:

> The principal function of this bureau is not to supply a channel through which government aid or private charity shall be dispensed, but to make the freedmen a self-supporting class of free laborers, who shall understand the necessity of steady employment, and the responsibility of providing for themselves and their families. Where employment is offered on terms that will provide for the comfortable subsistence of the laborers, removing them from the vices of idleness and from dependence on charity, they should be treated as vagrants if they do not accept it. . . . While the freedmen must and will be protected in their

rights, they must be required to meet these first and most essential conditions of a state of freedom, a visible means of support, and fidelity to contracts.[187]

The conception of freedom promoted by the bureau emphasized less the rights of freedpeople than their obligations and responsibilities—steady employment and fidelity to labor contracts. This vision of freedom contrasted radically with that held by blacks themselves, for whom freedom implied independence and landownership. The very terms of black freedom, as defined by the ideology of free labor, confirmed their status as a permanently subordinate labor force.

The function of the Freedmen's Bureau as an instrument of labor control, therefore, derived to a great extent from its commitment to the free-labor ideology, embodied in the contract system. Eric Foner's assessment of the Freedmen's Bureau provides a useful point of departure for examining this issue. Foner argues that

> the Freedmen's Bureau was not, in reality, the agent of the planters, nor was it precisely the agent of the former slaves. It can best be understood as the agent of the northern free labor ideology; its main concern was to put into operation a viable free labor system in the South. To the extent that this meant putting freedmen back to work on the plantations, the Bureau's interests coincided with those of the planters. To the extent that the Bureau demanded for the freedmen the rights to which northern laborers were accustomed, it meant an alliance with the blacks.[188]

However, in promoting the free-labor ideology, the bureau, while not the *agent* of planters, did in fact serve the *interests* of planters as against those of former slaves.

Consider the fundamental asymmetry in how the

policy of the Freedmen's Bureau, guided by the ideology of free labor, related to the conflicting objectives and class interests of planters and freedpeople. Planters sought to maintain the plantation system and gang labor, while blacks sought independence and land of their own. The Freedmen's Bureau, committed to getting blacks back to work on the plantations, resolved this conflict entirely to the advantage of planters. This was the case, not because of any explicit identity of interests, but rather because the bureau's adherence to the free-labor ideology happened to coincide with planters' commitment to the plantation system much more so than with blacks' interest in becoming independent farmers. No doubt the bureau often acted on the behalf of freedpeople, but it acted on the behalf of freedpeople conceived as a subordinate agricultural labor force, not as a people struggling to gain independence. The bureau served the interests of both planters and freedpeople, but only as those interests conformed to the requirements of the plantation system, an economic arrangement that served their respective interests quite unequally. Indeed, the policy of the Freedmen's Bureau sometimes seemed to be so much on the side of the planter class that some freedpeople, its ostensible benefactors, criticized the presence of the bureau and advocated its withdrawal from the South.[189] In what was perhaps an overly harsh judgment, the New Orleans *Tribune* in 1867 accused the agents of the Freedmen's Bureau of being "the planter's guards, and nothing else."[190]

Conclusion

Planters believed that only by maintaining the gang-labor system could they ensure the rigorous control over the black labor force that plantation agriculture required. Proof of the strength of planters' commitment to the plantation system and gang labor can be found both in their words and in their actions, in what planters said about the requirements of profitable agricultural production with free black labor and in what they did to try to ensure the continued subordination of blacks. Planters believed that wages were an insufficient inducement and that blacks would not work unless compelled; they repeatedly asserted that plantation agriculture could not survive on the basis of free black labor and that strict controls over the labor force were necessary. What planters said about the labor question was reflected also in their deeds: in the unwillingness of many planters to accede to the abolition of slavery, in their use of force and deception to maintain their former slaves on the plantations, in their efforts to organize employer cartels, in their call for the enactment of legislative measures to control black labor, in their reliance on long-term, detailed labor contracts, and in their resort to organizations like the Ku Klux Klan as a means of maintaining control over the labor force.

The determination of planters to create an alternative system of forced labor to take the place of slavery was more than matched by the determination of freedpeople to resist the restoration of the antebellum plantation system. The postwar scarcity of labor made it possible for blacks to mount effective opposition to the plantation system. Labor scarcity opened up alternative opportunities to freedpeople, enhanced their bargaining power, and afforded them the leverage to make demands of their own, as well as to resist the demands of their employers. The presence of northern authorities in the South also contributed to the effectiveness of black resistance. Though military officials and agents of the Freedmen's Bureau functioned to facilitate labor control, they also served to guarantee freedpeople certain minimal rights. Thus planters were constrained in the sorts of responses they could adopt in the presence of black recalcitrance. Though the Freedmen's Bureau shared the planters' interest in maintaining the plantation system, it restricted the use of the coercive power that was perhaps necessary for the preservation of that system. Planters in the postwar South, consequently, were unable to contain effectively the resistance of blacks. Despite their efforts to restore a forced-labor system in southern agriculture, planters found it increasingly difficult to resist black pressure to abandon plantation agriculture and gang labor.

Chapter 3 · Forty
Acres
and
a Mule

In October of 1865, the freedpeople of
Edisto Island, South Carolina, learned that the land they
had farmed during the war and now regarded as their own
was about to be restored to its rebel owners. They sent a
letter of protest to General O. O. Howard, commissioner of
the Freedmen's Bureau. "Land monopoly is injurious to the
advancement of the course of freedom," wrote a committee
of three, "and if Government Does not make some
provision by which we as Freedmen can obtain A Homestead, we have Not bettered our condition."[1] This judgment reflected the sentiment of former slaves throughout
the South. Most freedpeople recognized that in order to
safeguard their newly won freedom they needed access to
means of subsistence independent of white landowners.
The possibility of landownership was the key to whether
they would gain independence or remain subservient to the
authority of their former masters.

For planters, on the other hand, black landownership
represented the paramount threat to the plantation system. Planters recognized, reported a Union army officer in
1865, "that if negroes are not allowed to acquire property

or become landholders, they must ultimately return to plantation labor, and work for wages . . . and they feel that this kind of slavery will be better than none at all."[2] Alternatively, if blacks were able to secure an autonomous economic existence, planters would be denied an exploitable labor force and the system of plantation agriculture would collapse. What was at stake in the ensuing conflict, therefore—to repeat a point made in the previous chapter—was the very nature of the class relations that were to structure the southern economy. Were freedpeople to become independent producers or a subordinate agricultural labor force?

Because of what it might have meant for the fate of freedpeople and the future of the southern economy, black landownership was one of the most significant possibilities pursued in the aftermath of slavery. This possibility shaped the aspirations and behavior of blacks after the war, and it inspired their resistance to plantation labor. That the vast majority of freedpeople were ultimately unable to realize the dream of "forty acres and a mule" in no way diminishes the historical significance of this possibility. The struggle of blacks to obtain land, their concomitant resistance to less desirable alternatives, and the conflict between planters and freedpeople over the issue of black independence contributed decisively to the course of events that eventually culminated in sharecropping.[3]

Federal Policy and Black Landownership

Both during and after the Civil War, the opportunity for blacks to become landholders was largely in the hands of the federal government. A brief survey of government policy and congressional legislation concerning southern lands, therefore, is necessary to assess the possibility of black landownership.

On August 6, 1861, Congress passed the first confiscation act, which rendered subject to forfeiture all property used in aiding the rebellion.[4] Lincoln permitted only a conservative interpretation of this act, though, and it pertained less to landed property than to captured slaves. Congress passed the second confiscation act on July 17, 1862. This act extended the provisions of the first by authorizing the confiscation of all Confederate property and freedom for the slaves of all persons engaged in rebellion. Under pressure from Lincoln, Congress added an explanatory provision declaring that no confiscated property would be forfeited beyond the life of its present owner. The government, therefore, gained no clear and permanent title to property seized under this act. In any case, of the southern lands under federal jurisdiction at the end of the war, only a small proportion was acquired under the provisions of the confiscation acts. These two measures, consequently, did not provide a practical means through which freedpeople might gain homesteads. Nor, of course, was this the intention of Congress; military and political considerations motivated the passage of the confiscation acts, not the desire to provide land to emancipated slaves. However, the first and second confiscation acts did have symbolic and practical significance. They represented an important initial step in the challenge to property rights in the South, and they brought the issue of confiscation and redistribution onto the political agenda.

A different classification of land was seized under the June 7, 1862, act "for the collection of direct taxes in insurrectionary districts within the United States." This act authorized the forfeiture of land for nonpayment of taxes and provided that it be sold at public auction. Land purchased under the provisions of the tax act, unlike that acquired under the confiscation acts, carried the permanent transfer of property titles.[5]

In 1863, the federal government seized 76,775 acres of land in occupied South Carolina for nonpayment of taxes. A commission established to dispose of this land reserved 60,296 acres for the government and put up for sale the remaining 16,479 acres. Edward Philbrick, representing a group of Boston businessmen, purchased approximately 8,000 acres, and a group of blacks, collectively, bought 2,000 acres. In 1864, most of the 60,000 acres of land previously reserved were also offered for sale. The government set aside 16,000 acres for exclusive purchase by blacks at a special rate of $1.25 per acre. Urged on by the sympathetic Union general Rufus Saxton, blacks tried to acquire most of the rest, through preemption, also at the special rate, rather than having to compete for it in public auction (where it was eventually sold at an average of $11 per acre). The tax commissioners responsible for supervising the land sales, after enlisting the support of Salmon P. Chase, Secretary of the Treasury, refused to accept the claims of preemptors though, and blacks lost another opportunity to acquire land. In the end, blacks were able to purchase only 2,276 acres at the special $1.25 rate, and another 470 acres were bought by a collective of blacks in competitive bidding.

The federal government gained possession of a more substantial amount of southern land under the provisions of the captured and abandoned property act passed by Congress on March 12, 1863.[6] In 1865, the Treasury Department, which exercised control over captured and abandoned land during the war, turned over 850,000 acres to the jurisdiction of the newly created Freedmen's Bureau.[7] The bill establishing the Freedmen's Bureau, passed on March 3, 1865, appeared to offer a genuine opportunity for blacks to acquire land. The section of the Freedmen's Bureau bill most relevant to the land question specified

> that the Commissioner, under the direction of the
> President, shall have authority to set apart, for the use of
> loyal refugees and freedmen, such tracts of land within
> the insurrectionary States as shall have been abandoned,
> or to which the United States shall have acquired title
> by confiscation or sale, or otherwise; and to every male
> citizen, whether refugee or freedmen as aforesaid, there
> shall be assigned not more than forty acres of such land,
> and the person to whom it was so assigned shall be
> protected in the use and enjoyment of the land for the
> term of three years at an annual rate. . . . At the end of said
> term, or at any time during said term, the occupants of any
> parcels so assigned may purchase the land and receive such
> title thereto as the United States can convey.[8]

This bill did not authorize outright grants of land, but it did hold out the promise that freedpeople would be able to rent land and have the subsequent opportunity to purchase it.

Yet the Freedmen's Bureau had jurisdiction over insufficient acreage to provide forty-acre homesteads to the thousands of blacks expecting to become landholders. Even if the bureau had been free to distribute to former slaves all of the land originally in its possession, forty-acre plots could have been provided to only slightly more than twenty thousand families, far fewer than the number hoping to set up independent homesteads.[9] This would have still constituted a promising beginning though. In fact, however, the bureau was not free to allot to blacks even the relatively limited acreage under its control. The captured and abandoned property act did not give the United States government guaranteed title to the land, for property seized under this act was subject to restoration upon confirmation of the loyalty of its owner.

The fate of land titles in the possession of the Freedmen's Bureau was ultimately decided on May 29,

1865, when President Johnson issued his general amnesty proclamation, restoring the property rights of most rebel landowners. The restoration of southern lands thwarted any hope that the Freedmen's Bureau would become an instrument of land redistribution. By the middle of 1866, of the approximately 850,000 acres of land originally under the authority of the Freedmen's Bureau, somewhat over half had already been restored, and most of the rest was returned to its original owners during the next couple of years.[10] Only in the early months of its existence did it appear as though the Freedmen's Bureau might become a means for the realization of the possibility of black landownership.

The policy introduced by General William T. Sherman in the occupied territory of South Carolina, Georgia, and Florida presented blacks with the most promising opportunity to acquire land.[11] Along its march to the sea, Sherman's army attracted a large number of refugee slaves. Their presence posed difficult management problems and interfered with military operations. On January 12, 1865, General Sherman and Secretary of War Stanton conferred with a local group of black ministers in an effort to arrive at a practical solution to the refugee issue. That meeting resulted in the enactment of "Special Field Order No. 15," which Sherman issued four days later. The significance of this order, as LaWanda Cox emphasizes, is that it was one of the few instances of federal policy that originated specifically from aspirations articulated by black people themselves.[12]

Administered by General Rufus Saxton, Special Field Order No. 15—as requested by the black representatives with whom Sherman and Stanton had met—established a reserve set apart for the exclusive settlement of refugee slaves. This reserve consisted of "the islands from Charleston south, the abandoned rice-fields along the rivers for thirty miles back from the sea, and the country bordering the Saint John's River, Fla." The order further stipulated that each family was allowed to "have a plot of not more than forty acres of tillable ground . . . in the possession of which land the military will afford them protection until such time as they can protect themselves or until Congress shall regulate their title."[13] For the time being, blacks were given "possessory" titles. News of Sherman's policy spread hope among slaves throughout much of the South that they would gain possession of their former masters' lands.

By June of 1865, under the auspices of Special Field Order No. 15, approximately forty thousand freedpeople had settled on over four hundred thousand acres of land. By the end of the summer, however, the former owners, with special presidential pardons in hand, were demanding restoration of their property.[14] Commissioner Howard and other Freedmen's Bureau officials resisted at first; they hoped that by delaying restoration congressional Radicals would gain time to validate the possessory titles to the land held by the black homesteaders on Sherman's reservation. But the president insisted upon the immediate restoration of southern lands, including those encompassed by Special Field Order No. 15, and commanded Howard to carry out his instructions.

While the Freedmen's Bureau finally acceded to the orders of the president, the freedpeople who had settled on abandoned plantations refused to acquiesce so easily. "We own this land now," said one former slave to the previous owner of the plantation. "Put it out of your head that it will ever be yours again."[15] In some cases, black landholders refused to leave when ordered to do so and armed themselves to prevent eviction. During the early months of 1866, however, under military supervision, blacks were forced to give up possession of the land and compelled either to work out a contract with the previous owners or to leave the area.[16]

The passage of the Southern Homestead Act in June 1866 created another avenue through which blacks might obtain land.[17] In contrast to most wartime measures, this act, sponsored by Congressman George Washington Julian, was designed explicitly to promote black landownership. In order to give blacks first access, the Southern Homestead Act restricted homesteading by former rebels until 1867; it also limited to eighty the number of acres that could be claimed by any single person, thus deterring speculation and encouraging settlement by small farmers. Freedpeople gained little though from the provision restricting access to homesteads until 1867. The southern states were not immediately prepared to begin administering the Homestead Act; information about available land had to be obtained, surveys taken, maps drawn, and land offices established—and all of this had to be done within six months if freedpeople were to enjoy privileged access. Most states were unable to get under way this quickly; Mississippi did not open up a land office until 1868!

The public domain in the states of Florida, Louisiana, Mississippi, Alabama, and Arkansas comprised almost fifty million acres of land—enough in principle to allow the majority of freedpeople to become independent landholders. The Homestead Act, therefore, appeared to provide a means for blacks to acquire land of their own, without requiring the confiscation of the southern plantations. That it managed to circumvent the controversial issue of confiscation explains how the Homestead Act, in contrast to other land-reform legislation, gained sufficient congressional support. The problem with this plan, however, was that much of the land in the public domain was not suitable for farming; planters already owned most of the quality arable land. The land available for homesteading was often heavily wooded or otherwise of poor quality and, though valuable perhaps, could not be adequately exploited without costly initial improvement, which was economically impossible for the vast majority of freedpeople. Most prospective black landowners preferred to settle on already improved land, where they could begin supporting themselves right away.

Most freedpeople, after weighing the advantages and disadvantages, did not regard the possibility of homesteading as an appealing or practical option. Besides requiring extensive supplies and a stake large enough to last until the land began producing, homesteading also entailed expensive transportation costs. Moreover, in order to take up homesteading, freedpeople would have to uproot their families, move to remote areas with uncertain opportunities, and expose themselves to violence from whites opposed to black people's owning land. Finally, because many freedpeople were bound to year-long labor contracts and subject to legal and extralegal sanctions against vagrancy, even those blacks who might have considered homesteading found it difficult to take advantage of the opportunity. Though more explicitly designed to promote the interests of freedpeople than wartime measures, the Southern Homestead Act fared little better in providing realistic opportunities for black landownership. Fewer than one thousand freedpeople ultimately received final certificates to land under the Southern Homestead Act.[18]

Northern Opinion on Confiscation and Redistribution

Thaddeus Stevens, a Republican congressman from Pennsylvania, maintained that land for freedpeople was "far more valuable than the immediate right of suffrage."[19] Even within his own party though, Stevens could claim little support for this position. With the exception of a handful of abolitionists and Radical Republicans, influential opinion in the North, while supporting citizenship rights for freedpeople, did not favor a policy of confiscating the plantations of the former slaveholders and redistributing them to the former slaves.[20]

The northern business press, in particular, was adamant in its opposition to such a policy. Business interests feared that the restoration of normal economic relations would be impeded by a prolonged and vindictive reconstruction, as would be entailed by any land-confiscation program. The *Commercial and Financial Chronicle*, a New York paper advertising itself as the representative of the "Industrial and Commercial Interests of the United States," repeatedly raised this issue in the years after the war. In the interest of facilitating economic reconstruction, the *Chronicle* proposed a conciliatory policy toward the South and praised President Johnson's program of rapid reconstruction and "early reconciliation of the Southern States." While accusing the president's critics of inciting economic turmoil, the *Chronicle* advocated a prompt return to normal relations through a program that endeavored to be "really practicable" rather than "ideally desirable."[21] The *Chronicle* even called for an end to debate about the policy of confiscation and redistribution. As long as political controversy left property titles in doubt, the *Chronicle* warned, labor and capital would be inhibited from immigrating to the South and economic normalization would be needlessly delayed.[22] The *Chronicle* supported a laissez-faire approach toward freedpeople and counseled against northern interference on the "Negro Question": "The power of the Union having broken down the false relations of master and slave, the true relations of the negro with the white citizen must be left to adjust themselves."[23] The freed slave, the *Chronicle* pronounced in an uncharitable tone, "will soon learn that he must work or perish."[24]

The opinions published in the pages of the *Chronicle* were typical of those promulgated by the northern business press in the immediate postwar years. Peter Kolchin, in a survey of business papers in the North between 1865 and 1868, found little support for Radical Reconstruction or for the policy of confiscation and redistribution.[25] The great majority of business papers approved of Johnson's moderate reconstruction measures, opposed his impeachment, and were decidedly hostile to the Radicals. The business press did not support special legislation to protect or assist freedpeople and expressed little concern about their fate, though business interests were naturally anxious that blacks get back to work again. Nor, certainly, did the northern business press favor the confiscation of the southern estates or grants of land to freedpeople. Northern businessmen found it difficult enough to accept, even as a war measure, the confiscation of southern slave property; there was little possibility of gaining their consent to the confiscation of landed property for the purpose of providing homesteads to freed blacks.

The business papers surveyed by Kolchin, as with the *Commercial and Financial Chronicle,* were primarily concerned that normal economic relations with the southern states be reestablished as quickly as possible. Northern businessmen, in particular, eagerly anticipated the revival of cotton production and the creation in the southern states of a market for northern goods and capital.[26] The policy of confiscation and redistribution, besides being anathema to the economic principles held sacred by northern business, presented a threat to these specific economic objectives as well. For if blacks possessed land of their own, they would certainly take up subsistence farming. This would limit both their potential as consumers of northern goods and their availability as laborers on cotton plantations.[27] The revitalization of cotton cultivation, northern financial experts predicted, might yield a further economic benefit as well. Because of its key importance as an export commodity, the renewal of cotton production might permit the United States to achieve a balance-of-trade surplus, which would make it possible to pay off the federal debt incurred during the war and to combat postwar inflation without inducing a depression.[28]

The influential ideology of free labor also weighed heavily against the policy of confiscation and redistribution.[29] Proponents of the free-labor ideology objected to land giveaways and extolled the virtues of hard work (as though this were unknown to ex-slaves). Though not opposed to black landownership in principle, they believed that freedpeople should acquire land through their own efforts—working their way up as wage laborers—and not through government charity. Even the *Nation*, a liberal periodical sympathetic to the interests of freedpeople, fell too far under the spell of the free-labor ideology to favor the policy of confiscation and redistribution.[30] For most influential interests in the North, such a policy entailed a violation of the sanctity of private property rights too grave to contemplate, no matter how traitorous the property holders in question.

The fear of the precedent that might be set by such a radical venture further militated against a policy of southern land reform. The *New York Times* warned that any justification for confiscating the land of the planter in Mississippi might also be turned against the manufacturer in Massachusetts:

> If Congress is to take cognizance of the claims of labor against capital . . . there can be no decent pretense for

> confining the task to the slave-holder of the South. It is a
> question, not of humanity, not of loyalty, but of the
> fundamental relation of industry to capital; and sooner or
> later, if begun at the South, it will find its way into the
> cities of the North. . . . An attempt to justify the
> confiscation of Southern land under the pretense of doing
> justice to the freedmen, strikes at the root of all property
> rights in both sections. It concerns Massachusetts quite as
> much as Mississippi.[31]

No revolution in class relations in the South could be undertaken without threatening the stability of class relations in the North. The fate of the southern black working class was tied to that of the northern white working class. Northern business, Du Bois observed, "did not want to appear to punish the South by taking any more of its already partly confiscated capital. They did not want to set an example of confiscation before a nation victimized by monopoly."[32] An interested observer from the South, similarly, discerned a fear among northern policymakers that "the spirit of agrarianism . . . evoked" by a policy of confiscation "will not be appeased by anything less than a general division of the spoils, involving the whole country in one common vortex of anarchy and lawlessness."[33]

Many southern plantations, both during and after the war, came under the control of northern planters and speculators, typically through leasing arrangements. This presented another obstacle to the program of confiscation and redistribution. According to historian Lawrence Powell, somewhere between twenty and fifty thousand northerners tried their hand at plantation agriculture during the war and in the Reconstruction period, most of whom by 1868 had given up and left the South.[34] Nevertheless, northern entrepreneurs had a substantial stake in southern land during the critical immediate postwar years, when the issue of confiscation and redistribution appeared on the national political agenda. The implication of this for the fate of the policy of confiscation was obvious: "Who in Congress, save the most ardent friends of the ex-slaves, would any longer take an interest in dissolving a pattern of land tenure in which northern wealth now had such a large and immediate stake?"[35] It was one thing to punish one's defeated enemies by confiscating their wealth, but quite another to trample on northern business interests just to provide former slaves with homesteads.

One is not left with the impression, after examining government policy and northern opinion with respect to the possibility of black landownership, that freedpeople had much of a real chance of acquiring homesteads through the agency of the federal government. Yet this was not how it seemed in the 1860s. The outcome of debates in the North about confiscation and redistribution and the fate of the various land policies carried out during and after the war—however they appear in retrospect—seemed quite uncertain at the time. Southern landowners certainly considered the threat to their property holdings as real. Many of the personnel in the occupying Union army and the Freedmen's Bureau also believed that a redistribution of the southern lands was a genuine possibility. And most important, freedpeople themselves were convinced that with the abolition of slavery they would receive "forty acres and a mule."

Forty Acres and a Mule

The restoration of southern lands and the effective resolution of congressional debates on confiscation and redistribution did not close the book on the possibility of black landownership. The determination of blacks to acquire land persisted, as did their opposition to the plantation system. By the end of 1865, most southern landowners probably shared the opinion of the governor of Mississippi, according to whom there was "a great deal more danger of 'Cuffee' than Thad Stevens taking over lands."[36] Blacks, both during and after the war, gave southern property holders good reason to fear this possibility. In some instances, slaves refused to wait for the victory of the Union army or for the authorization of the federal government and took it upon themselves to divide up the plantations and property of Confederate landowners.[37] A Union army officer told an audience in New York of "numerous cases where the freedmen have laid claims to the lands of their former masters and have quietly informed them that they held title under the United States government."[38] Not all freedpeople announced their claims to land so quietly. In one case, a group of former slaves led by Abalod Shigg, acting on the belief that they had a right to the land, appropriated two plantations along the Savannah River and maintained possession of them until evicted by federal troops.[39]

The source of the expression "forty acres and a mule" cannot be definitely established, although it probably originated from Sherman's Special Field Order No. 15. Whatever the derivation of this specific phrase, though, the idea that freed slaves were to receive grants of land from the government was no mere wishful fantasy. The possibility symbolized by the expression "forty acres and a mule" was confirmed to blacks by several independent sources, which helps to explain the prevalence and persistence of this belief. Many blacks became convinced they would gain possession of the property of their former masters by the federal government's wartime land programs and the rumors of confiscation they engendered. Black people's own sense of what they had a right to expect also encouraged them to embrace the slogan "forty acres and a mule." In defending their claim to the plantation lands, freedpeople sometimes invoked their own version of a labor theory of value. "We has a right to the land where we are located," explained a Virginia freedman. "Didn't we clear the land, and raise de crops ob corn, ob cotton, ob tobacco, ob rice, ob sugar, ob everything. And den didn't dem large cities in de North grow up on de cotton and de sugars and de rice dat we made?"[40] Inspired by the evident justice of such a policy, freedpeople proclaimed their expectation of "forty acres and a mule" in an increasingly confident and combative voice. "It's de white man's turn ter labor now," said a black preacher to an assembly of field hands. "He ain't got nuthin' lef' but his lan', an' de lan' won't be his'n long, fur de Guverment is gwine ter gie ter ev'ry Nigger forty acres of lan' an' a mule."[41]

Some blacks first learned that northern victory might mean the confiscation of southern plantations from the apprehensive discussions among their own masters and from public announcements about the threat of land redistribution made by Confederate leaders seeking to rally property holders around the war effort. In March of 1865, for example, the Confederate Congress, in its last address, declared that the penalty for losing the war would be "the confiscation of the estates, which would be given to their former bondsmen."[42] Public speakers in Texas also spread the warning that "if the southern people were beaten, all the lands and property would be taken from them and given to blacks."[43] Slaves, always on the lookout for clues as to how the war might affect their status, were at least as quick to pick up on this message as were southern whites.

Although federal policy toward black labor during the war contributed to the preservation of the plantation system, some of the wartime land and labor programs undertaken by northern authorities also strengthened blacks' expectations of "forty acres and a mule." Thousands of blacks, for example, farmed independently on land set aside under Sherman's Special Field Order No. 15, however precarious and short-lived their tenure. In certain other cases, blacks were permitted a relatively autonomous existence on abandoned plantations. In Davis Bend, Mississippi, for example, blacks, under the protection of the Union army, succeeded in establishing an economically self-sufficient and independently governed community, though Confederate landowners regained possession of these plantations after the war as well.[44] Elsewhere, too, for varying lengths of time, blacks during the war managed to live and work under circumstances that provided them with considerable autonomy; such experiences shaped their conception of freedom. Examples of blacks' gaining independence and land during the war, although relatively rare, were still common enough to excite the expectations of slaves throughout the South and to lend substance to the dream of "forty acres and a mule."[45]

Agents of the Freedmen's Bureau, at least during the early months of its operation, and soldiers in the invading Union army also fostered among blacks the expectation that they would receive grants of land from the government or gain possession of their home plantations.[46] One Union soldier, for example, told a freedman in Virginia to take an acre of his former master's land for each time he had been whipped.[47] Black soldiers and other black leaders played an especially important role in spreading the promise of "forty acres and a mule" and constituted a powerful force in support of land redistribution. Reports appeared in the white press throughout the South telling of black soldiers providing weapons to former slaves and inciting them to seize the plantations by force should the government renege on its promise to provide them with homesteads.[48] Southern whites, however, anxious for an excuse to rid the South of black soldiers, typically exaggerated the threat represented by their presence. While it was true that black soldiers were especially insistent in their demand for land and encouraged other black people to act likewise, there is not much evidence that they were prepared to lead a violent insurrection to gain control of the plantations.

The records of the Freedmen's Bureau and the Union army, the reports of travelers and journalists in the South, and the testimony of both southern whites and blacks all confirm the prevalence among freedpeople of the belief that they were soon to gain possession of the lands of their former masters. "The impression is universal among the freedmen," reported an assistant commissioner of the Freedmen's Bureau in 1865, "that they are to have the abandoned and confiscated lands, in homesteads of forty acres, in January next."[49] Sidney Andrews, reporting from South Carolina in the fall of 1865, also found "among the plantation negroes a widely spread idea that land is to be given them by the government."[50] This "widely spread idea"—part hope, part expectation, and part demand— was also deeply rooted. Agents of the Freedmen's Bureau, sent out to persuade blacks to sign annual labor contracts, found it nearly impossible to disabuse freedpeople of the idea that the government intended to provide them with forty-acre homesteads.[51] In one case, a black audience, told by an agent of the Freedmen's Bureau that the government was not planning to provide them with land, accused him of being a rebel in disguise, "dressed in blue clothes and brought . . . here to lie to us."[52] A correspondent for the *Nation* reported, similarly, that "not one in ten" believed him when he told black people that the government did not intend to give them grants of land.[53]

Blacks' expectations of land redistribution were particularly intense during the period from the end of the war until the beginning of 1866—a time accordingly of great uncertainty and anticipation. Though for several years after the war these expectations persisted, peaking annually around Christmas as the past season's labor contracts expired and as blacks looked forward to the new year, optimistic of a great change in their status. In 1867, the passage of the Reconstruction Act, Thaddeus Stevens's revival of the confiscation issue in Congress, and the commencement of state constitutional conventions in the South renewed blacks' hopes and further aggravated planters' efforts to maintain the plantation system.[54] When rumors that the large plantations were to be confiscated surfaced once again in 1868, some blacks, in anticipation, purchased boundary markers in order to stake out their forty-acre tracts.[55] So persistent were these expectations that Charles Nordhoff—in 1875—found that many Louisiana blacks still believed that the government planned to provide them with 'forty acres and a mule.'[56]

The prophecy of "forty acres and a mule," despite the fact that it remained an unrealized dream, was certainly real in its ramifications. The expectation among blacks that they were to receive grants of land from the government disrupted the plantation system, made it nearly impossible for planters to procure an adequate and reliable supply of laborers, and was reportedly "at the bottom of much idleness and discontent."[57] One Georgia planter stated, in 1865, that "he hadn't been able to hire a nigger for next year, or to hear of a neighbor who had hired one. The black vagabonds," he explained, "all expected their masters' lands at Christmas."[58]

Even more ominous to southern whites was the possibility that the unfulfilled desire of blacks for land would lead them to appropriate the plantations by force.

"In some places they openly announce the fact that the lands will be divided amongst them," reported a Mississippi newspaper in 1865. "In others they assert . . . that if they are not divided peaceably they will fight for them."[59] Especially in 1865, but for several years after the war as well, the fear among southern whites that blacks would turn to violence and revolution to acquire land was pervasive. It was "quite possible," one planter wrote in 1867, that blacks might take possession of the plantations and "eject the proprietors."[60] One reporter was told by a white man "of much apparent intelligence" that "the negroes have an organized military force in all sections of the State, and are almost certain to rise and massacre the whites about Christmas time."[61] Whenever blacks' expectations intensified, as they usually did around Christmas, southern whites sounded warnings of black insurrection.[62] Rumors that blacks would riot on Christmas day led the Georgia assembly in 1865 to impose the death penalty "for any combined resistance to the lawful authority of the state" and extended prison terms for inciting "riot, conspiracy, or resistance."[63]

Freedom and Landownership

"The height of the freedmen's ambition," reported John Trowbridge in 1865, "was to have little homes of their own and to work for themselves."[64] The desire of blacks to settle on land of their own and to control their own labor was more than just ambition, for freedpeople perceived the independence and autonomy that landownership made possible as constituting the very essence of freedom.[65] The reason the former slaves wanted to own "a little piece of land," observed a northern visitor to the South in 1865, was "to be *free*, to control his own time and efforts without anything that can remind him of past sufferings in bondage."[66] Blacks realized that freedom—in this sense—was by no means an inevitable concomitant of emancipation. Just as planters presumed that the abolition of slavery did not prohibit the continued subordination of blacks under a modified system of forced labor, so too did freedpeople recognize that they were not truly free simply because they were no longer slaves. Many blacks were consequently skeptical about the prospects of freedom without landownership: "What's de use of being free if you don't own land enough to be buried in," declared one former slave. "Might juss as well stay slave all yo' days."[67] Freedpeople understood that without access to means of subsistence independent of the plantation system, they would remain at the mercy of their former masters and, consequently, would be little better off than they had been under slavery. "Gib us our own land and we take care of ourselves," one freedman explained, "but widout land de ole massas can hire us or starve us, as dey please."[68]

In the interview with General Sherman and Secretary of War Stanton that led to the enactment of Special Field Order No. 15, twenty church leaders representing Savannah's black population, with former slave Garrison Frazier as their spokesman, explained to their white audience how they interpreted freedom: "The freedom . . . promised by the proclamation, is taking us from under the yoke of bondage, and placing us where we could reap the fruit of our own labor, take care of ourselves, and assist the government in maintaining our freedom." To achieve this objective, Frazier emphasized, freedpeople needed "to have land, and turn it and till it by our own labor. . . . We want to be placed on land until we are able to buy it and make it our own."[69] Another freedman expressed a similar conviction, once again drawing attention to the connection between freedom, landownership, and self-sufficiency: "I want some land; I am helpless," he declared to an army officer in 1865, "I cannot help myself unless I get some land; then I can take care of myself and my family; otherwise I cannot do it."[70]

Because land gave them the opportunity to reap the fruit of their own labor and to take care of themselves—because it thus made them truly free, blacks were willing to go to great lengths to establish themselves as independent proprietors. The former slaves, one planter observed, "will almost starve and go naked before they will work for a white man if they can get a patch of ground to live on, and get from under this control."[71] A respondent to Loring and Atkinson's 1868 survey of agricultural conditions in the South reported, similarly, that freedpeople have a "dislike to being controlled or working for white men. They prefer to get a little patch where they can do as they choose."[72] And if they could not immediately purchase "a little patch," blacks sought to rent land. Freedpeople regarded renting as the next-best alternative to landownership, just as they considered the postbellum gang-labor system as the next-worst alternative to slavery. Renting, like landownership, made it possible for blacks to "do as they choose" and to preserve their much-valued independence.

Blacks embraced a vision of freedom that was indelibly stamped by their experience under slavery as a subordinate race deprived of the right to control their own labor. The conception of freedom that they promoted, accordingly, represented the antithesis of slavery—the antithesis of a system that compelled them to labor under the authority, and for the profit, of another man. This conception of freedom was incompatible with both slavery and with the postbellum plantation system; and it was at odds with the northern free-labor ideology as well. What blacks sought, indeed, was not freedom *of* the market, but freedom *from* the market, or, more precisely, freedom from the plantation-labor market. The free-labor ideology and the annual-contract system endowed blacks only with the limited right to choose the planter to whom they would transfer control over their labor. Although they took whatever advantage they could from their right to mobility in the labor market, most blacks regarded the freedom associated with the postwar plantation system as a sorry alternative to the freedom conferred by landowner-ship. A black man from Louisiana told one reporter that as long as he had to work for planters, he was not really free, but land, on the other hand, "was a great thing for a man, and made him free and his own man."[73] This was precisely what worried southern whites. "There is nothing which makes a man so free, so independent, and so lordly in his aspirations," warned a Democratic leader from South Carolina, "as ownership of land."[74]

The desire of freedpeople for homesteads of their own, therefore, was neither the reflection of an irrational "land thirst" nor the product of a strict economic calculus. It was not from some whimsical conceit that black people sought to acquire land; nor necessarily was it from an expectation of the economic benefits to be gained from landownership relative to alternative land-tenure arrangements. Rather, freedpeople were attracted to the possibility of landownership because of the independence and freedom it promised. F. L. Cardoza, a black delegate to the Constitutional Convention of South Carolina in 1868, made this connection explicit, while at the same time attacking the southern plantation system.

> One of the greatest slavery bulwarks was the infernal plantation system, one man owning his thousand, another his twenty, another fifty thousand acres of land. . . . What is the main cause of the prosperity of the North? It is because every man has his own farm and is free and

independent. Let the lands of the South be similarly divided. . . . Now that slavery is destroyed, let the plantation system go with it. We will never have true freedom until we abolish the system of agriculture which existed in the Southern states.[75]

The ambition of blacks to have their own homesteads, as Eric Foner emphasizes, "reflected a desire for autonomy" and was not "simply a quest for material accumulation and social mobility."[76] This rendered the conflict of interests between planters and freedpeople all the more incapable of being negotiated to a mutually satisfactory compromise. The possibility of landownership represented an alternative that was qualitatively different from the plantation system, and thus left little room for freedpeople and planters to bargain with one another. Consequently, for example, even those fortunate landowners who could afford to pay premium wages often found it difficult to procure an adequate labor supply, for blacks were looking for something beyond just an economic return. The autonomy and independence that blacks prized were not readily traded in for the promise of higher wages.

Planter Opposition to Black Landownership

Planters "say that if you suffer the colored people here to own land they cannot get any laborers," a black man from Mississippi explained, "for where a colored man owns a piece of land, as many as can do so will go to their own land, and that will defeat them from getting labor."[77] Blacks who farmed on land of their own, as this freedman recognized, presented a problem for planters not only because their labor was withdrawn from the plantation market, but also because the example of freedpeople as independent proprietors encouraged other blacks to "go to their own land." Freedpeople farming on land of their own were a disruptive influence, rendering other blacks all the more dissatisfied with plantation labor and difficult to control.[78] Black landownership undermined labor discipline, jeopardized the future of the plantation system, and thus posed a threat to the fundamental interests of white landholders. Planters were determined, therefore, to prevent freedpeople from owning land. They sought to avoid the "fatal mistake" committed previously by the British government of "allowing the emancipated negroes to become owners of the soil" and permitting them to settle down "in easy indolence, content to live upon pumpkins and whatever a bounteous nature might lavish at his feet." To prevent such an outcome in the American South, a contributor to *De Bow's Review* argued, the white man must remain the exclusive proprietor of the land.[79] If southern whites could maintain a monopoly on landownership, planters would have a chance to preserve the plantation system. If, on the other hand, blacks became independent landholders, they "will not be worth anything" and the plantation system could not survive; a black man "will not work for anybody else when he gets property of his own."[80]

Numerous witnesses called before the Joint Committee on Reconstruction in 1866, as well as many visiting journalists and northern officials stationed in the South, confirmed that planters were adamantly opposed to the possibility of black landownership. "The object which the freedman has most at heart is the purchase of land," General Rufus Saxton testified, but "it is the policy of the majority of the farm owners to prevent negroes from becoming landholders. They desire to keep the negro landless, and as nearly in the condition of slavery as it is possible for them to do."[81] The alternative, planters feared, was that blacks "will become possessed of a small freehold, will raise their corn, squashes, pigs and chickens, and will work no more in the cotton, rice and sugar fields."[82] Without an adequate labor supply all the valuable land that planters owned would go to waste, and they would be deprived of their means of economic existence. "I own these lands," a Georgia planter declared, "and, if the niggers can be made to work, they'll support me; but there's nothing else that I know anything about, except managing a plantation."[83] But planters realized that if blacks had any choice at all, they would avoid plantation labor. Blacks could "be made to work" only if alternative possibilities, especially landownership, were closed off to them.

Planters were also opposed to blacks' renting land.[84] In the first place, planters regarded rental arrangements as bad business. According to one planter, land rented to freedpeople "is ruined beyond recovery."[85] "Those who rent their lands to negroes, never realize any profit," another landowner claimed, "and the negroes never make a support."[86] A veritable plague of troubles threatened to descend upon the planter foolish enough to rent land to former slaves: the "quality of the soil begins at once to depreciate from improper usage and careless cultivation; the teams decline to the poorest condition; the crops produced are an inferior quality."[87] Southern planters could not imagine that black labor, without the controlling influence of white supervision, would produce anything but economic ruin. "Rent never, under any circumstances," admonished a Georgia planter. "Negroes left to their own judgment, and their own volition must fail."[88]

Planters expected that adverse social and moral consequences would also result from allowing blacks to farm independently on rented land. Such land "soon becomes the safe harbor of all the depraved negroes in the vicinity; the vicious habits of the women and men alike increase owing to their removal from the control of the proprietor; thievish and superstitious practices are more common and open, and brawls and quarrels arise more often than elsewhere."[89] Renting land to blacks would liberate them from the civilizing influence of white authority, planters believed, and, lacking that influence, blacks would revert to the savage and barbarous state to which they were by nature inclined. The New Orleans *Tribune*, in several editorials in 1869, scoffed at these charges. The real objective of planters in refusing to rent land to blacks, the *Tribune* proclaimed, "is to keep the colored people in subjection, so that their wages, their votes, their movements may be controlled by the whites."[90]

Planters' complaints about the uneconomic and immoral habits of black renters drew less from actual experience than from their own preconceptions about black labor. Nevertheless, planters had good economic reasons for being opposed to renting land to blacks. Black renters, in principle, enjoyed considerable autonomy, which was, of course, precisely why they preferred such an arrangement. They were free to control their own labor, set their own work schedule, and select their own mix of crops. By renting blacks land and turning over to them the key cultivation decisions, however, planters were in danger of losing control, not only over the black labor force, but over the process of agricultural production as well. As compared to the gang-labor system, for example, which maximized planters' ability to control the labor force, renting land to blacks threatened to diminish significantly the managerial prerogatives of white landowners, and consequently their economic returns. It was a dangerous concession to permit blacks such autonomy. One planter in South Carolina, disturbed by the willingness of some landowners to rent land to blacks, warned that it would "be hard ever to recover the privileges that have been yielded to the negroes."[91]

The continuing commitment of most planters to maintaining the plantation system led them to oppose rental agreements. Renting land to blacks threatened to reduce the already limited supply of plantation laborers, encouraged other freedpeople to demand rental arrangements, and created a haven for blacks dissatisfied with the plantation system. Never rent to a black man, recommended one planter, for the black renter "is naturally inclined . . . to settle off to himself where his chickens and family will not be interrupted; and where he will not be compelled to work so hard. The settlements become dens for the reception of those who will not work and who are offended with their employers."[92] By permitting rental agreements, planters would only exacerbate the problem of labor control. Planters worried that opening up the possibility of renting land to blacks would add to the competitive pressures among themselves for labor and would increase the ability of blacks to play employers off against one another in bargaining for labor arrangements. Indeed, one landowner attributed the postwar labor shortage to the fact that "some of the landowners have rented lands to negroes, to farm upon their own responsibility."[93]

It was not enough for the planter to refuse to sell or rent land to his former slaves; it was also necessary that neighboring landowners subscribe to the same policy. In South Carolina, and many other southern states as well, planters passed resolutions not to sell land to blacks and adhered to "gentlemen's agreements" against renting land to freedpeople.[94] Planters in Virginia also resolved not to sell or rent land to blacks, proclaiming that "negro labor without the direction and guidance of white men would be a failure."[95] In Mississippi, where for a time the Black Codes legally prohibited blacks from owning land, "even the renting of small tracts" to blacks "is held to be unpatriotic and unworthy of a good citizen."[96] Planters were largely successful in their efforts to prevent blacks from renting land. One black man, among the few fortunate enough to discover someone who would rent to him (his former master had refused), told a northern reporter that, although he thought that renting was a good idea, he was pessimistic about the likelihood of many blacks being able to take advantage of the opportunity because of the opposition of landowners.[97] And in Louisiana, Charles Nordhoff found that, although many blacks wanted to acquire small plots of land, few were able to do so because of the unwillingness of landowners to rent or sell, even though they retained huge amounts of acreage not under cultivation.[98]

Besides trying to establish agreements among themselves, planters sometimes resorted to more violent means to prevent blacks from purchasing or renting land. In South Carolina, according to one report, "many black men have been told that they would be shot if they leased land and undertook to work for themselves."[99] Instances of violence inflicted upon blacks trying to farm independently were widespread enough for freedpeople to take such threats very seriously. In the early part of 1869, for example, the New Orleans *Tribune* reported the murder of three black men who dared to live by themselves on rented land.[100]

Local whites reckless enough to rent or sell land to freedpeople might also find themselves subject to violence. A thirty-five-year resident of Louisiana, who had violated the implicit pledge to not rent land to blacks, received the following threatening notice from disapproving neighbors:

> We have been informed that you are 'lowing niggers to squat about on your land; or, in other words, you are

renting niggers land. One of our committee told you that you would be burnt out, but you would not pay any attention to him. Now, sir, your gin-house is burnt for renting niggers land. If this is not sufficient warning we will burn everything on your place. If that don't break it up we will break your neck. If that don't break it up, we will shoot the niggers.[101]

In the Mississippi Valley area, one reporter observed, "the feeling against any ownership of the soil by the negroes is so strong, that the man who should sell small tracts to them would be in actual personal danger."[102] In another case, a white man, after hearing threats to burn his house down, broke off an agreement to rent land to blacks.[103] "It would be a bold man now who would hint at the idea of renting land to negroes," one observer declared. "Such a person would only subject himself to personal violence. The central, controlling idea is, to get the negro upon the plantation; once there, to place him as nearly in a condition of slavery as is possible."[104]

Planters sought to force blacks back onto the plantations by restricting alternative means of subsistence. Along with preventing blacks from renting or purchasing land, this also required the enactment of legislative measures limiting blacks' access to open lands. Given the somewhat loose definition and enforcement of property rights in the South and the bountiful nature of much of the land, the danger, noted one planter, was that freedpeople could "do with very little bread—live on fish and oysters, coons, &c., &c. There being therefore but little necessity for labor, very little work is done by the negroes."[105] In response to this potential threat to the plantation system, legislatures in many of the southern states enacted laws designed to tighten up the enforcement of property rights—laws against the use of unenclosed and unimproved lands, tougher legal measures against trespassing and foraging, and restrictions on hunting and fishing on "common" lands. As Steven Hahn points out, "Planters recognized that customary use rights, along with the availability of public domain in some states, jeopardized labor supply and discipline and, by extension, the revitalization of the cotton economy." Thus, in order to restrict blacks' access to the land, southern planters "began to press for stricter definitions of and stronger safeguards for private property."[106]

Thus, it was not exclusively the poverty of freedpeople that prevented them from acquiring land. The efforts of planters to restrict blacks' access to alternatives outside of the plantation system played a significant independent role in obstructing black landownership. The vast majority of blacks were, of course, too poor to purchase land outright. Still, provisions could have been made to allow blacks to lease or purchase land on credit, using the land itself as collateral.[107] A few blacks, furthermore, did in fact possess the means to buy at least small plots of land from money accumulated while working on abandoned plantations during the war. More significantly, many soldiers came out of the war with considerable savings and a strong desire to purchase land. In Louisiana in 1865, for example, twenty black regiments, pooling their bounty money, offered to buy all the confiscated and abandoned land in the state.[108]

So while lack of money was certainly an impediment to blacks' acquisition of land, it was neither an insuperable obstacle nor the only obstacle; and having adequate finances by no means guaranteed that land could be obtained. Ransom and Sutch present some important evidence on this point. Given the unusually strong desire of blacks for land, it would be expected, if there were no restrictions on black landownership, that a greater share of their wealth, as compared to whites, would be invested in land. Based upon data from the manuscript tax rolls for Coweta County, Georgia, in 1878, Ransom and Sutch find that "for each and every wealth class, black owners of real estate held a smaller fraction of their wealth in land than did their white counterparts." "Clearly," they conclude, "something other than mere poverty must explain the low level of black landownership." That something else, they suggest, was the opposition of southern whites, who "denied blacks the opportunity of becoming a landowning class."[109]

The ability (or even desire) of southern whites to deny freedpeople access to land was not absolute. Some blacks, though not a great number, were able to hang on to the land that they had obtained during the course of the war; a few were successful in acquiring land under the provisions of the Southern Homestead Act; some were able to rent or purchase land from desperate or sympathetic southern landowners; and some were able to acquire land with the assistance of northern friends.[110] According to the best estimate, though, less than 5 percent of the black population was able to obtain land in the first few years after the war.[111]

Conclusion

Most freedpeople were unable to establish an independent economic existence outside of the plantation system. Unable to buy or rent land, the vast majority failed to gain the freedom they hoped emancipation would bring. Most had no choice but to continue working for their former masters. But even as freedpeople were forced back onto the plantations, the dream of landownership and the desire to maximize their independence persisted. "While land ownership, more than anything else, embodied their specific conception of freedom,"

Thavolia Glymph argues, "it was the conception, in the end, that mattered. When denied land, their struggle to define labor relations continued to incorporate that conception of freedom."[112]

Thus, while planters were successful in keeping blacks from acquiring land, they had not yet necessarily won the war to maintain the plantation system. Planters' victory in the battle against the dream of "forty acres and a mule" was partial and incomplete, as they failed to extinguish blacks' desire for independence and freedom. Even when the immediate prospect of obtaining land was obstructed, the struggle for independence continued, as blacks fought to achieve a land-tenure arrangement that enhanced their chances for autonomy. Planters, therefore, had little time to savor their victory over the possibility of black landownership, for they still faced the problem of wresting obedient service from a discontented labor force that persisted in pressing its demand for freedom.

Chapter 4 · Economic
            Reconstruction
            and Southern
            Immigration

            Blacks' determination to gain eco-
nomic independence jeopardized the future of plantation
agriculture in the South. Their continuing refusal to
submit to the plantation regimen and the concomitant
scarcity of labor forced planters to consider an alternative
possibility. For the first several years after the war, in an
effort to buttress the plantation system, southern landholders sought to increase the agricultural labor supply by
promoting Chinese and European immigration to the
South. Through this strategy, planters hoped to diminish
their dependence on black labor and, by putting freedpeople into competition with foreign workers, to pressure
blacks into acquiescing to the plantation system.

       With the end of the Civil War and the abolition of
slavery, immigration became one of the most widely
discussed and seriously pursued possibilities for recon-
structing and revitalizing the southern economy.[1] Debates about the merits and purposes of immigration filled
the pages of southern newspapers and periodicals.[2] Southern states legislated expenditures and allocated funds to
establish immigration bureaus and commissioners. Pub-

lic and private immigration agencies were set up throughout the South. Farmers formed associations to promote and lobby for immigration. Local governments passed special laws offering incentives to immigrants. A variety of pamphlets and brochures advertising the advantages of the southern states to prospective immigrants were circulated in the North and in Europe. Immigration agents were sent overseas. The first postwar issue of *De Bow's Review*, one of the most influential planter periodicals, contained three articles heralding the advantages of southern immigration.[3] And throughout the postwar years, *De Bow's Review* regularly included a special section devoted to the "Department of Immigration and Labor," which reported on the business and progress of immigration agencies and on the arrival and employment of immigrant workers.

Northern as well as southern whites extolled the virtues of immigration to the South. The *Commercial and Financial Chronicle* of New York, for example, regarded immigration, of both labor and capital, as a necessary condition for successful economic reconstruction in the southern states.[4] Northern businessmen even established agencies in New York and New England for the purpose of supplying immigrant laborers to southern planters.[5] Government officials in the North promoted this possibility as well. Theodore Peters, traveling throughout the South as an agent of the Department of Agriculture, estimated that the abolition of slavery had created a "vacuum . . . for labor so large that a million of laboring people would now find profitable employment." Peters recommended that federal and state governments address the great need for labor in the South by establishing programs to encourage immigration.[6]

The possibility of southern immigration is important for several reasons. First, the effort to attract immigrants to the South, the high expectations fostered in anticipation of their arrival, the experiences with the relatively few immigrant laborers that were eventually lured into the southern states, and the conflict between those favoring and those opposing immigration influenced the process and outcome of economic reconstruction. The discussions and debates surrounding the issue of immigration, in addition, shed further light on how planters perceived the economic situation in the postbellum world and how they regarded the "labor problem" in particular. What planters had to say about immigration reveals much about their interests, their conception of free black labor, and their experience with the postwar gang-labor system. An exploration of the possibility of southern immigration, therefore, will illuminate the problems planters faced in trying to preserve plantation agriculture and will help to identify the considerations that led them to abandon gang labor and consent to the adoption of sharecropping.

The historical significance of the possibility of southern immigration derives precisely from its failure. The inability of white landholders to increase the supply of plantation labor through immigration reduced the alternatives left open to planters, weakened their bargaining position, and compelled them to reconsider the usefulness of black labor. With the alternative of southern immigration effectively foreclosed, planters found it increasingly difficult to resist freedpeople's demand for greater autonomy. This helped prepare the way for the rise of southern sharecropping. The issue of southern immigration in this respect illustrates the usefulness of describing and analyzing the conflict between planters and freedpeople in terms of the idea of constriction of possibilities.

Slavery and Southern Immigration

There was relatively little immigration to the South prior to the Civil War.[7] In 1860, only 15 percent of all European-born citizens of the United States resided in the fifteen slave states. Most of these lived in one of the border states (Missouri, Maryland, and Kentucky) or in New Orleans. The rest of the South in 1860 contained less than 6 percent of all European immigrants. Many of these, moreover, resided in urban centers and other localities where slavery lacked a significant presence. The immigrant population was relatively less attracted to areas of the country where slavery predominated.[8]

Indeed, prior to the war, planters proclaimed as one of the advantages of slavery precisely that it acted as a barrier to immigration. "One of the great benefits of the institution of African slavery to the Southern states," declared Edmund Ruffin, "is its effect in keeping away from our territory, and directing to the north and northwest, the hordes of immigrants now flowing from Europe."[9] Whether judged beneficial or not, commentators from both the North and the South, before and after the war, agreed that the existence of slavery had impeded southern immigration. With this obstacle to immigration now eliminated, many postwar observers anticipated a large movement of white immigrants into the South. "The barrier of slavery being now removed," wrote C. L. Fleishman in 1866, "I see no difficulty whatever why the current of emigration cannot be turned into the Southern channel."[10]

Many observers believed that slavery had not only inhibited immigration, but had prompted the emigration of nonslaveholding whites as well. Thus, the existence of slavery produced a twofold depletion of the white population, both by driving out native whites and by discouraging prospective immigrants. De Bow drew attention to this phenomenon in an 1866 issue of his *Review.* He cited the 1850 census, which showed that six times as many people had emigrated from the South to the North and West as had emigrated from the free states to the South.[11] Charles Nordhoff, writing shortly after the war, argued that the extent of the emigration from the southern states during slavery was even more disturbing than the numbers indicated, for the South, he believed, was also losing its best citizens. Furthermore, Nordhoff argued, this immigration to the North violated the presumed natural propensity of the human race to migrate southward: "The horror of slavery . . . has sufficed to conquer even this strong instinctive tendency."[12]

Southern whites interested in promoting immigration also had to confront an ideological obstacle. Slavery's defenders often claimed a unique relationship between the character and constitution of the black race, on the one hand, and the southern climate and the demands of cotton cultivation, on the other. White laborers, presumably, could withstand neither the climate of the South nor the physical demands of plantation agriculture.[13] As part of their continuing effort to sell the South to potential settlers, therefore, the proponents of immigration were compelled to reconsider the question of the suitability of white labor for southern agriculture.

J. C. Nott of Alabama addressed this problem in great detail in an early issue of *De Bow's Review.*[14] According to Nott, different races were "peculiarly adapted to certain climates," but each had a "certain degree of pliability of constitution," an ability to adjust, within limits, to climates for which they were not naturally suited. Nott was optimistic, naturally, that whites possessed a greater "pliability of constitution" than did blacks (another manifestation of the former's presumed superiority), great enough in fact that whites could adequately serve after all as agricultural laborers in the South. Illustrating more than anything else the "pliability" of ideology, Nott drew a reassuring conclusion: "Whites can live, labor and make cotton in our climate."[15]

Not everyone agreed, however, that white laborers were fit for southern agriculture. The "miasmatic climate"[16] of the South and the expectation that European laborers "would languish in the hot Southern sun"[17] led some planters to question the advisability of white (especially northern European) immigration. Instead, they recommended the immigration of Chinese or perhaps southern European laborers, who, presumably, could more easily and surely adapt to the southern climate.[18]

Southern Immigration and the Plantation System

Most southern whites in the immediate postwar years saw considerable merit in the idea of promoting immigration to the South. Nearly everyone agreed that southern immigration would have a beneficial impact on the region's economy; indeed, many speculated that the southern economy could be revived only through immigration. However, while agreeing on the need to attract immigrants, southern whites were deeply divided over the purposes of such immigration. Was the intent to prop up the plantation economy or to promote a "New South"? Were immigrants to be brought in as plantation laborers or independent proprietors?

The conflict surrounding the issue of immigration brought to the surface a long-standing division among southern whites concerning the future of plantation agriculture and the southern economy.[19] Most former slaveholders, frustrated by labor scarcity and black recalcitrance, regarded immigration as a means for salvaging the plantation system. They expected immigrants to replace their former slaves as a permanently subordinate laboring class or to serve as a supplement to the black labor force. Planters "yet cling to the idea of wielding the products of large bodies of land," the New Orleans *Picayune* protested, and "desire only laborers; and if not able to get white men, are willing to take Chinese, Hindoos or any other sort of people, out of whom labor can be bought or coaxed."[20]

Planters faced opposition from other southern whites who regarded immigration as a key ingredient of a larger reform movement that would put an end to the hegemony of plantation agriculture. These advocates of economic change saw the persistence of the large antebellum landholdings as constituting a barrier to both southern immigration and economic progress. The abolition of slavery gave the critics of the plantation system an opportunity to press their case for a "New South." "Now that slavery no longer exists," declared a Georgia newspaper, "it has become a social necessity to break up and abandon the plantation system."[21] One critic of the southern "land aristocracy," a white resident of Mississippi, suggested that the subdivision of the plantations, besides being a "social necessity," would improve the efficiency of cotton production as well.

> In my opinion, a division of those large plantations into small farms, to be sold or rented out to white emigrants, who would be working independently, would produce a larger [cotton] crop than in 1860, and secure peace and prosperity to the country. What we have to contend now, is against the establishment of a land aristocracy, the substitute of slaveholders' aristocracy, and that is one of the main reasons why they do not encourage emigration unless such as they will control.[22]

Some southern whites were optimistic that, with the emancipation of the slaves and the "impossibility of concentrating large bodies of laborers," the plantation system would collapse on its own accord and inevitably give way to a more decentralized system of agricultural production. "Capital being unable to monopolize labor, it will no longer monopolize land, which, without labor, is of comparatively little value."[23] Constrained by the shortage of labor, planters, so it seemed, would have no choice but to put up their plantations for sale. This would place the South in an especially advantageous position to attract an immigrant population, especially since land in the North and West was becoming increasingly scarce and expensive. However, most planters were not so readily prepared to give up on the possibility that they might yet "monopolize labor."

Critics of the plantation system and reformers heralding a New South looked upon immigration as a means of populating the southern states with an "industrious and improving purchaser," with a thriving "middle class" of independent farmers, merchants, artisans, and the like.[24] "We desire," exhorted E. C. Cahell, a congressman from Florida and former resident of Mississippi, "earnestly desire, the immigration of honest industrious *white* men. Especially do we invite, *cordially invite*, those having means to become proprietors of the soil."[25] A Shreveport critic of plantation agriculture proposed, similarly, that the proper strategy for economic reconstruction "is not in immigration of laborers, but of land buyers. Not in carrying on large plantations, but small farms."[26] In Louisiana, "a lively and vocal group of agrarian reformers" led by the editor of the Franklin *Planters' Banner*, Daniel Dennett, also advocated abandoning the plantation system in favor of a diversified agricultural economy. Dennett, a Jeffersonian advocate of small farms, urged the plantation owners to sell off their excess acreage to entice "frugal, conscientious immigrants to come into Louisiana with the idea of eventually becoming landowners."[27]

Among the most vocal advocates of economic reform was John A. Wagener, the state commissioner of immigration for South Carolina. Wagener also favored diversification and an agricultural economy comprised of small farms; and he too called upon planters to facilitate immigration by selling some of their idle land. A frequent critic of the plantation system, Wagener knew that immigrants would not be attracted to the South unless provided with an opportunity to settle on land of their own. Unfortunately, he told an audience in Newberry, South Carolina, planters were altogether "biased in favor of that time honored [plantation] system," and they were opposed to the immigration of any laborers except those meant for plantation agriculture.[28] The principal impediment to immigration, Wagener declared, was "the tenacity with which the large land-owner clings to his useless, idle, surplus acres."[29]

The critics of the plantation system recognized what planters refused to: that without the prospect of becoming independent landholders, immigrants would not be attracted to the South. While for planters, immigration was necessary to save the plantation system, for its critics, the abandonment of the plantation system was necessary to entice immigrants. "If southern people expect white immigrants to come here and live, and cultivate their lands as mere hirelings," declared a white Mississippian, "they had as well abandon the delusion."[30] The "only way to obtain good labor," wrote a contributor to *De Bow's Review*, "is to offer them the power of owning land."[31] Planters, however, needed a stable and permanently subordinate labor force; they had no interest in creating opportunities for landownership and upward mobility; nor certainly did they see any advantage in southern immigration if it required them to sacrifice their plantations.

Whether the fundamental problem was conceived as scarce labor or surplus land reflected the divergent economic interests of southern whites. For landholders committed to the maintenance of the plantation system, the real problem was labor scarcity, not the existence of large amounts of uncultivated land. The solution, therefore, was not to break up the large landholdings, but to increase the size of the plantation labor force. For the advocates of economic reform, on the other hand, the problem of labor scarcity resulted from a surplus of idle land; the solution was to make such land available for purchase, which would in turn draw immigrant farmers to the South. A speaker at a meeting of the Richmond County, Georgia, Agricultural Society expressed the position of the agrarian reformers:

> Let us dispose of our *surplus* lands as speedily as possible; and, to this end, we must do all in our power to encourage the immigration of industrious laborers from Europe. . . . We should divide our overgrown plantations with such of these people as are able to purchase; and to those who are not, we can give such profitable employment as will soon enable them to secure for themselves comfortable homes, and thus identify themselves with us and our future, socially and politically.[32]

The availability of surplus land, from this perspective, was a great inducement "to immigrants desiring to secure cheap and comfortable homes": the "land cries out for labor."[33] The owners of the land, however, cried out for a class of laborers to replace their former slaves, not laborers desiring cheap homesteads.

Although many planters did lease their plantations to northern businessmen in the years after the war, most refused to sell their land, even in the face of desperate economic circumstances.[34] One journalist suggested to a traveling companion in Virginia that, because planters were short of capital and their slaves gone, farms should be available at low rates. "They should be," the other man responded, "but your Southern aristocrat is a monomaniac on the subject of owning land. He will part with his acres about as willingly as he would part with his life."[35] Even planters despairing of the possibility of ever again bringing their lands under cultivation were reluctant to put any up for sale. "Scarcely any [Alabama landowner] seemed to regard their chance of cultivating their lands by free negro labor as hopeful," one reporter wrote, "and the most had a vague, uncertain idea that in some way or another they would have to give up their lands. Still there were scarcely any sales, and prices had found no settled standard."[36] Public sentiment in Alabama was opposed in particular to selling land to "Yankees"; and throughout the South generally, according to Whitelaw Reid, there prevailed an antagonism to allowing "newcomers" to purchase land.[37] Planters in Louisiana, one historian found, refused to break up the plantations "even to obtain labor superior to the Negro, or to enhance the general value of real estate by increased settlement."[38]

Those who controlled the land ultimately held the upper hand on the issue of immigration. Southern planters' conception of the purposes of immigration prevailed. According to John Dennett, reporting from the South in 1865 and 1866 for the *Nation*:

Most Southerners who were much interested in the question seemed rather to look upon the expected immigration of white men as a means of supplying

> Southern landholders with a laborious and obedient
> peasantry than as the incoming of a class of men who
> soon would cease to be hireling laborers and become
> landholders themselves.[39]

The advocates of small farms lacked control over the crucial resource that, if no other obstacles to southern immigration existed, might have made the South more attractive to prospective settlers—namely, land. Meanwhile, those who controlled the land saw little economic advantage in encouraging the immigration of independent farmers, especially if it meant the abandonment of plantation agriculture.

Although freed slaves shared with New South reformers an interest in breaking up the large plantations, white critics of the plantation system were by no means the allies or friends of black people. At least some planters envisioned a possible future for blacks in the South, if only as a permanently subordinate labor force. For most reformers and critics of the plantation system, on the other hand, "there was no place for the Negro, either as landowner or agricultural laborer."[40] Not all white proponents of economic diversification and yeoman farming shared this antagonism toward blacks; some saw the common interests of small farmers of all races served through the subdivision of the large plantations. Most, however, viewed the presence of free blacks in the South as a hindrance to immigration and advocated their colonization.[41]

Planter Opposition to Southern Immigration

Most planters favored immigration because they believed that an increase in the labor supply was necessary for the preservation of the plantation system. However, a minority of planters—no less committed to the maintenance of plantation agriculture—dissented from this analysis. They argued that the southern plantation economy could survive and prosper without immigrant laborers, and that a policy of promoting immigration to the South would actually be harmful to the interests of the landholding class. The most vocal and forceful critic of southern immigration was David Dickson, a prosperous Georgia planter. Dickson's opposition to southern immigration and his evaluation of the problems posed by emancipation sparked an informative debate carried out in the pages of the *Southern Cultivator* in the late 1860s.

Dickson opposed immigration for several reasons. First, he was not persuaded by the popular conviction that the black race was doomed to extinction; and he believed that black people in large numbers would inevitably continue to reside in the South. The resulting problem of social control, he argued, could be resolved only if the former slaves were placed under the authority of white employers. Immigration, however much it might bear on the "labor question," did not adequately address the "Negro problem." "The negro," Dickson argued, "we have here with us, and we cannot get rid of him if we would.... The only way to make it tolerable for them to live amongst us, is to give them *employment*. With full employment, they will steal less, be more law-abiding, and a less nuisance in every way."[42] Second, counseling patience, Dickson suggested that the natural increase in population would more than provide for the future needs of the South, making immigration unnecessary and harmful to the interests of planters, especially if it required subdividing the large estates.

Third, economic disorganization in the South, according to Dickson, derived not from labor scarcity but from northern interference: "Give us our liberties and constitutional rights, with our best men to represent us in all departments, and we can make as much cotton as the world wants." Dickson predicted that economic prosperity for the South could be had "without an outside man or dollar. Good government would do more to develop this country than all the men and money in the world."[43] Fourth, Dickson defended the especially controversial position that immigration, on strictly economic grounds, would be detrimental to the interests of the planter class. He maintained that, while a reduction in the cost of labor would follow from an increase in its supply, a decrease in the price of cotton would also result. Dickson managed to find a silver lining in the dark cloud of labor scarcity. "We want a scarcity of labor," he argued, so "that there may be a scarcity of cotton, and correspondingly good prices."[44] Finally, besides appealing to the self-interest of planters, Dickson also sought to enlist the support of other white southerners against the policy of immigration: "Do those who have no land, wish competitors in labor, and in the land market?"[45]

Dickson's critics scoffed at his suggestion that the best way to deal with freedpeople was to give them employment. If Dickson were in Mississippi, explained one planter,

> he would find that a large and rapidly increasing mass of this negro population would not so willingly accept the proffered *"employment,"* which he would give them as a correction of the evils flowing from their sudden emancipation. Both in this State and Louisiana, there is an increasing disposition, on the part of this people, to become *landholders* and *tenants,* and not *hirelings,* seeming to be anxious to rid themselves of all supervision on the part of the white race, and to look upon it as a sort of continued badge, or remembrancer, of their former condition of servitude.

Landholders, this planter declared, because of the unwillingness of blacks to serve as obedient hirelings, could no longer rely upon the labor of their former slaves for cotton cultivation in the South; "Asiatic" immigrants would have to be brought in as replacements.[46]

S. W. Trottie of South Carolina also defended the policy of immigration against Dickson. The scarcity of labor and the abundance of land in the South, Trottie observed, were driving up the price of the first and driving down the price of the second. As a result, "there will soon be no laborers, but all proprietors. And when all are homesteaded, what will become of the present landholder, the upper strata of society?"[47] Trottie continued this attack in a later issue, charging that the opponents of immigration consisted mainly of those planters who were "peculiarly blessed" with high-quality land and sufficient capital, permitting them to pay the high wages needed to attract laborers. "But where there is one Dickson, there are one hundred bankrupt farmers. . . . Mr. Dickson's heavy profits are owing to the scarcity of labor, and the one hundred failures which we have assumed to stand against his success, are also owing to the scarcity of labor."[48] The secret to Dickson's ability to retain a labor force, Trottie contended, was that he paid twice as much as his neighbors; laborers, consequently, sought his employment. But the corresponding solution for the less well-off planter, Trottie argued, was "the multiplication of laborers."

> Now the multiplication of laborers to an ample extent, would be simply an extension of the relationship existing between Mr. Dickson and his laborers. Let the laborer know that as soon as he is discharged, there is another ready and anxious to take his place, and a difficulty in his finding employment elsewhere, and there will be thrown

about him an influence calculated to check licentiousness
and vice, and morally elevate him.

Thus "will be inaugurated a counter revolution . . . by
which the landed aristocracy will in a measure, be
reinstated to their position of independence and influence."[49]

Planters needed to secure a stable and reliable labor
force, but their ability to do this was constrained by the
imperative of economic profitability. For those very few,
especially well-off planters who could afford to pay
uncustomarily high wages, it was possible (if Dickson's
case can be considered indicative) to procure a dependable
labor force. Since few planters could bear the cost of doing
this, the supply of cotton would remain low and prices
consequently would be high, thus accommodating the
relatively greater pay for labor. Yet the more planters able
to take advantage of this alternative, the less the payoff,
for the supply of cotton would increase and prices would
go down, undermining the economic logic of this strategy.

No matter, however, for this option was not available to most landholders. For the majority of planters,
high wages as the price for a stable supply of labor was not
a desirable alternative; nor could most have afforded to
adopt this program even had they wanted to. In fact, the
vast majority of planters after the war were unable to pay
cash wages at all and were compelled to compensate their
labor force with a share of the crop. In addition, as some of
the contributors to this debate recognized, many blacks
were adamant about not wanting to go back to work in the
cotton fields under white supervision, no matter what the
wages.

From the perspective of his critics, Dickson's opposition to immigration looked like a plot to eliminate or at
least disadvantage the average planter; despite his refer-

ences to patriotism, Dickson's proposal seemed suspiciously self-serving. "There is only one remedy," replied a planter from Alabama, referring to the problem of labor control, "and that is to so *flood* the country with laborers, that they shall exceed the demand. My *rich* neighbor then, will have no advantage of *poor* me."[50]

For the average planter then—for whom black labor was hard to find at all, expensive when available, and difficult to control when under contract—immigration seemed to be the only reasonable alternative. The more that planters were aggravated by black resistance to the plantation system, the greater their psychological investment in the possibility of southern immigration. The more they resented free blacks, the higher their expectations for the labor of Chinese and European immigrants.

Chinese Immigration to the South

The scarcity and uncertainty of free black labor led many southern whites to the conclusion drawn by a Georgia planter: "The preservation of cotton in the South may depend on it securing . . . another race of laborers."[51] Most planters who agreed with this assessment favored the introduction of Chinese immigrants into the South as replacements for the black "race of laborers" now ruined by emancipation.[52] Let's "drive the niggers out," a white resident of Mississippi proclaimed, "and import coolies that will work better, at less expense, and relieve us from this cursed nigger impudence."[53] For other proponents of Chinese immigration, the purpose was less to "drive the niggers out," than to force them back onto the plantations. A Kentucky newspaper optimistically predicted that by bringing Chinese laborers into the South "the tune . . . will not be 'forty acres and a mule,' but . . . 'work nigger or starve.' "[54]

Planters had good reason to believe that Chinese

immigration might be a practical alternative. Every year thousands of Chinese immigrated to the United States seeking work, more than one hundred thousand between 1850 and 1870. In addition, experiments with Chinese labor had already been successfully carried out in other parts of the world, and these precedents lent the possibility of Chinese immigration an aura of realism. The use of "coolie" labor by the French and British in the West Indies, for example, was widely cited by southern whites as being particularly relevant to the case of the postbellum South. Planters also considered importing Chinese laborers from Cuba, where they were reported to be good workers and obedient. More important, southern whites were encouraged by accounts of Chinese laborers in the western United States, where they were employed especially in mining and railroad construction. Planters frequently drew on these examples when discussing the merits of using Chinese laborers on southern plantations.[55]

Planters envisioned a nearly inexhaustible potential in the possibility of Chinese immigration. China, wrote George Gift, a leading proponent of the movement to bring Chinese laborers into the South, is "a vast country, overflowing with millions of surplus population, eager to emigrate."[56] One Alabama planter calculated "that you can bring over for a song" millions of "coolies" from China. "It will take three of 'em to do the work of two niggers," he advised, "but they'll live on next to nothing, and clothe themselves, and you've only got to pay 'em four dollars a month. That's our game now."[57] A planter from South Carolina ventured an even more fanciful estimate of the potential for Chinese immigration.

> I say let them come—the more the better. We don't need
> them by the thousands or few millions, but the hundreds of

millions. The South, from Mason Dixon's line to Mexico, could profitably employ, perhaps 250 million. Let them come, and the sooner the better. They will do the work that the freedmen won't do and the white man can't do.[58]

The Chinese, planters believed, were plentiful and anxious to immigrate. Indeed, the coincidence of vast amounts of "fertile soil" but no reliable labor force, on the one hand, and the presence of "numberless" and apparently idle Chinese, on the other, suggested to one observer the workings of divine providence.

> The fervid rays of the summer sun paralyzes the energies of the European laborer, and by an unwonted convulsion in the social organism, the negro has been arrested in his labors, and doomed to extermination. We may be sure that God did not create this vast extent of fertile soil for a waste. Nor did he bring upon it the highest order of manhood to ignore its value and neglect its cultivation.
>
> For many years it has been a puzzle to determine the designs of providence in regard to these numberless people [the Chinese]. . . . It has been left for us, in this favored region, to unravel the great mystery, and to discover the wonderful adaptation of means to ends—here is the soil, there are the laborers.[59]

Though many advocated ridding the South of black people altogether, probably most planters regarded Chinese immigrants as a supplement rather than an alternative to black labor. The introduction of Chinese laborers into the South, planters expected, by augmenting the existing plantation labor supply, would make it possible to procure reliable workers at affordable wages. In addition, planters anticipated that the competitive pressure of another "race of laborers" would undermine the power of free blacks to resist plantation labor and would bring

them back under the authority of the southern landholders.[60] According to a Georgia planter:

> Chinese immigration would operate beneficially in
> preventing the industrious negro from relaxing from
> industrious habits, owing to the bad example of the idle
> and intemperate; while the latter would see the necessity
> of reforming, as they no longer commanded the labor
> market, and must therefore work or starve; while the
> improved general industry would operate beneficially on
> the rising generation.[61]

Planters also hoped that immigration, by breaking
the monopoly that blacks possessed in the labor market,
would compel them to refrain from politics and restore to
southern landholders the power to control labor. Planters
found that labor was scarce and unreliable not only
because freedpeople sought alternatives to plantation
labor, but also because blacks became increasingly preoccupied with politics during the period of Reconstruction.
Blacks participated in political rallies and meetings, they
attended Republican conventions, they flocked to political lectures and debates, they joined organizations like
the Union League, and they mobilized in order to gain the
right to vote. Planters attributed much of their inability to
regain control over the black labor force to this outbreak
of political activism.[62] "Muscle is abundant—the power
to control it is lacking," observed a South Carolina
planter. "Old Ned has 'laid down the shovel and the hoe,'
and has applied his muscle to the hinges of the ballot-
box."[63] However, if they were placed into competition
with Chinese immigrants, blacks "may find it to their
interest to quit stealing and going to the Legislature, and
go to work in the cotton fields where they belong."[64]
Planters saw in Chinese immigration a means both for

regaining their ability to command the labor force and for putting an end to the threat of "Negro domination."[65]

Planters imagined Chinese laborers to be just about perfect for plantation agriculture.[66] This is not at all surprising, for the qualities of the Chinese seemed to be inferred, more than anything else, from the needs of wishful planters. The stereotype of freedpeople—lazy, unreliable, demanding, irresponsibly forsaking work for politics—served as a counterpoint in favorable contrast to which was drawn the stereotype of the Chinese. Chinese laborers were presumed to be everything that free black laborers were not. Planters' characterizations tell us nothing about the Chinese, but they do reveal much about planters' own interests and desires and about their conception of the proper behavior and role of labor.

Chinese laborers were described as being "early risers, industrious and intelligent"; they were said to be frugal, thrifty, hardworking, and satisfied with low pay.[67] "I never saw a Chinese pauper; I never saw a Chinese who was a drunkard; I never saw one idle," reported a visitor to California. "Like a hive of bees they are always busy."[68] The Chinese, furthermore, "never meddle with politics" and were invariably peaceful.[69] In contrast to white immigrants, the Chinese, planters believed, had no interest in becoming landholders and thus could be truly relied upon as field hands.[70] "If we invite foreign emigrants at all," declared one planter, "let them come from China, as laborers for *wages*, under the supervision of Southern planters."[71]

Chinese laborers were also thought to be especially qualified for cotton cultivation. Loring and Atkinson, in their 1868 assessment of labor conditions in the South, reckoned that "there is probably no race so well fitted to meet all the requirements of cotton cultivation as the Chinese." The Chinese have "nimble and dexterous fingers," perfect for picking cotton, they can live easily and cheaply on "rice and other vegetable food," and they "will thrive" under climatic conditions too harsh for white laborers.[72] Chinese laborers compared favorably to blacks as well: more easily controlled, "more skillful in the use of their hands and muscles," more "industrious," "more apt to learn," and more inclined to take instructions. In addition, planters also praised the Chinese for their "imitative capacity" and for being especially "docile and obedient."[73]

Not all planters favored Chinese immigration, however, or believed that they would prove efficient and reliable as plantation laborers. Some planters doubted the feasibility of bringing thousands or millions of Chinese laborers into the South. Others expressed concern about importing into the southern states yet more "incongruous races" from Asia.[74] Some planters, similarly, worried about the effect on traditional moral values and religious beliefs of introducing an alien culture into the South.[75] Cultural differences, some feared, might also lead to problems of labor control. One planter was troubled about not knowing how to deal with such an alien labor force: the Chinese "are not like the negro, who is satisfied with plenty of 'hog and hominy,' and a shelter to turn the rain," he explained.[76]

In addition, some planters were skeptical that Chinese laborers could be employed profitably in the southern cotton fields, or that they could be easily managed, or that they would prove dependable as a permanently subordinate labor force. Some believed that wages and transportation costs would be too high.[77] Others argued that even if Chinese immigrants could be initially enticed into the South, they would not be content to remain. The Chinese do not immigrate to America to become permanent settlers, critics suggested, but rather are "soujourners"; they come with the intention of accumulating wealth and eventually returning home.[78] Furthermore, a northern newspaper speculated that since the Chinese have such a strong attachment to their homeland, they would soon become homesick and "having constitutionally less love and tenacity of life, [the Chinese] become melancholy, and are seized with an irresistible propensity for suicide."[79] Others feared that the Chinese might not be quite as servile as some southern whites expected. If they were not seized by a "propensity for suicide," they might be seized by a propensity for rebellion. "John is at home in a riot," warned a correspondent to the *Southern Cultivator*.[80] "The Chinese laborer," added another, "will never suit our purposes, unless we are prepared to have a standing army on each plantation."[81] Finally, in Alabama, Democrats were concerned that Chinese immigration would give rise to a "negro-Republican-Chinese coalition."[82]

Northern opinion was far more unequivocally opposed to Chinese immigration to the South. The *Commercial and Financial Chronicle* of New York, for example, though generally sympathetic to the policy of southern immigration, strongly advised against the immigration of Chinese laborers. The *Chronicle* warned that the introduction of Chinese into the South would ignite controversies about their political status not yet resolved even with respect to freed blacks.[83] The U.S. commissioner of agriculture in 1867 also worried about the consequences of bringing another "inferior race" into the country:

> The introduction of Asiatics to meet the requirements of cotton production is to be depreciated, not only because such labor is unskilled and far inferior to negro labor; but it will add to the complications produced by the jealousies

and prejudices of races widely differing in character, taste, and traditional customs. The assumed disadvantage in the presence of one inferior race cannot be neutralized by the introduction of another.[84]

The U.S. Congress, too, was strongly opposed to Chinese immigration, seeing in such a policy a devious attempt to reestablish slavery and the slave trade.[85] Some in the North also anticipated the dangerous possibility that Chinese immigration would bring political control in the southern states back to planters, who presumably would be able to control the votes of Chinese citizens.[86] Southerners sympathetic to Chinese immigration re- garded these criticisms as just further evidence that the North was determined to keep the southern states in a condition of economic and political subservience.[87]

The critics of Chinese immigration had little to worry about, though, for few Chinese laborers were tempted by the opportunity to replace black workers on the southern plantations. "The impression on my mind," stated a Chinese merchant, "is that the Chinese laborer cannot better his condition by emigrating to the South to work in the cotton fields or on sugar plantations at what must necessarily be a low figure of compensation, and in competition with the negro population."[88] A citizen from Georgia, formerly a resident of California, found that "the Chinese in San Francisco were a good deal amused at the idea of coming to the South to work at customary negro wages."[89] According to the report of the Chinese consul in San Francisco, Chinese laborers on the West Coast were receiving wages two to four times higher than what southern blacks were typically paid. There was little economic incentive, therefore, for the Chinese to immi- grate to the South.[90]

During the decade and a half after the Civil war, in

fact, very few Chinese immigrants took up residence in the South. The Chinese population in the United States numbered 105,465 in 1880. Fewer than 1 percent of these lived in the fifteen southern states. Louisiana had by far the largest Chinese population, with a mere 489 in 1880.[91] Especially when measured by the tens of millions of Chinese laborers desired and anticipated by southern planters, the possibility of Chinese immigration constituted a dismal failure. Even the relatively few Chinese who settled in the South proved disappointing as agricultural laborers; most quickly deserted the plantations and turned to other economic pursuits.[92] By the early 1870s, there remained little interest in importing Chinese laborers into the South.[93]

White Immigration to the South

When freedpeople refused to labor obediently and diligently on the plantations, planters attributed this to what they presumed to be the characteristic laziness and improvidence of the black race. They never seriously considered that their difficulty in securing a reliable labor force might have to do with the exceedingly undesirable labor conditions of plantation agriculture. Thus, it was remarkably easy for planters to imagine that they could induce white immigrants into taking the place of their former slaves. Their racial views did not constrain planters to regard blacks as the only eligible candidate for plantation labor. Many planters fully expected "to get these Germans, Swedes and Swiss, so as to supersede black labor" on the plantations.[94] The laboring class, as conceived by planters, did not consist exclusively of "alien" or "inferior" races. Thus, for planters skeptical about the practicability of Chinese immigration or opposed to introducing another "incongruous" race into the South, the possibility of white immigration seemed to be the only way to preserve the plantation system. The idea of attracting white immigrants into the South, according to an 1867 report, was "seriously occupying the minds of our people."[95] In the words of a Georgia planter: "We shall have to have control of the free nigroes or import white men to do the work."[96]

Freedpeople, complained the Mississippi *Sentinel*, refused to enter the plantation labor market and preferred to settle on land of their own. "Steps must be taken then to provide against these contingencies," the *Sentinel* advised. "Labor must be imported from Germany, Switzerland, or the North."[97] As with the Chinese, the objective of white immigration was just as much to put pressure on blacks as to replace them on the plantations. By placing freed blacks into competition with white laborers, planters believed, they could regain some of the control they possessed as slaveholders. According to one report, such was "the language of scores of men."[98] Planters anticipated that "the competition of thrifty immigrants," besides adding to the plantation labor supply, "would stimulate the Negro"[99] and would force "down the price of black labor."[100] "Competition," a writer for the *Texas Almanac* declared, "will dissipate many of the freedmen's conceited notions and lower their growing pretentiousness."[101]

The purpose of labor control might also be served by just threatening to displace black laborers with white immigrants. This was apparently what William J. Sykes, a white resident of Mississippi, had in mind. Speaking before the freedpeople of Lowndes County, Sykes counseled them to "beware of becoming politicians," and encouraged them to engage in honest labor and fulfill all contracts. Sykes offered the following warning:

> Whilst the white men who own the lands would be
> seriously injured by your failure to comply with your

contracts, you would be the greatest sufferers, because they have more means of support than you have. Your interests and theirs are the same. There are men now ready to import foreign laborers to take your places, and to put you out of employment. *This is your real danger.* It may be avoided. Show yourselves faithful to your contracts this year.[102]

White Alabamians, similarly, used the threat of foreign immigration in an attempt to discourage blacks from participation in the Freedmen's League, which, planters maintained, was keeping wages unnaturally high. This "leaguing," railed one of the Alabama papers, "is a game that two can play at. If they assume to dictate, we will oust them; and supply their places with better laborers, whom we can import from the North."[103]

Relatively few Europeans immigrated to the South after the war, refuting predictions that the abolition of slavery would open a gateway to massive immigration. In fact, fewer immigrants resided in the southern states in 1870 than in 1860.[104] Nevertheless, planters did manage to carry out a few experiments with white immigrants. Irish, Italian, Dutch, Swedish, Scottish, and especially German immigrants all saw some employment on southern plantations after the war; but planters' experiences with white immigrants proved universally disappointing.[105] Even when they were willing to accept employment on the plantations, white laborers were just as costly as black laborers. They could be just as demanding and recalcitrant, and they too objected to slavelike working conditions, especially the use of overseers, and insisted upon the opportunity to become landholders.[106] "Germans leave their country not merely to find work as day laborers," one New York observer pointed out. "They all aim to become landowners, and that chance must be very *conspicuously pointed out to them,* or they continue the beaten tract westward."[107]

The agrarian reformers and critics of the plantation system, for precisely this reason, preferred white immigration, and especially the immigration of German laborers, who were regarded as being "vastly superior" to blacks: but "it is not as laborers for us, that the Germans will profit us most, it is rather as laborers for themselves, on our land, either rented, sold or given to them. We want our country filled up with a good breed of men."[108] Planters were not interested in filling up the country "with a good breed of men" however; they wanted reliable plantation laborers. In South Carolina, for example, planters were prepared to assist immigrants coming from Germany, but only on the condition that the latter "consent to take a secondary position," that they agree to accept permanently the role of a subordinate laboring class.[109] Planters found few German immigrants willing to go along with this requirement. "It is useless for our planters to turn to Germany," advised a Louisiana resident. "No country in Europe has a peasantry so sturdily fond of social independence. They clanise, but they will not labor in gangs—not even in the west; certainly not in cotton fields."[110] German immigrants, planters eventually realized, would not serve the needs of plantation agriculture. "If the Germans should come, they would not consent to engage as laborers for wages in cotton farms," an Alabama resident declared, "and so far as making cotton is concerned, the farmers would be no better off."[111]

By the end of the decade, most planters had soured on the possibility of white immigration. They recognized that white immigrants could "never be relied upon to supply the gang labor required for the cultivation of large estates." Most European immigrants who came to the

South "turned their attention to the cultivation of the soil with their own hands," but what the South really needed, as far as planters were concerned, were immigrants "at the plow handle."[112] Any white laborers worth having, lamented the editors of the *Southern Cultivator*, sought to become landowners themselves, hence white immigrants could not, especially in the long run, solve the plantation labor problem.[113] Planters, one historian observes, ultimately found that "most of the foreigners attracted to the section proved even less content than Negroes to remain plantation laborers."[114]

As planters abandoned the possibility of white immigration, they came to the reluctant conclusion that, as far as the demands of southern cotton cultivation were concerned, the labor of free blacks was superior to that of European immigrants. "Swedes, Germans, and Irishmen had been imported, but the Swedes refused to eat cornbread, the Germans sloped away north-west-ward in the hope of obtaining homesteads, and the Irishmen preferred a city career," an Englishman reported from Virginia. "It seems," he concluded, "the South will have need of Sambo yet awhile."[115] Planters too began having second thoughts about the relative worth of free black labor. "I guarantee," declared a Georgia planter in 1869, "that any lazy thieving negro, well managed, will be of more use to any planter, than any German laborer that I have ever seen, and I have seen several in this community, and have worked some myself."[116] This conclusion, no doubt, was influenced by the fact that no viable alternative to black labor had emerged. "I am now done with white labor," declared a South Carolina planter in 1869. "They have been a great many immigrants brought to this district, very few of whom have been worth their board. I think this immigration business one of the grandest humbugs of the day."[117]

Conclusion

For planters, immigration held out the possibility that, despite black resistance, landholders would be able to preserve the system of plantation agriculture. The policy of immigration was a response to the failure of labor control, and it was also a tactic of labor control itself, a way of forcing free blacks to accede to the demands of the plantation system. Freedpeople correctly understood the intention of this policy: "to bring foreigners to your country, and thrust us out or reduce us to a serfdom intolerable."[118]

Planters' interest in immigration reflected their experiences with, and attitudes toward, free black labor. Planters advocated immigration because they resented the independence that blacks now claimed and because they were unable to control the black labor force. They constantly complained about the disobedience and insubordination of freedpeople and hoped that immigration would provide them with an alternative labor supply. On the other hand, planters also complained about the shortage of black labor and hoped that immigration would fill the labor vacuum. Thus, planters pursued the possibility of immigration both because of their increasing hostility toward freedpeople and because of a decline in the effective supply of black labor.

Planters' turn to immigration and their contradictory thoughts about free black labor reflected the difficult situation in which they found themselves. They continually bemoaned the presence of free blacks and advocated their colonization out of the South. At the same time, planters lamented the shortage of black laborers and competed for their employment. Planters found immigration so appealing because it seemed to address both aspects of the "Negro Problem": the presence of *free* blacks and the shortage of *laboring* blacks. From the perspective of planters, immigration promised to resolve a multitude of problems. Where labor was scarce, immigration would make it plentiful again. Where blacks were demanding, immigration, by breaking their monopoly of labor, would make them accommodating. And if blacks proved useless as free laborers or insurrectionary as a free subordinate class, as many whites expected, immigration would make possible their colonization, while still permitting the maintenance of the plantation system.

The subsequent failure to attract a significant number of immigrants willing to serve as a permanently subordinate labor force put the future of the plantation system in doubt. As evidence mounted that immigration would not even begin to supply planters' needs and as they failed to make the threat of immigration credible, they were forced to reconsider the usefulness of black labor and to ponder means for making it more available. Ironically, while originally intended to discipline the black labor force or drive blacks out of the South altogether, efforts to encourage immigration, because of their palpable lack of success, wound up putting pressure on planters and demonstrating their continued dependence on their former slaves.

Chapter 5 · Economic
            Reconstruction
            and Black
            Colonization

Despite the scarcity of labor, southern whites in the immediate aftermath of slavery frequently advocated black colonization, the relocation of the black population outside of the South. "If any grand colonization project should be started," a reporter for the *Nation* wrote in 1865, "the Southerners would all favor it, as they say now all they want is 'to get shet of them'; that is, to get them out of the country."[1] Given the prevailing racial ideology in the white South, this was not necessarily a disingenuous or irrational reaction to the abolition of slavery. Many planters fully expected that free black labor would not prove viable anyway and hoped to procure an alternative supply of labor through immigration. In addition, whites throughout the southern states feared that emancipation would inevitably give rise to a race war and regarded the colonization of free blacks as necessary for peace and social order. Whether convinced that free black labor was worthless or concerned about the threat of black insurrection—or whether simply as an expression of a more rudimentary hostility toward black people— southern whites took seriously the possibility of ridding the South of the former slaves and gave strong support to proposals for black colonization. In Virginia, for example, a candidate for Congress in 1865 was expected to receive a "strong vote" in his district because of his outspoken position in favor of "the emigration and colonization of the Negro population."[2]

Planters specifically, however, were understandably equivocal in their support for colonization. In fact, most planters were prepared to accept the continued presence of black people in the South—if they could be made to work and safely relegated to a permanently subordinate position. There would be no need for colonization, planters maintained, if their power to manage the labor force and exercise effective authority over the black race were restored. A Confederate major, shortly after the war, presented a succinct analysis of the "Negro question" that captured precisely the viewpoint of most southern planters: "If you of the North want now to conciliate and settle the South, you must do one of three things: re-establish slavery; give the old masters in some way power to compel the negroes to work; or colonize them out of the country, and help us to bring in white laborers!"[3] To the extent that planters doubted their ability to either "re-establish slavery" or "compel the negroes to work," colonization appeared to an eminently reasonable policy. The fact that planters advocated colonization as frequently and vociferously as they did is, in itself, a telling indication of the effectiveness of black resistance to the plantation system. Even so, reflecting the difficult situation in which they found themselves, planters remained uncertain about the possibility of black colonization. While they deeply resented the presence of free blacks in the South and hoped to see them deported, planters also had great need for their labor. Planters' ambivalence about the prospect of free black labor is revealingly expressed in the observation that every planter "would be glad to have the entire black race deported—except his own laborers."[4]

Even though the possibility of black colonization typically involved more wishful thinking and tough talk than concrete action, it deserves an important place in the story of economic reconstruction and the rise of sharecropping in the postwar South. What planters had to say about colonization provides valuable evidence regarding their interests, their views on free black labor, and their thoughts on the problem of economic reorganization. An exploration of the possibility of black colonization will illuminate the reasoning and experiences of southern planters and free blacks as they confronted one another with competing visions of a new economic order. Furthermore, as with southern immigration, the historical importance of the possibility of black colonization derives also from its failure; for the defeat of this possibility, and the fact that the southern states were destined to remain the home of millions of black people, made it all the more pressing for planters to make some accommodation with their former slaves.

It is not too surprising that southern whites turned to this possibility in the postwar years, for the idea of black colonization has been a significant presence throughout American history. Proposals for black colonization attracted considerable interest just prior to, and during, the Civil War in particular, when the Lincoln administration and the Republican party played a leading role in the movement to deport freed blacks. The history of the colonization movement prior to the abolition of slavery provides the context necessary for fully appreciating the significance of this possibility in the postwar South.

The Colonization Movement Before the Civil War

Colonization projects in the United States began as early as the 1600s and 1700s, when crimes and rebellious acts committed by blacks were punished by deportation.[5] Proposals for the systematic and large-scale removal of black people, however, were not seriously entertained until the 1770s and 1780s, when colonizationists were motivated, in part, by the desire to Christianize Africa and to obstruct the slave trade by creating a buffer zone along the African west coast. Toward the end of the 1780s and into the 1790s, however, this missionary interest gave way to more pressing domestic concerns. During these years, the upper South, particularly Virginia, experienced a growth, through immigration and manumission, in the population of free blacks. This raised the specter of race war, as most whites assumed that free blacks would neither be granted full equality in America nor submit peacefully to a permanently subordinate status. The resulting potential for violence and insurrection could be removed only by deporting the free black population. This marked a shift in the platform of the colonization movement. After 1787, Winthrop Jordan notes, the primary motive of the colonizationists "was not to get Negroes over to Africa but to get them out of America."[6] As a result of both real and imagined slave insurrections—especially the successful slave revolt in St. Domingue (now Haiti) in the 1790s and the Gabriel Prosser plot in Virginia in 1800—the objective of the colonization movement narrowed even further. After 1800, Jordan argues, "the colonization movement became in much larger measure an effort to free America from the danger of slave insurrection."[7]

The fervor for colonization diminished somewhat in the early 1800s, when the African slave trade closed and antislavery agitation declined.[8] But the founding of the American Colonization Society (ACS) in 1816 and 1817 resurrected the colonization movement. Through its political lobbying and intellectual influence, through the authority of its official publication (the *African Repository*), and through the creation of a black colony along the African west coast (Liberia)—the ACS played the central role in the colonization movement in nineteenth-century America.[9]

The immediate aim of the ACS was to remove free blacks from the United States and relocate them in Africa. Presumably, blacks and whites would both benefit from this separation of the races. Colonizationists believed that it was impossible to eradicate race prejudice, that blacks could never achieve equality in the United States, and that only by settling in another country, apart from whites, could black people hope to better their condition and enjoy the fruits of freedom and liberty. White America would gain from colonization too, for the deportation of free blacks would rid the country of a dangerous presence and a source of national divisiveness.[10]

With respect to the crucial problem of slavery, though, the ACS did not maintain a unified or consistent position, and some members favored avoiding this controversial issue altogether. However, some colonizationists actively supported slavery (indeed, some owned slaves themselves) and regarded the colonization of free blacks as a way of removing a disruptive element and stabilizing the institution of slavery.[11] In contrast, many members of the ACS supported colonization precisely because of their opposition to slavery; they believed that, without some plan for removing free blacks, emancipation would be neither socially desirable nor politically viable. But even when it came out against slavery, the ACS maintained a conciliatory posture and tried to appeal to southern slaveholders with a program combining gradual emancipation and colonization.[12] This greatly underestimated the extent to which planters possessed a specifically economic stake in the preservation of slavery. The strategy adopted by the ACS assumed, incorrectly, that planters' commitment to slavery derived primarily from their apprehension about living alongside a large free black population. But as it turned out, the promise of colonization was not enough to transform planters into abolitionists—although abolition, as we shall see, transformed many planters into colonizationists.

The ACS experienced limited success in recruiting blacks and encouraging settlement in Liberia. Prior to 1860, several thousand free blacks relocated in Africa, although some of these were forced to accept deportation as a condition of manumission.[13] But most free blacks opposed the idea of colonization and expressed hostility toward the American Colonization Society in particular. "On the whole," Louis Mehlinger concludes from an examination of the attitudes of free blacks toward African colonization, "the movement never appealed to a large number of intelligent free people of color."[14]

While trying to gain political support by appealing to all possible groups and interests, the ACS succeeded only in antagonizing nearly everyone—free blacks, slaveholders, and abolitionists alike. Internal conflicts, financial difficulties, and bad press from disillusioned emigrés further contributed to the failure and decline of the ACS in the 1830s and 1840s. In the 1850s, as the conflict over slavery intensified, as fears and expectations of eventual emancipation increased, and as conditions worsened for free blacks in the North, the colonization movement experienced a resurgence—with black people themselves taking much of the initiative.[15] Influenced by a new black nationalism and increasingly impatient with their white allies in the antislavery movement, many free blacks began to reconsider the merits of colonization. Black advocates of emigration still shunned the American Colonization Society, though, and most preferred resettlement somewhere in the Western Hemisphere rather than in Africa. Yet, while growing in appeal during the 1850s, the idea of colonization probably never attracted anything approaching a majority of free blacks; most opted to continue the struggle for equality in the land they considered their rightful home. And with the onset of the Civil War and the renewed hopes it engendered, the momentum of the colonization movement among free blacks was checked.[16]

The Lincoln Administration and Black Colonization

Lincoln's views on emancipation and colonization were consistent with those of the American Colonization Society. He preferred a system of gradual emancipation with compensation to slaveowners and colonization of blacks beyond the borders of the United States. Lincoln's most famous statement in support of colonization was presented in August 1862, before a small gathering of free blacks from the District of Columbia. Lincoln stated that much mutual suffering and divisiveness resulted from two such physically dissimilar races living together. He further argued that even with the abolition of slavery, black people could never hope to attain equality with whites. "It is better for us both, therefore to be separated," Lincoln declared. He acknowledged that most free blacks would probably not see much immediate advantage in colonization, but urged his audience not to take such a "selfish view of the case." If free blacks were willing to make the sacrifice and volunteer for colonization, Lincoln suggested, they might smooth the way for the abolition of slavery. Just as the promise of colonization was used to persuade slaveholders to agree to emancipation, so too did Lincoln use the promise of emancipation to persuade free blacks to agree to colonization. Lincoln concluded his address by describing the virtues of Central America as a possible location for black colonization, emphasizing especially the prospects there for coal mining.[17]

Other rationales for colonization found a hearing in the Lincoln administration. In 1862, the Reverend James Mitchell, subsequently appointed commissioner of emigration, warned that the prospect of an increase in "the mixed breed bastards" posed a threat to the family, to the nation, and to white supremacy. The problem of miscegenation could be avoided, Mitchell argued, only through the colonization of the black population.[18] The 1862 House report on emancipation and colonization also played on white fears of racial "intermixture," defending colonization as serving "the highest interests of the white race."

> Much of the objection to emancipation arises from the opposition of a large portion of our people to the intermixture of the races, and from the association of white and black labor. The committee would do nothing to favor such a policy; apart from the antipathy which nature has ordained, the presence of a race among us who cannot, and ought not to, be admitted to our social and political privileges, will be a perpetual source of injury and inquietude to both. This is a question of color, and is unaffected by the relation of master and slave. The introduction of the negro, whether bond or free, into the same field of labor with the white man, is the opprobrium of the latter; and we cannot believe that the thousands of non-slaveholding citizens in the rebellious States who live by industry are fighting to continue the negro within our limits even in a state of vassalage, but more probably from

a vague apprehension that he is to become their
competitor in his own right. We wish to disabuse our
laboring countrymen, and the whole Caucasian race who
may seek a home here, of this error. . . . The committee
concludes that the highest interests of the white race,
whether Anglo-Saxon, Celt, or Scandinavian, require that
the whole country should be held and occupied by those
races alone.[19]

The committee on emancipation and colonization
extolled the advantages of colonization for the domestic
economy as well. The deportation of blacks, the committee report predicted, would encourage immigration from
Europe, result in the beneficial substitution of free labor
for slave labor, lead to higher wages for white workers,
and bring prosperity to previously backward sections of
the country.[20] The United States would profit not only
from the removal of blacks, but from their resettlement as
well. The committee anticipated that the colonization of
blacks in Central America would open up new commercial opportunities and would facilitate the creation of a
"colonial system" similar to that enjoyed by Great
Britain.[21] Black colonization, the committee suggested,
would place in Central America a race of people particularly suited to the climate and yet of a sufficient level of
civilization to maintain stable governments. In short, the
report of the committee presented black colonization as a
useful instrument of American colonialism.

It may therefore be well imagined what would be the
result of planting five millions of American negroes . . . in
a country . . . protected by our power and directed by our
intelligence, and stimulated to exertion by those motives
which the wants of civilization, which they have acquired
among us, have never failed to supply. . . . If we add to this
the certain result of extending our power and influence,

through their instrumentality, over the millions of people who already inhabit these regions, we shall be able to form some conception of the value to our commerce which the foundation of such a colony would confer.[22]

Finally, as Wisconsin senator James R. Doolittle declared, the colonization of blacks in Central America was sanctioned also by both Divine Providence and the "natural laws of climate."[23]

All this talk in support of colonization involved more than just idle speculation. The Lincoln administration in the early 1860s undertook two practical experiments in black colonization. The first involved Lincoln with Ambrose W. Thompson and the Chiriqui Improvement Company. Thompson's company controlled several hundred thousand acres of land, ostensibly rich in coal, located in a northern province of Panama. That black emigrés could immediately begin supporting themselves by mining coal especially favored Chiriqui as a site for colonization. During the course of 1861 and 1862, several key members of Lincoln's administration recommended the Chiriqui colonization project. In September of 1862, Thompson and the government signed a provisional contract, and the president appointed Kansas senator Samuel Clark Pomeroy to evaluate the Chiriqui location and oversee the process of colonization. But by late September, most of Lincoln's advisers and cabinet members were becoming distrustful of Thompson and increasingly opposed to the Chiriqui project, though Lincoln persisted. Heated protests against black immigration from the governments of Honduras, Nicaragua, Costa Rica, and other Central American countries finally put an end to the Chiriqui project. In addition, Chiriqui coal was subsequently discovered to be worthless, and Thompson's motives and claim to the land were found to be questionable. The Chiriqui colonization project went down to defeat without a single colony-bound ship leaving harbor.[24]

The second experiment in colonization undertaken by the Lincoln administration resulted in a more disastrous outcome. The proposed site for this colonization project was the island of à Vache, which belonged to the government of Haiti. Initially, the intermediary for this project was businessman Bernard Kock. On December 31, 1862, the government made a contract with Kock to transport five thousand emigrants at fifty dollars a head to the island of à Vache. The contract was annulled when doubts were raised about Kock's honesty and competence. The project proceeded, however, when three New York businessmen, Leonard W. Jerome, Paul S. Forbes, and Charles K. Tuckerman (who turned out to be Kock's associates), came forward to assume the contract. In the spring of 1863, 453 prospective colonists set sail from Fortress Monroe. Kock (back in charge again), drawing on the funds designated to provide food and shelter for the black colonists, purchased "handcuffs and leg-chains" instead and built "stocks for their punishment."[25] In addition, Kock managed to confiscate the money of the colonists, while also refusing to pay them for the labor they performed while on the island. Many colonists died from disease and others fled to Haiti. Less than a year later the government, while trying to avoid embarrassing publicity, sent a relief ship to return the survivors to the United States. So ended Lincoln's second colonization project.[26] That same year Congress repealed all appropriations for black colonization. Whether Lincoln's interest in colonization endured these defeats is an issue of some debate among historians.[27]

The rhetoric in support of black colonization, despite the failure of these projects, served important political purposes for the Republican party. Many northern Republicans hoped that the promise of colonization would not only reduce fears of emancipation in the North, but would also diminish opposition to the abolition of slavery in the South, thus bringing the war to a rapid close.[28] In 1862, for example, Missouri senator Francis P. Blair declared that the war arose not from any "love of slavery," but rather from dread of racial equality. In order to ease fears of "amalgamation," Blair proposed that the races be separated.

> The outbreak, as I have already said, sprang from the convictions in the common mind in the disturbed region that the negroes were to be liberated and put upon an equal footing with the whites. The mere idea of this amalgamation was instrumental in producing the rebellion. . . . The idea of the separation of the races is a complete antidote to that poison.[29]

The committee on emancipation and colonization, also in 1862, advanced a similar position:

> It is believed that the most formidable difficulty which lies in the way of emancipation in most if not in all the slave States is the belief, which obtains especially among those who own no slaves, that if the negroes shall become free, they must still continue in our midst, and so remaining after their liberation, they may in some measure be made equal to the Anglo-Saxon race.[30]

Colonization, Robert Zoellner writes, "was to act as a sugar coating for the bitter pill of emancipation."[31] Lincoln and the Republican party sought to convince both northern and southern whites that—while they were staunchly opposed to slavery, a commitment tempered by respect for property rights—they did not favor social and political equality for blacks. The enemies of slavery were not necessarily the friends of black people.[32]

By speaking out in favor of black colonization, Republican leaders in the North sought to fortify themselves against another politically sensitive issue. The onset of the Civil War and the prospect of emancipation fostered considerable anxiety in the free states, especially in the Midwest, that the North would be overrun by freed blacks emigrating from the South.[33] In order for the Republican party to conduct the war effectively and sell the policy of emancipation, it had to assuage fears of a massive migration of blacks—fears strategically exploited by northern Democrats and southern slaveholders. One strategy adopted by Republicans, demonstrating that their opponents were not the only ones adept at playing on racial prejudice, was to turn the argument around: the abolition of slavery, they countered, would result in a migration into the South of free blacks from the North.[34] But in addition to this rhetorical device, Republican leaders turned to the policy of colonization as a way of further shoring up their position on the impending "Negro question." The need to appease an apprehensive northern constituency became especially pressing with the passage of the Confiscation Acts, with Lincoln's decision to introduce the Emancipation Proclamation, and with increasing evidence that the war was indeed becoming a war against slavery.

With the failure of wartime colonization schemes, northern Republicans hoped that, as a last resort, the freed slaves could be compelled to remain in the South. Accordingly, the Lincoln administration stepped up programs to employ refugee slaves on abandoned plantations and to utilize them for military purposes, e.g., building fortifications. In addition, and more dramatically, the Union army began to enlist blacks as soldiers. According to one historian, this "systematic mobilization of the blacks in the South moderated the racial fears of the Midwest. . . . No longer was the administration merely relying on climate and sentiment to hold Negroes in the South; it had developed a positive means for containing them there." The policy of "employing and caring" for refugee slaves on abandoned plantations in the South "had effectively sealed the vast majority of them in the region. . . . In this way, the threat of a great migration was destroyed."[35] This policy, and the value (subsequently demonstrated) of both black laborers and black soldiers, along with Union victories at Gettysburg and Vicksburg and a surging economy in mid-1863, eased the way for northerners to accept the destruction of slavery as a legitimate war goal.[36]

With the end of the Civil War, the issue of black colonization in the North lost some of its political urgency. Northern interest in the deportation of the black race did not disappear entirely though. The American Colonization Society, for example, continued its operation into the postwar era, and even anticipated new opportunities opening up with emancipation.[37] In the aftermath of slavery, however, the primary locus of interest in black colonization shifted to the white South.

White Perspectives on Colonization in the Postwar South

In *The White Savage*, Lawrence J. Friedman identifies two competing racial ideologies in the white South. Adherents of the "proslavery ideology," on the one hand, favored "a social order of integrated subservience." These southern whites, whom I will call integrationists, believed that it was their responsibility to look after, and provide guidance to, the "inferior" black race. Their image of the South made room for black people but envisioned them holding a subordinate status only, a status of tutelage comparable to that of children. Exclusionists, on the other hand, refused to include any place at all for blacks in their vision of the South, even as a permanently subservient laboring class. Instead, they "demanded the expulsion of all blacks from white society" and supported the policy of colonization.[38] As one disgruntled rebel said about the former slaves, outspoken in his support for the exclusionist cause: "They all ought to be drove out of the country."[39]

Embracing the ideology of paternalism, an ideology that denied to black people the capacity for independent agency, integrationists presumed that the fate of the black race rested entirely in white hands. "The Freedmen of the South are a powerful element for good or evil," a Georgia resident proclaimed, "and it is our duty, as the superior race, to educate and direct them."[40] Integrationists thus acknowledged an obligation to oversee the continued "elevation" of the black population and to ensure that it did not "revert to barbarism or utterly perish from the face of the earth." The responsibility of the white race toward the black race did not end with the abolition of slavery. "The negro is among us," a South Carolina planter observed in 1869. "He is here and we cannot help it, and the destiny that placed him here, has placed him here for a wise and good purpose." For this critic of colonization, the black person was "the proper, legitimate and divinely ordained laborer of the South"; he urged his neighbors to comply with the "great duty" of impressing this lesson upon the former slaves.

> Let us teach him that his power lies in his muscles, and that the proper field for its exercise, is in the cotton fields of the South. . . . This is our first great duty. We owe it to ourselves, we owe it to the negro, and we owe it to the country.[41]

Black people, integrationists emphasized, were not to blame for the war, and they should not be allowed to die or relapse into savagery. Nor should they be faulted for the adversity and disruption resulting from northern interference. "The negro had no agency in establishing his freedom," explained a North Carolina convention delegate, "and we must not condemn him for that which he made no effort to produce."[42] Neither, integrationists maintained, did the turmoil of Reconstruction justify banishing black people from the South. Rather, as one opponent of colonization stated, the white South must persevere in the "great work" of molding the black race into "effective hirelings."

> The South had already proved itself their greatest benefactor, by rescuing them from barbarism and heathenism and blessing them with the light of a pure christianity. It now remains to complete the great work by elevating them to the status of intelligent, industrious and effective hirelings. Let us not shrink from this arduous, but benevolent, enterprise.[43]

The integrationist perspective posited a happy fit between altruism, obligation, and economic self-interest. By making freed blacks into industrious workers, and thus facilitating the restoration of the plantation system, southern whites would at the same time fulfill their duty toward the black race and demonstrate their own benevolence. Despite the self-serving features of this ideology, however, integrationism attracted only a minority of the white population in the postwar South.

Instead, the end of the Civil War left most southern whites feeling more bitter than dutiful toward the former slaves. The fear and uncertainty arising from an unprecedented "Negro problem" also stirred up support among white southerners for the ideology of exclusionism and the possibility of black colonization. Hostility toward free blacks inspired much of this interest in colonization, but it was fueled also by the humiliation of defeat and resentment toward northerners. Virginia planters, for example, threatened to do all within their power to drive blacks away and "to make the government odious for freeing them."[44] Such expressions of vindictiveness toward the federal government often accompanied declarations calling for black colonization. Since northern interference created the "Negro problem," it seemed only right that the government assume responsibility for resolving it. "Now that you've got them ruined, take the cursed scoundrels out of the country"—this, one journalist found, was the opinion held by most whites in the interior of Mississippi.[45]

Skepticism about the prospect of ever "elevating" freedpeople to the status of "effective hirelings" gave added support to the possibility of black colonization. The prevailing sentiment among southern whites in the years following the war, according to one report, was "that 'if we cannot have them as slaves, take them away; we don't want them.' "[46] Even planters faced with a serious shortage of labor came out in favor of colonization, as John Dennett discovered while reporting from the South in 1865 and 1866.

> Within the past month I have heard a good deal said in favor of colonization, and said by owners of large plantations, who might be expected to desire a crowded labor-market. Speak to them about the vast expense, and other practical difficulties in the way of removing a whole nation from the country in which it has lived for generations, and which it loves, and one will say the Government may have all his share in the public lands to

pay it for taking away his niggers; another that he will
gladly bear a heavier tax than has yet been imposed on him
as part of the expense, and that his acquaintances all say
the same thing; and all cite Andrew Jackson's removal of
the Indians as a case in point.[47]

During the immediate postwar years, as one historian
observed, the "racial antipathy" of planters "warred with
their labor force requirements."[48] The motive of "spite,
ill-will, and disappointment" frequently took precedence
over planters' need for black labor.[49] Despite "the fact
that all the planters are complaining about the insuffi-
ciency of labor," reported one observer, most southern
whites considered free blacks a "nuisance" and "would
gladly be rid of his presence, even at the expense of his
existence."[50] This widespread desire among southern
whites to remove blacks from the South if they could not
be retained in bondage was, one black man responded,
"really interesting": "If you cannot rob the Negro of his
labor and of himself, you will banish him."[51]

Some southern whites favored the colonization of
blacks not despite the labor problems that would result
from their absence, but because of the troubles caused by
their presence. "Blacks have ceased to be producers, and
the whites cannot support them," General Alfred Dockery declared in an 1865 speech urging colonization;
consequently, he advised, "it would be better for both
races that they be separated." As an alternative to the
colonization of blacks outside the borders of the country,
Dockery recommended that freedpeople, like the Indians,
be resettled in segregated reservations.[52] Not everyone in
the South, however, was so resistant to acknowledging
the inevitable dependence of the southern economy on
black labor. The economic wisdom of black colonization
was questioned, for example, in an editorial published in

the Charleston *Daily Courier:* "Is not the black man still a valuable component of the state? Is not his brawny arm necessary to develop our resources and would not the sudden withdrawal of the entire negro population be an actual calamity?"[53] But even planters desperate for labor had little to gain from the continued existence in the South of the "black man" and his "brawny arm" if the latter refused to work. "The people would rather get rid of them [freedpeople] if there were any possible means of doing so," declared a white Virginian. "They are a nuisance, in the present state of affairs. They will not work."[54] In North Carolina "as everywhere," Sidney Andrews reported hearing the "complaint that the free negro will not work"; and despite the considerable demand for labor, Andrews discovered that "strange as it may seem, the people are warm colonizationists."[55] There was, of course, nothing "strange" about this at all, for if "the free negro will not work," planters had no use for them and their colonization represented no great loss.

The frequent accusation that black people would not work and should therefore be deported drew an angry response from freedpeople. "They have no reason to say we will not work," replied a black soldier opposed to colonization, "for we raised them and sent them to school and bought their land. Now it is as little as they can do to give us some of their land—be it little or much."[56] But like this soldier, most blacks did not want to work for their former masters, but rather intended to farm on land of their own. From the perspective of whites, however, this made them no less suitable as candidates for colonization than if they had refused to work altogether.

While planters were primarily concerned with the problem of labor control, other southern whites favored colonization because they perceived the free black population as a threat to social order. Many were anxious that the continued safety of the white population was in jeopardy; only the separation of the races could ensure its preservation.[57] Slavery was a system of racial domination and control, in addition to being a mode of labor exploitation. More specifically, southern whites commonly believed that the institution of slavery functioned to contain the otherwise barbarian impulses of the black race.[58] With the release of blacks from bondage and their removal from the civilizing influence of white authority, many feared that a war between the races would inevitably erupt. Judge Sylvannum Evans, for example, in a speech given while campaigning for Congress in 1865, charged that "the cause of continued strife and tumult" was the presence of "the vagrant freedmen." "I am sure we do not want the scenes of St. Domingo and Hayti repeated in our midst," Evans warned. "I believe such will be the case if they are not removed. If elected I shall urge the general government the duty of colonizing the negroes."[59] The choice, declared a white Virginian, was for blacks to be either "extirpated" or sent back to Africa.

> These unfortunate creatures thus set at liberty en masse I fear are preparing great trouble as well for the whites as for themselves . . . unless the government makes a timely and firm interposition, in a conflict between the two races. Should this be the case, the race must unavoidably be extirpated. . . . Africa was the point toward which the whole work tended, and this is the point where it must end if the negro is to be really benefited.[60]

For a New Orleans resident, however, there was no choice at all; the "only way" to deal effectively with the threat of black insurrection, he proposed, was "to kill the niggers off, *and* drive 'em out of the country."[61]

Some southern whites expected that the problem

posed by the presence of free blacks would eventually take care of itself; the separation of the races would occur through "natural" processes, rendering any colonization program unnecessary. There was, for example, some anticipation that blacks would depart from the South voluntarily. In his testimony before the Joint Committee on Reconstruction, the Reverend Dr. Robert McMurdy predicted that, upon being placed into competition with white laborers, free blacks would gradually leave the country and immigrate to the West Indies.[62] Similarly, a contributor to De Bow's Review from the District of Columbia suggested that the white race, "from their superior capabilities," would multiply faster than the black race and soon acquire ascendancy. Blacks, as a result, "will gradually but certainly tend from the temperate regions of the South to the terras calientas, until the colored race, like a dark fringe, will border the shores of the Southern Atlantic and the Gulf of Mexico."[63]

Especially widespread among southern whites was the belief that blacks, under the rigor of freedom, were doomed to extinction. "The past history of the negro," declared a physician from Alabama, demonstrates that "freed blacks cannot be relied upon as an agricultural population, and that emancipation must ultimately result in their extermination. . . . Like the Indian and other inferior races, he may expect to be driven out by the superior intelligence, energy and perseverance of the whites."[64] The Nation reported that this was a "nearly unanimous" belief. Southern whites expected that "the colored race is destined to speedy extinction, crowded out of existence by competition with the superior race."[65]

Others believed that, competition from whites aside, the black race would die off from its own natural indolence and from an inability to survive without the supervision and guidance of white authority. "The guardianship of the

latter [southern whites] having been withdrawn," wrote the
Memphis *Avalanche*, "the former [freed blacks] will rap-
idly lapse into semi-barbarism and gradually disappear. . . .
The negro race is doomed."[66] Such ominous predictions
were sometimes used to justify the program of black
colonization: if they were relocated out of the South, the
black race might yet be saved from extermination. "Unless
the colored people were removed to Texas, or some South
American country," proclaimed one Norfolk resident,
"they would surely die out by reason of their laziness and
shiftlessness."[67] John Rock, a black critic of colonization
writing prior to the war, ridiculed the myth that blacks
could not take care of themselves and would be doomed to
extinction if set free: "Do you imagine that the Negro can
live outside of slavery? Of course, now, they can take care
of themselves and their master too; but if you give them
their liberty, must they not suffer?"[68]

Besides exclusionism and integrationism, Friedman
also refers to a third racial ideology, whose "only promi-
nent proponent," he argues, was William Gannaway
Brownlow, the governor of Tennessee during Reconstruction. While sometimes appearing to be a fervent exclusionist, Brownlow, like the integrationists, also maintained a high regard for the paternalistic relationship
between blacks and whites that presumably obtained in
the antebellum South. According to Friedman, Brownlow's apparent adherence to competing doctrines, rather
than signifying any inconsistency, "applied different
principles to different Negroes." The ideology of exclusionism applied to "insolent" blacks, while the ideology
of integrationism targeted "servile" blacks. This ideological flexibility, Friedman observes, allowed for the "integration of the docile and the exclusion of the defiant."[69]

Yet, rather than being rare, evidence indicates that
among planters specifically a variant of the position

adopted by Brownlow was quite prevalent in the postwar years. Planters did not necessarily fall into either the exclusionist or integrationist camps exclusively; their position on black colonization was based less on ideology than on practical considerations. On the one hand, to the extent they doubted that integration on the basis of black subordination could be effectively restored, planters favored the option of deporting their former slaves and thus adhered to the ideology of exclusionism. On the other hand, planters seemed willing to forgo demands for colonization if they could somehow reestablish their authority over the black population. That is, to the extent they envisioned the possibility of recreating something approaching the master-slave relationship, planters adhered to the ideology of integrationism.

Many planters, therefore, still held out the possibility that blacks might yet be able to live in the South and make a useful contribution to the southern economy—if, through legislative measures, for example, they were subjected to a strict system of social control. A lawyer from Raleigh, for example, proposed that blacks be placed "under the control of the Legislature," which, he advised,

> ought to provide against vagrancy; adopt measures to
> require them to fulfill their contracts for labor, and
> authorize their sale, for a term of years for breaches of
> order. Either do that, and so protect us against an intolerable
> nuisance, or colonize them out of the country.[70]

From this perspective, legislative control over the black population, by replicating certain of the characteristics of slavery, represented an alternative to colonization. Such legislative measures could even be construed as being beneficial to blacks. "The Negro," one southern white explained, "is doomed to undergo extinction. . . . The race will first become a pauper and then disappear. Nothing but the most careful legislation will prevent it."[71] A legislative substitute for the authority of the white master might save the black race from extinction. The editors of the *Carolina Times*, similarly, recommended that "the only course to keep the Negro from dying out or relapsing into barbarism" is the enactment by the legislature of "a compulsory code of enforced labor."[72]

For perhaps even most planters then, the paramount consideration in reflecting on the possibility of black colonization was not the ideological conflict between exclusionism and integrationism, but rather the prospect for reestablishing social control: control over a labor force believed to be naturally indolent and incapable of responding to market incentives, and control over a presumably inferior and savage race prepared for insurrection or destined for extinction. Since planters could not be sure how the "Negro question" would finally be resolved, they also expressed equivocation and uncertainty about the desirability of black colonization. From the perspective of most planters, the question of whether or not free blacks should have a future in the South depended upon the resolution of more fundamental issues: whether the preservation of social order was possible given the continuing presence of free blacks, and whether the black population could fulfill the labor force requirements of plantation agriculture. In the final analysis, planters welcomed the continued presence of black people in the South only if they were subjected to a strict system of control.[73]

Black Perspectives on Colonization in the Postwar South

The possibility of black colonization attracted white adherents almost exclusively and thus, to the extent that it depended upon the voluntary emigration of southern blacks, had absolutely no chance for success. Southern blacks after the war were even less inclined than free blacks before and during the war to give their support to any colonization schemes. "I saw none of the negroes," Whitelaw Reid reported, "either residing in Savannah or from the country, who had any desire to be colonized away from their present homes." Freedpeople, he wrote, "utterly revolt" from the idea of being relocated out of the South.[74] "What's the use to give us our freedom," protested one freedman, "if we can't stay where we were raised, and own our houses where we were born, and our little piece of ground?"[75] While many freedpeople certainly wanted to live apart from whites, especially from their former masters, they did not desire racial separation to occur at the expense of a southern homeland.

> Ask them if they would like to live by themselves, and they would generally say "Yes"... but further inquiry would always develop the fact that their idea of "living by themselves" was to have the whites removed from what they consider their own country.... They believe in colonization; but it is in colonization on the lands they have been working.[76]

Thus blacks opposed colonization not from a desire to live alongside southern whites, of course, but rather because they believed they possessed a right to the land on which they had lived and worked for so many generations, and they looked forward to the opportunity to acquire southern homesteads. Freedpeople claimed a positive right to a homeland in the country of their birth. "This is your country, but it is ours too," stated a resolution by a convention of freedpeople in South Carolina in 1865. "You were born here, so were we; your fathers fought for it, but our fathers fed them."[77] In Virginia, also in 1865, a black convention made the following public resolution:

That as natives of American soil we claim the right to
remain upon it, and that any attempt to remove, expatriate,
or colonize us in any other land against our will is unjust, for
here we were born, and for this country our fathers and
brothers have fought, and we hope to remain here in the full
employment of enfranchised manhood and its dignities.[78]

In contrast, the idea of colonization looked like a plot to
deprive them of their newly won freedom and defraud
them of their promised "forty acres and a mule." "If we
can get lands here and can work and support ourselves,"
explained a black man testifying before the Joint Committee on Reconstruction, "I do not see why we should go to
any place that we do not want to go."[79] Indeed, the
inability of advocates of black colonization after the war
to recruit prospective emigrants was due, in part, to the
expectation among freedpeople that they would gain
possession of the plantations.[80]

Within a decade of the abolition of slavery, however,
southern blacks were more seriously entertaining the
possibility of emigrating out of the South, if not to a
foreign country, at least to the West. The end of Reconstruction and the rise to dominance again of the Democratic party in the South threatened the political and civil
rights that black people had won in the years immediately
following the war. Their economic situation deteriorated
too, as sharecropping continued to evolve into an oppres-
sive debt-peonage system. Thus, later on in the century
many blacks, for both political and economic reasons,
began reconsidering the possibility of colonization.[81]

Emigration of Southern Whites

One South Carolina planter, "utterly disgusted"
with his former slaves, longed to "some day be in a land
that is purged of them."[82] This planter hoped for a future

in which the free black population would be removed from the South or would disappear through extinction. For some southern whites, however, emigration rather than black colonization appeared to be the most promising route for achieving a homeland "purged" of free blacks.[83] Humiliated by defeat, faced with the loss of their antebellum world, and confronted by an impossible "Negro problem," several thousand white southerners in the years after the war chose to leave the South altogether, and many thousands more gave this possibility serious consideration. "O, what a fall is here," declared the New Orleans *Tribune* in a biting editorial on the white emigration movement. "Has it come to this? Those who but a few years ago were the lords over the poor negroes . . . now talk of colonizing elsewhere!"[84]

Even before the war, southern whites had given some thought to expanding southward and extending their domain into the countries of Latin America. With the defeat of the Confederacy and the abolition of slavery, the possibility of white emigration ceased being a matter of mere speculation; southern whites actively began to mobilize around the program of emigration. Emigration agents traveled to destination countries to report on conditions firsthand and make necessary arrangements for resettlement. Southerners with more of an adventurous spirit journeyed to inspect the opportunities for emigration themselves. Prospective emigrants also organized associations, groups, and companies throughout the South. According to one account, every southern state had at least one "society for the promotion of emigration," and in most states numerous such organizations were established.[85] Emigration societies and companies— the Southern Emigration Society of Edgefield, South Carolina, for example—functioned to locate and identify possible sites for relocation, to gather and distribute information, to mobilize support among southern whites, and otherwise to facilitate the process of migration.

Proponents of southern emigration also circulated pamphlets and books advertising the advantages offered by residence in Brazil or Mexico. *The Emigrant's Guide to Brazil*, by Lansford Warren Hastings, *Ho! for Brazil*, by General W. W. Wood of Mississippi, and *Brazil, the Home for Southerners*, written by Ballard S. Dunn, a priest from New Orleans (the latter two both published in 1866) were among the most popular examples of this propaganda literature. Southern whites showed renewed interest in prewar travelers' reports from Latin America as well. The advantages of relocation were also extolled by the first wave of emigrants in personal letters and communications, which were often printed in southern newspapers and periodicals.[86]

Government officials and influential figures in Latin American countries greeted the possibility of southern emigration with considerable enthusiasm. Brazil and Mexico, in particular, actively campaigned to encourage the immigration of southern whites. Both countries advertised in southern newspapers, courted emigration agents, entertained representatives of southern colonization societies, and offered a wide variety of assistance, inducements, and incentives to prospective emigrants. And Americans in both Brazil and Mexico were granted official or quasi-official status in governmental departments concerned with immigration. Authorities in Brazil optimistically predicted that one hundred thousand families from the South would eventually immigrate to that country.[87]

These efforts to promote southern emigration had a significant impact. In 1865, according to an estimate from the New York *Herald*, fifty thousand southerners were ready to emigrate to Brazil alone; many thousands more, anticipating favorable reports, were also preparing to leave; still others wished they could join the movement, but finally lacked the resolve or the financial resources necessary to undertake such a journey.[88] The reality of the emigration movement did not quite match these estimates. Nevertheless, several thousand whites—including a significant number of planters—did in fact leave the South shortly after the war in search of new homes in foreign countries. And many more than this, had they the means, probably would also have gone.[89] For others, moreover, the decision to remain in the South was not an easy one. An Alabama planter told John Trowbridge that he had actually settled on emigrating to Brazil, but in the end he got only as far as Mobile when he decided to remain in the South, despite feeling like a "foreigner" and an "alien."[90]

The motives of those who elected to join the exodus from the South were varied. The political turmoil and uncertainty resulting from the defeat of the Confederacy motivated many southern whites to leave the country. Some were anxious about war reprisals and northern vengeance, while the threat of "Negro domination" or "Yankee rule" drove others away. Many more were motivated by the fear of black insurrection, by the loss of their labor force, and by a general hostility toward free blacks. Major Joseph Abney, president of the Southern Colonization Society established in 1865, gave this explanation for deciding to forsake the South in favor of residence in Brazil:

> The future is enveloped in clouds and darkness . . . and now at one fell dash of the pen, to set free the negroes who constituted three fourths of all the property that remained to us, and nearly the whole of the laboring power of the country, and quarter them among us, where they will defy

our authority, remain a subject of continual agitation for
fanatics, engender a festering wound in our side, and
discourage and utterly hinder the introduction here of a
better class of laborers, is enough . . . to drive any people
to despair and desperation.[91]

Some who chose the possibility of emigration did so
because they lacked confidence in free black labor and
were attracted by opportunities for reestablishing slavery
in a new locale. Brazil and Mexico were especially
attractive sites from this perspective, for slavery still
existed in Brazil, and labor codes in Mexico appeared to
give employers sufficient power to establish something
approximating a system of indentured servitude.[92] Mat-
thew Fontaine Maury, for example, an influential proponent of emigration, believed that the "Virginia gentlemen" and the "Southern gentry" were destined to become
"hewers of wood and drawers of water to their conquer-
ors" if they remained in the South. The alternative
promoted by Maury was to recreate antebellum life in
Latin America, to found a "New Virginia" in Mexico.[93]

Despite all the possible motives and apparent advantages for leaving the South, the vast majority of southern
whites chose to remain. Those determined to maintain
their residence in the South were alarmed by the prospect
of white emigration and lobbied hard against the emigration movement. They feared that a further depletion of
the white population would only make matters worse,
adding to threat of "Negro Domination." The southern
press frequently criticized emigration projects and urged
whites to remain and make do in the South.[94] *De Bow's
Review*, for example, although expressing sympathy for
whites choosing to leave the South, nevertheless editori-
alized against emigration.[95] Critics argued that emigration would only make it more difficult for the native

white population to regain control in the South. Northern newspapers also came out against emigration, and the federal government tried more official means for obstructing southern emigration, for example, by prohibiting the operation of emigrant agents from Latin American countries.[96]

Some emigrants left originally with the intention of eventually returning. By the early 1870s, however, even most of those who had intended to relocate permanently had also returned to the South. Economic distress, tropical disease, native hostility, social and political turmoil, and the difficulty of gaining title to land were among the most important reasons for the failure of southern emigration. Economic opportunities in most areas of Latin America, especially the possibilities for recreating the antebellum world, were not great. Emigré planters, for example, found Brazilian slaves no less difficult to control than free blacks.[97] The failure of the possibility of white emigration meant that southern whites were not going to be able to escape the presence of free blacks.

Chapter 6 · The Rise
of
Southern
Sharecropping

The years following the abolition of slavery witnessed a confusing proliferation of labor arrangements in southern agriculture.[1] The most significant development in the postwar economy during this period of disorder and transition was the subdivision of the plantations as units of agricultural production. With this transformation, which began to occur as early as 1868, sharecropping and tenancy displaced the centralized plantation system favored by planters.

Under the postwar plantation system, blacks worked together in gangs or squads, received standardized wages, and lived in the consolidated slave quarters. Sharecropping established a more decentralized system of agricultural production. The large plantations, previously run as single production units, were divided into small plots of land, typically ranging from thirty to fifty acres each. These plots were leased on a yearly basis to individual families, who operated as the primary unit of production. Freedpeople abandoned the old slave housing and took up residence in separate family cabins located on their designated plots of land. Each family at the end of the season received as compensation a share of the crop, usually one-third to one-half; sharecroppers were responsible for feeding and clothing themselves, while the landlord supplied all the farming provisions. Although planters undoubtedly relinquished some of their control over the labor force with the breakdown of the plantation system, sharecropping by no means entirely freed black laborers from landlord supervision and management. Planters' interest in the crop gave them a strong incentive to oversee cultivation practices and to ensure maximum labor effort. Decisions about the crop mix remained in the hands of planters. And, of course, landlords could exploit their right to refuse to renew the lease at the end of the season as a means of exerting pressure on sharecroppers.

Sharecropping emerged after several years of turmoil and uncertainty, as ex-masters and ex-slaves contended to create a viable replacement for slavery. Yet, paradoxically, neither planters nor freedpeople promoted sharecropping, neither set out to establish it, and neither even gave it much consideration until 1868. Sharecropping originated from the struggle between planters and freedpeople, but it was an outcome that neither advocated, anticipated, or actively pursued. This helps to understand one curious aspect of the narrative presented thus far: the previous chapters include hardly a word about sharecropping. This silence reflects the fact that sharecropping was not on the historical agenda during the immediate postwar years. Planters and freedpeople, along with federal authorities and interested parties in the North, each sought to influence the course of social change, but none of them lobbied for or promoted this specific labor arrangement. Sharecropping was not implicated in the most significant developments and struggles occurring between the years 1865 and 1867; debate and conflict over other alternatives and possibilities held center stage. Yet somehow what transpired during this period prepared the way for, and culminated in the rise of, sharecropping.

The concept of constriction of possibilities is employed here to characterize and analyze the complicated and circuitous process that led planters and freedpeople finally to adopt sharecropping. From this perspective, sharecropping arose from the conflict between planters and freedpeople as they each struggled to achieve outcomes beneficial to their interests and to prevent outcomes harmful to their interests. A standoff resulted such that both planters and freedpeople found themselves in unfavorable circumstances. Freedpeople remained dependent on planters, because of the latter's virtual monopoly of land, and planters remained dependent on their former slaves, because of the latter's virtual monopoly of labor. Each tried, unsuccessfully, to break the monopoly possessed by the other. Blacks attempted to acquire their own land or gain access to means of subsistence independent of the plantation system. Planters endeavored to establish a new system of forced labor in southern agriculture, and they sought to acquire an alternative supply of labor through immigration. Many landowners, increasingly exasperated by black resistance to the plantation system, supported proposals for colonizing the black population; and some planters, out of resignation and despair, seriously considered leaving the South themselves. Ultimately, both planters and freedpeople had the power and resources to prevent the other from realizing their most desired aims, and neither had the capacity to realize their own. Blacks managed effectively to subvert the system of gang labor, but were unable to achieve genuine economic independence. Planters, benefiting from the unwillingness of the federal government to undertake a program of land reform in the South, managed to prevent blacks from gaining land, but were unable to preserve the plantation system or restore the power and authority they possessed as slaveholders.

This chapter continues the narrative, focusing specifically on the transition from the plantation system and gang labor to sharecropping. Much of this chapter analyzes planters' views on various labor arrangements, aiming to discover what they thought about sharecropping and why they eventually adopted it. Contrary to neoclassical theory, this evidence will show that planters were not drawn to sharecropping because of its perceived advantages and efficiencies, but because black resistance left them with little choice. Freedpeople's struggle to overturn the gang-labor system compelled planters to adopt this more decentralized labor arrangement as a concession to the demand for greater economic autonomy. However, this chapter will also argue that, while black initiatives played a key role in its adoption, it would not be accurate to say that freedpeople favored sharecropping or that it arose because blacks demanded it; sharecropping after all fell far short of the dream of "forty acres and a mule." In the end, neither planters nor freedpeople were enthusiastic about sharecropping, which in significant respects failed to meet the interests and expectations of either. That they nevertheless found themselves bound together in this unfortunate compromise lends support to the interpretation suggested by the idea of constriction of possibilities.

Sharecropping and Tenancy

Sharecropping was a form of wage labor, where the landlord compensated the laborer with a share of the crop at the end of the season. Tenancy, in contrast, was a form of renting, where the tenant compensated the landlord with a share of the crop. The tenant, in principle, unlike the sharecropper, maintained control over the process of production, dominion over the land and crop, and greater freedom from landlord supervision. The tenant enjoyed the privileges of a renter, while the sharecropper possessed the rights of a hired laborer only. This put tenancy a step up from sharecropping on the so-called agricultural ladder.[2] Southern courts recognized the distinction between these two labor arrangements and delineated their legal ramifications. According to a South Carolina court of appeals:

> The fundamental distinction between the relationships of landlord and cropper and landlord and tenant is in the fact that the status of a cropper is that of a laborer who has agreed to work for and under the landlord for a certain proportion of the crop as wages, but who does not thereby acquire any dominion or control over the premises upon which such labor is to be performed, the cropper having the right merely to enter and remain thereupon for the purpose of performing his engagement; whereas a tenant does not occupy the status of a laborer, but under such a contract acquires possession, dominion, and control over the premises for the term covered by the agreement, usually paying therefore a fixed amount either in money or specifics, and in making the crop performs the labor for himself and not for the landlord.[3]

Tenancy, furthermore, could take at least three different forms: (1) "standing rent" or "fixed-share rent," in which the tenant paid a certain amount of the crop to the landlord, e.g., a specified number of bales of cotton; (2) "share tenancy," sometimes also called "the third and fourth arrangement," where the tenant paid as rent a certain proportion of the crop to the landlord, typically one-third of the grain and one-fourth of the cotton crop; and (3) "cash rent," where the tenant paid a specified amount of money, per month or per year, as rent on the land.

My focus in this chapter is on the transition from the plantation system employing gang labor to the decentralized family-farm system of agricultural production. I use the term sharecropping exclusively to refer to this system, ignoring the distinction between it and tenancy. This is appropriate here, partly because, while tenancy may have been more common among white farmers, the vast majority of blacks operated under sharecropping. In addition, for reasons discussed below, tenancy was similar enough to sharecropping, especially considering the more significant contrast to gang labor, that separate analyses for these two labor arrangements are not necessary in the present context. A brief consideration of the distinction between sharecropping and tenancy, however, is worthwhile for the additional light this will shed on the workings of postbellum southern agriculture.

However clearly established in law, the distinction between sharecropping and tenancy tended to break down in practice; this distinction, furthermore, was not clearly recognized or acted upon by landlords and laborers. Indeed, the very nature of sharecropping invited confusion. As A. F. Robertson observes, "There is an interesting ambiguity about sharecropping, which is often revealed in subjective evaluation: the supplier of labour may choose to regard it as a form of tenancy, while the supplier of land may consider it as a labour hire arrangement."[4] Contracts rarely stipulated explicitly whether an arrangement was sharecropping or tenancy. Landlords and laborers, therefore, were not necessarily cognizant of the specific arrangement to which they had agreed, and they each often held different notions about their rights and obligations. As a result, the responsibilities of the contracting parties, rather than being conclusively established by written agreement, were subject to day-to-day conflict and negotiation.

Even within the courtroom the distinction between sharecropping and tenancy tended to blur. While the courts did not have a problem drawing this distinction in the abstract, they did, as Harold Woodman points out, "have trouble deciding whether a particular contract or oral agreement created a landlord-tenant or a landlord-cropper relationship."[5] Usually, the courts regarded an arrangement as tenancy when workers furnished their own stock, farm implements, and other provisions, with the landlord supplying only the land and dwellings; sharecropping was assumed to exist when workers provided only labor and the landlord supplied everything else. But as Charles Mangum observes, clear-cut cases by these criteria were rare: "Most of the cases are complicated by the fact that the landlord and tenant each supplies in whole or in part some of the other things which are needed for the effective use of the land."[6] The distinction between sharecropping and tenancy was "at best, only a theoretical one," M. B. Hammand adds, "for all possible combinations of these two systems have existed since the war and still continue to exist in the leading cotton states."[7] Thus, while the legal ramifications of the two contrasting systems in their pure forms were clear enough, whether any particular arrangement constituted sharecropping or tenancy was by no means always evident, either to the courts or to landlords and laborers themselves.

The enactment of crop-lien laws shortly after the end of the war further obscured any practical distinction between sharecropping and tenancy. Both sharecroppers and tenants required rations and farming supplies during the course of the season (tenants were not so well stocked that they could maintain self-sufficiency for an entire year). Local supply merchants appeared throughout the plantation South after the war to meet this need. These merchants (a role sometimes assumed by landlords themselves) advanced provisions to farmers during the year and gained a lien on the crop as security for their loans. Under the crop-lien system, furthermore, merchants desiring to protect their investment had an incentive to supervise the labor force, direct the cultivation process, and participate in production decisions concerning, for example, the selection of the crop mix. Since tenants and sharecroppers often found themselves still in debt at the end of the season, they became increasingly subject to the control of their merchant-creditors. The crop-lien system and the rather permanent indebtedness of laborers, therefore, undermined whatever relative autonomy and independence the tenant might have otherwise enjoyed. In practice, as a result of the development of the crop-lien system, tenants were often reduced to the status of sharecroppers.[8]

Ultimately, the contrast between sharecropping and tenancy did not have tremendous practical significance and was not particularly relevant to the experience of freedpeople. Of far greater importance was the difference between these two arrangements, on the one hand, and the plantation system, on the other. Both sharecropping and tenancy increased the autonomy of the labor force as compared to either slavery or the postwar gang-labor system, but neither of these arrangements freed black laborers from the control of white landowners. The focus of this analysis, therefore, is on the transition from gang labor to the decentralized family-farm system of agricultural production usually referred to as sharecropping, the most prevalent and characteristic labor arrangement for blacks in postbellum southern agriculture.

Money Wages, Share Wages, and Sharecropping

Writing in *De Bow's Review* in 1866, Percy Roberts identified three distinct "Systems of Hire": (1) the "system of money wages"; (2) the "share system," "reserving the exclusive management of affairs in the hands of the planters"; and (3) the "cropper" system, "which consists in dividing the land among the laborers in certain proportions, giving the latter control of themselves."[9] The "system of money wages" and the "share system" were both associated with gang labor and differed only in how the labor force was compensated: cash payment versus a share of the crop. The "cropper" system or sharecropping, Roberts recognized, brought a significant departure in the mode of labor organization, involving the abandonment of gang labor and the decentralization of the plantation as a unit of production.[10]

Loring and Atkinson's 1868 survey of agricultural practices in the South, using terminology similar to that employed by Roberts, asked planters to evaluate the relative merits of the "wage system" and the "share system." In a footnote, Loring and Atkinson remarked on the more recent emergence of a third labor arrangement in which the plantation was divided up into lots of fifty acres or so and farmed by squads of laborers or families; this they called the "tenant system for freedmen" and observed that it "is sort of a connecting link between the old gang plantation system and the small farm or peasant system."[11] This new system, of course, was sharecropping.

During the first several years after the war, while operating under the gang-labor system, planters frequently commented on these different "systems of hire," discussing in particular whether it was preferable to compensate the labor force with money wages or share wages. Although this debate focused on systems of labor compensation, it illuminates planters' thinking about the management and organization of the black labor force more generally; and it shows planters' enduring preoccupation with the problem of labor control. What planters said concerning share wages versus money wages can be used to infer their perspective on the adoption of sharecropping. For example, when planters objected to the share system as a method of payment, they were also certain to oppose sharecropping proper (as their specific criticisms make clear). For planters, sharecropping only added to the disadvantages of the share system by pairing this imperfect method of payment with a decentralized mode of labor organization that significantly reduced their ability to control and supervise the labor force. An analysis of this debate will help to demonstrate that planters regarded sharecropping as contrary to their interests, but were forced to agree to this system because of black opposition to gang labor.

The Wage System and the Share System

In an address before the Pomological and Farmer's Club of Society Hills, South Carolina, W. H. Evans presented a systematic analysis of the relative merits of the share system and the wage system. This address was reprinted in the *Southern Cultivator* in 1869 and was also reprinted, in a slightly edited form, in Loring and Atkinson's report, also published in 1869.[12] Evans's analysis, therefore, received widespread publicity and attention; and it is the best single contemporaneous source, written from the planters' perspective, on the relative merits of the money-wage system and the share-wage system. Evans's essay also provides considerable indirect evidence on how planters viewed sharecropping.

The summary of Evans's analysis presented below,

including occasional references to Loring and Atkinson's additions, discusses in turn the advantages and disadvantages of the share system of payment, the advantages and disadvantages of the wage system of payment, and a concluding evaluation of the relative merits of these two modes of labor compensation. Other contemporaneous sources on the wage system and the share system will then be examined to corroborate the conclusions drawn by Evans and by Loring and Atkinson.

The Share System of Payment: Advantages. The share system of payment, according to Evans, possessed several apparent advantages. First, the share system "gives the laborer a motive to protect the crop." Second, it "stimulates industry by giving the laborer an interest and pride in the crop." Because of these incentives to labor, the share system appeared to be an especially advantageous arrangement, especially given the concerns planters had about the dependability of free black labor. Along with most southern planters, however, Evans doubted that black people were psychologically capable of responding properly to the incentive features of the share system. Only "a comparatively small part of the laborers of the country," Evans argued, "are influenced by these stimulants." Planters believed that economic inducements in themselves would have little effect on the performance of the black labor force; the only sure means to improve the quality of black labor was through the application of more stringent managerial controls. According to Evans, therefore, the incentive characteristics of the share system of payment did little to recommend it as a "system of hire" with free black labor.

Third, since landlords and laborers shared proportionally in gains and losses, the share system "does not subject the farmer to loss from a failure of or a decline in the value of his crop." Evans also expressed skepticism about this apparent advantage, questioning in particular whether the risk-sharing function of the share system was likely to have much beneficial impact in the future. The extreme fluctuations in crop values experienced during the 1866 and 1867 seasons, Evans predicted, would be unlikely to occur again. Thus, planters could expect no real gain from risk-sharing.

Evans acknowledged that the share system of payment did possess one genuine advantage. It "is regarded by the laborer as a higher form of contract and is thereby more likely to secure labor." Loring and Atkinson maintained, similarly, that the share system "secures laborers for the year, with less likelihood of his breaking the contract, a thing he sometimes likes to do when the hard work begins." Because it was less objectionable than the wage system, blacks were more willing to sign and adhere to labor contracts under the share system. According to Evans and Loring and Atkinson, this was the main consideration leading to the adoption of share wages. This analysis suggests, therefore, that the share system did not arise because the system itself embodied features inherently advantageous to landowners. For planters, the wage system of payment was an intrinsically preferable arrangement. But the share system of payment had one advantage, which turned out to be crucial: freedpeople were more willing to work for share wages than money wages. The decisive advantage of the share-wage system, therefore, rather than constituting an immanent characteristic of this arrangement, was a by-product of black resistance and the conflict between freedpeople and planters.

The Share System of Payment: Disadvantages. The share system of payment, according to Evans, also possessed certain disadvantages. First, because laborers were compensated by a share of the crop at the end of the year, "discharging hands when they become inefficient or refractory" presented special problems; disobedient employees could not be so easily dismissed. This "evil," Evans emphasized, "is in fact inherent in the system and must go far towards condemning it as a general form of contract." Thus, while the deferred-payment system associated with share wages might encourage the labor force to remain at work during the entire year, it also decreased the flexibility of employers to hire and fire according to their own discretion. And since payment could also be deferred under the money-wage system, without any corresponding loss of flexibility, there was no real advantage in relying on share wages to compensate the labor force.

Second, the share system made it difficult to carry on "general work of improvement on the farm," for the labor force had no incentive to do any work that did not directly contribute to improving the quality or yield of the crop. Planters were forced to pay additional wages in order to procure other labor services from their employees. Finally, under the share system of payment there was the "annoyance and perplexity of harvesting and dividing the crop." According to Loring and Atkinson, the share system had the further drawback that employees working under this arrangement tended to regard themselves as partners; thus, share agreements had the disadvantage "of having the laborers dictate methods of cultivation according to their own notions, which are seldom right ones."

The Wage System of Payment: Advantages. An important advantage of the wage system, according to Evans, was that it "gives the farmer control over his labor, by enabling him to discharge his hands when they become inefficient." Second, in contrast to the share system, the wage system "stimulates industry and enterprise on the part of the farmer." Under the wage system, Evans explained, "every improvement and increase of the crop inures entirely and directly to the employer; while a failure is his loss only. These considerations lead naturally to a liberal system of manuring, the full application of animal power, and the use of improved agricultural implements—the three leading conditions of success." Third, by paying wages, the farmer was induced to economize labor, which cheapened the cost of production. This, Evans proposed, had the further beneficial consequence of "making labor so abundant as to give capital a reasonable and natural control." In fact, Evans attributed the existing shortage of labor in the South to the presence of the relatively inefficient share system of payment. Fourth, according to Evans, the wage system "enables the farmer to carry on a general system of improvement." When paid wages, laborers were clearly defined as hirelings, and planters were better able to direct and control the labor force without challenges to their authority or demands for additional compensation.

The Wage System of Payment: Disadvantages. Evans regarded the wage system as having only minor disadvantages. First, he feared that it might lead to a "competition for labor which may carry wages so high as to be ruinous to the farmer." Loring and Atkinson pointed out, however, that since "the same laws of supply and demand govern both systems" the share system is in this respect no more preferable. Second, the wage system, according to Evans, "involves far greater labor in supervising and protecting the crop." Evans argued that rather than being a disadvantage this was among the most favorable qualities of the share system: "Indeed if it have the effect of compelling closer attention on the part of the proprietor, it will prove of the highest advantage."

Evans concluded his analysis by encouraging planters to adopt the money-wage system. But, he warned, if "hands are employed for wages, and then left to take care of themselves," this would result in the worst of all possible labor arrangements. The "very essence" of the wage system, Evans advised, "lies in constant and active supervision" exercised with a degree of "moral force." He ended his address on a note of hope: "I trust the day is not distant when any respectable land owner will be ashamed to admit that he is cropping with a class of ignorant and indolent laborers."

Loring and Atkinson were even more unequivocal in their support for the wage system over the share system. Indeed, they considered the wage system—"*as a system*"—to be without disadvantages. Yet at one point in their summary of the responses to their survey, Loring and Atkinson stated that the "balance of preference seems to be in favor of giving the laborer a share of the crop." This conclusion, however, is inconsistent with Evans's analysis, inconsistent with Loring and Atkinson's own recommendations, and inconsistent with the extracts from planters included in their report. What Loring and Atkinson actually meant to say here was that the share system was more *prevalent* than the money-wage system, not that planters expressed a positive preference for it; the preferences responsible for the widespread adoption of the share system were entirely those of the black labor force. This becomes apparent from the comments by planters cited in Loring and Atkinson's survey. According to one respondent, for example, "The universal opinion would be against the share system and in favor of wages in money, if not for the difficulty in getting the services according to contracts." Thus, while the money wage system was widely favored—"*as a system*"—planters could not make it operate effectively in practice: they could not procure a reliable labor force. "Money wages . . . are best," one planter declared, "if the hands could be kept at work; [but] there being no restraint, they quit when they please, go off to the villages, hunting, fishing, or sleeping, especially in the summer, when labor is most needed." Another respondent was more direct in explaining why he adopted the share system: "I prefer wages . . . but a share in the crop is the universal plan; negroes prefer it and I am forced to adopt it. Can't choose your system. Have to do what negroes want. They control this matter entirely." Loring and Atkinson ultimately put the matter of planters' apparent preference for share wages in perspective, when they noted that along with the adoption of the share system "comes constantly, we might say always, the expression of a preference for paying wages, as giving the farmer control over his labor, and for other reasons stated above." Loring and Atkinson concluded with this counsel:

> The conclusions arrived at are, therefore, that the return to the wages system, the enactment and enforcement of strict laws, compelling the carrying out of contracts, and an honest treatment of the freedmen, will do much to increase the quantity and improve the quality of the labor now in the South.

Planters' Views on the Share System of Payment

The testimony and analysis supplied by Evans and Loring and Atkinson suggest that, while most planters preferred the money-wage system, they were forced to adopt share wages at the insistence of the black labor force, who were determined not to serve as mere hirelings. This conclusion is confirmed by other evidence as well. In a discussion of the evolution of labor arrangements in the postwar South, A. E. Lightfoot, writing in *De Bow's Review*, recounted that in 1867 freedpeople demanded a share of the crop: "They demanded it, and, of course they got it. If a planter demurred to accede to it, he immediately found himself without hands."[13] Lightfoot blamed the inability of planters to resist these demands on their failure to act in concert and form strong associations. Similarly, an 1867 editorial in the *Southern Cultivator* explained the adoption of the share system of payment as a product of the "stress of circumstances" rather than the voluntary choices of planters:

> It appears then, that all classes except a highly favored few, are compelled to resort to a temporary expedient which their judgment condemns, to obtain the means of procuring labor to work their lands at all. Hence while everyone condemns the policy of paying for labor by a share of the crop there are comparatively few who are not driven by stress of circumstances to the adoption of this mode of compensation.[14]

Nor can its prevalence be attributed to the fact that the share system, once in operation, proved to be a relatively successful and profitable arrangement. "The usual custom in this country is to work on shares," a correspondent to the *Southern Cultivator* reported in 1868, "and failure has universally followed."[15] An agent of the Freedmen's Bureau from North Carolina dispatched a similar report: "In many cases the system of sharing the crops is in vogue. This system has operated badly, and the freedmen have been advised against it. They appear, however, to prefer it."[16] In general, officials of the Freedmen's Bureau favored money wages and strongly advised against the share system of payment.[17]

What planters found especially objectionable about the share system was the implication of partnership between themselves and their laborers. It seemed to planters that under the share system of payment, blacks were transformed from hired laborers into virtual business partners. "Why," inquired the editors of the *Southern Planter*, "should a planter admit as partners in his business his daily laborers any more than the merchant or mechanic?" Planters, accordingly, were admonished to economize and sacrifice so they might be able to pay wages "and thus *control* the product of his soil, as well as all the operations conducted thereon."[18] A contributor to the *Southern Cultivator* expressed similar outrage: "The almost universal practice is, to hire the laborer by giving him a part of the crop—thereby making him a partner in the farming business. What an idea! Profound ignorance associated in business with intelligence."[19]

Planters also complained that the share system gave them less than total control over the production process. This, a noted Georgia planter emphasized, was contrary to good business practices:

> I have not found it advantageous to hire laborers, white or black to crop on shares. A farmer should have full control of the management of his crops to manage it successfully, and this you can hardly do, when your laborers are partners. They claim rights, and often assert them in the mode of cultivation, &c.—it leads to contentions and troubles.[20]

Where the share system was in operation, wrote a respondent to Loring and Atkinson's survey, "the hands feel themselves to be part owners and entitled to dictate."[21] The money-wage system, on the other hand, put the planter clearly in charge. "Don't you think a better plan would be to hire for wages and feed," one planter suggested. "By this system the farmer could control the labor, and have everything done his own way."[22] Under the share system, by contrast, where the principle of "co-partnership" obtained, black laborers, a Georgia planter observed, "have a right, and in the fullness of their conceit, exercise that right, to have a say in everything." With share agreements, he further predicted, "your plantation will run down and be turned out of doors in three years."[23] Thus, the disadvantage of the share system from the perspective of planters, as their numerous complaints testify, was that it led black laborers to consider themselves as, and demand the rights of, partners. The corresponding advantage of the money-wage system was that black laborers were less likely to form any illusory conceptions of partnership or make claims to managerial prerogatives.

One of the purported advantages of the share system, emphasized by adherents of the neoclassical approach, was that it gave laborers an interest in the crop and thereby encouraged their care and hard work. Some northern observers also cited this as a potential benefit of the share system.[24] But from the perspective of most planters themselves, giving laborers an interest in the crop had something of the character of a double-edged sword. While having an interest in the crop might encourage laborers to work more diligently (though there was widespread doubt about this too), it was from having such an interest that blacks demanded the rights of partnership. Planters found that under the share system the black labor force felt it was their prerogative to have a say in the choice of cultivation practices and the management of the labor process. Black laborers under the share system refused to accept the unilateral authority of the landowner. "Virtually [the share system] is a partnership between capital and labor," stated the pseudonymous "Southerner," "deleterious to capital and prejudicial to production."

> When freedmen are hired for a part of the crop, in plantation parlance, it is their crop, and with unmitigated stupidity they feel pretty much at liberty to neglect it, if doing so suits their convenience. . . . The freedman enjoying an interest in thc crop not only conceives himself privileged to neglect it, but considers that he has a right to a voice in its management, and sometimes takes it upon himself to disregard instructions.[25]

The problem with giving laborers an interest in the crop, from the perspective of planters, was that they took their interest seriously: "If I gave them a part of the crop," explained one planter, "they would consider themselves as much interested as I was, and would work when they pleased and as they pleased."[26] The same difficulty was noted by a Georgia resident: "When a man agrees to hire half interest in a crop he gives the laborer an equal right to dictate whether it shall be plowed deep or shallow, or whether it shall be plowed at all or not."[27]

Planters doubted, furthermore, that giving laborers an interest in the crop, besides the disadvantages associated with the implication of partnership, was sufficient to procure diligent labor. Indeed, giving black laborers an interest in the crop only brought to the surface what planters presumed to be their natural indolence:

> Our usual manner of hiring them or rather taking them as partners, encourages their natural propensity to idleness, makes them averse to any interest in the farm but the crop, and not *burdened* enough with that, to make them *voluntarily* plant, cultivate and harvest the crop as it should be done.[28]

The remedy suggested by this Arkansas planter was "to hire for wages, and let the laborer have no interest but that of *doing his duty or else get no pay*." The added advantage of the wage system was that "labor can be *controlled* and *used* the *year* round." Dickson Evans, a South Carolina planter, similarly maintained that "part of the crop is not sufficient to insure faithful service. *Nothing short of the continual presence of the owner or manager will do this.*"[29] This conclusion was repeated by planters throughout the South. Black laborers, declared the daughter of a Georgia planter, "required constant personal supervision."[30] Thus, giving laborers an interest in the crop did not necessarily reduce the costs of supervision, because planters did not believe that an interest in the crop was an adequate stimulant to black labor. So, the purported virtue of the share system emphasized especially by neoclassical economists was frequently regarded by southern planters as constituting no advantage at all, since black laborers required constant supervision anyway, or as being positively disadvantageous, since having an interest in the crop encouraged laborers to think of themselves as partners.

Nor were planters necessarily impressed by the risk-sharing function of share wages. Under the share system, "Southerner" observed:

> Apparently each party is involved in the risk of seasons and prices, and shares equally in the good or ill luck of seasons and prices, and share equally in the good or ill luck which may be assigned to Providence; but practically the results are prejudicial to the planter, for he had far greater interests at stake than the freedmen, and many other risks besides those of seasons and prices.[31]

Many planters believed that they would be better off

assuming all the risk themselves, for then they would be encouraged to supervise diligently and make use of the most advanced planting practices, in the expectation of reaping for themselves the full benefits from increased productivity. Moreover, planters also doubted that it was a wise policy to share gains and losses with their black laborers, for the latter were not motivated to be prosperous or inclined to protect the interests of their employers:

> The loss, as far as pertains to themselves, they [black laborers] are willing to bear, regardless of consequences; and as to their employer, they are indifferent whether he incurs loss or not. His personal adversity or prosperity is no concern of theirs; they work solely with an eye to self-benefit, and if the result of the year's operations is bankruptcy to him, they are apathetic.[32]

Planters would have been likely to favor the share system for its risk-sharing function only if they believed the labor force could be motivated by economic incentives to maximize productivity; and planters clearly did not believe this to be true for free blacks. Indeed, for planters, the risk-sharing characteristic of the share system would likely mean not that laborers would share in their gains, but that they would share in their laborers' losses. The problem with attributing the adoption of the share system to its risk-sharing function is that it fails to take seriously—in understanding the motivations of planters — their views on the quality and character of black labor.

Planters also complained that under the share system the laborer, whose compensation depended solely on the crop yield, was willing to work on the crop only and refused to engage in other chores around the plantation (e.g., ditching, fencing, etc.), from which he or she received no additional compensation. Giving the laborer an interest in the crop might have the advantage of encouraging more diligent crop-related work, but it also had the disadvantage of discouraging the laborer from doing any work not directly related to the crop. Respondents to Loring and Atkinson's survey often made this complaint. "No improvements could be made under this system," noted one planter. According to another, "It is impossible to get any work done cheerfully outside of the cotton and corn field."[33] Similarly, planters complained that under the share system "the laborer is released as soon as the crop is gathered, although they are hired for the year."[34] Northern observers also expressed concern about this aspect of the share system.[35]

Some planters also worried that black laborers were incapable of comprehending the nature of the payment system under a share agreement. Thus, they would be dissatisfied with the yearly fluctuations in remuneration resulting from variability in factors such as weather and cotton prices, unrelated to labor effort.[36] The *Nation*, which regarded the share system as an "unfortunate necessity," also made this point, emphasizing in addition how planters might be able to take advantage of blacks under such an arrangement: "It would be very unreasonable to expect the great mass of negro laborers, just emerging from the barbarism and ignorance of slavery, to work faithfully and persistently for a share of a crop of uncertain value, payable at a distant date by men who have up to this time defrauded them of their natural rights."[37] There was some concern then, both in the South and in the North, that the deferred-payment method associated with the share system would fail to incite hard work, and that the variability in compensation at the end of the season would produce discontent and conflict.

In conclusion, planters regarded the share system of payment as an inferior arrangement and preferred the money-wage system because it afforded them greater control over the labor force. Many planters lacked the cash and access to credit required to operate the money-wage system, however. Yet, the evidence presented above suggests that this was not the main reason planters agreed to share wages; and even when they possessed the necessary financial resources, planters were unable to implement the money-wage system.[38] Planters, ultimately, could not overcome black resistance to money wages; freedpeople, attracted by the prospect of gaining more independence and power, compelled planters to adopt the share system. The situation for planters was soon to get even worse. In the years to follow, they were forced to accede to a method of agricultural production that coupled this objectionable share system of compensation to an even more objectionable mode of labor organization.

The Rise of Southern Sharecropping: Planters

It is worth repeating that what uniquely characterized southern sharecropping was not the use of share wages to compensate the labor force, but the subdivision of the plantations into plots of land worked by individual families. Any theory of sharecropping is bound to be misleading, therefore, if it targets its explanation on the share system of payment rather than this transformation in the mode of labor organization. Some research, for example, attributes the rise of sharecropping to the lack of capital and credit in the economy of the postbellum South, which left planters with insufficient cash to make use of money wages.[39] The confusion here is obvious. While planters' inability to raise money might explain their increasing reliance on the share system of payment, this does not explain why landholders abandoned gang labor and agreed to subdivide the plantations into family farms. The shortage of capital and credit in the postwar South cannot account for the rise of sharecropping.

The demise of the gang-labor system and the emergence of sharecropping have also been ascribed to the economic setback experienced by planters resulting from poor cotton crops in 1866 and 1867. According to Vernon Wharton, this "seems to have been the deciding factor that made share-cropping by far the most prevalent system in Mississippi." Planters "were determined never again to come to the end of a season with large claims for cash wages."[40] Once again, while this might have contributed to planters' increasing reliance on share wages, it cannot explain why they introduced sharecropping as a replacement for gang labor. But perhaps planters, discouraged by adverse economic conditions, decided out of desperation to experiment with a radically new mode of labor organization. Such a hypothesis seems implausible though; given their doubts about free black labor, planters could not possibly have anticipated an increase in economic efficiency or an improvement in the crop yield from a system that decreased their ability to manage and control the labor force.

Ransom and Sutch also criticize the hypothesis that planters abandoned the gang-labor system because of poor harvests in the early postwar years:

> It is unlikely that a technique of production that had evolved and developed over sixty years of experience would have been abandoned simply because of one or two years of losses. Planters of the South had seen hard times before without abandoning the plantation system. But they began to do so in 1867–1868. The difficulties we have been discussing here were significant, not because they soured the planter on the practicality of using wage labor, but because they placed him in a weak position to resist

another powerful force: dissatisfaction of blacks with the old system.[41]

Ransom and Sutch present a persuasive account of how freedpeople effectively resisted planters' efforts to preserve the gang-labor system. Their conclusion, however, downplays the role of black resistance: "It is important to emphasize that the blacks could not so easily have overthrown the plantation regime had the landowners felt substantial losses would accompany the fragmentation of the unit of production."[42] Thus, for Ransom and Sutch, blacks were victorious only because planters expected no significant economic harm to result from the adoption of sharecropping. They base this contention on the argument that the postwar plantation system did not realize any economies of scale and, therefore, was no more efficient than the decentralized sharecropping system.[43] Other economists dispute this thesis, maintaining that planters did indeed have a rational economic incentive to preserve gang labor.[44]

However precise the calculations of present-day economists and whatever their computations reveal about the economic efficiency of the plantation system, the important question here is how planters themselves assessed the relative merit of gang labor as compared to sharecropping. Given their "sixty years of experience" with the plantation system, along with their conviction that black labor required constant supervision, it is highly unlikely that planters could have arrived at the conclusion that no significant loss would result from the abandonment of gang labor. Nor is such a conclusion consistent with the evidence presented here and in previous chapters, which clearly documents planters' strong commitment to the plantation system; nor is such a conclusion supported by what planters themselves had to say about the transition from gang labor to sharecropping specifically. The explanation initially put forward by Ransom and Sutch is more convincing: sharecropping was adopted because of the "dissatisfaction of blacks with the old system."

Sharecropping did not appear until several years after the war. Typically planters moved from money wages or, more commonly, share wages to sharecropping around 1868.[45] A correspondent to *De Bow's Review*, in an article published in 1869, gave this description of sharecropping's origins:

> With the year 1868, was commenced a system of labor which cannot fail in the end to utterly abolish the system so long adhered to in the South. Many men, owning large tracts of poor land, found it impossible to procure labor at any price, by which a margin was left for profit. In this strait, the idea suggested itself of cutting the plantation up into numerous small farms, or rather patches, and of renting these to negroes. To one acquainted with the characteristics of the race, it is no matter of surprise that this temptation proved irresistible. Every negro who procured one of these patches saw himself at once in the light of an independent planter, placed upon an equal footing with his former master, and, looking into the future, beheld himself a landed proprietor.[46]

According to this account, planters adopted sharecropping because they found it impossible "to procure labor at any price" under the plantation system. Blacks, evidently, refused to enter into labor contracts or demanded wage levels that threatened profitability. Desperate to somehow get laborers working on their land, planters responded by making a major concession: they divided the plantations up into "numerous small farms." According to an 1870 editorial in an Alabama newspaper, this development occurred over the opposition of planters, as a consequence of blacks' resistance to the plantation system and their desire to establish independent homesteads. Sharecropping, the Selma *Southern Argus* reported, was "an unwilling concession to the freedmen's desire to become a proprietor. . . . It is not a voluntary association from similarity of aims and interests."[47]

A contributor to the *Southern Cultivator*, and an especially harsh critic of the system, explained sharecropping as an unintended and "pernicious" deviation from the share-wage system.

> The tendency of the share system, has been to drift into the mere system of cropping—that most pernicious of all systems under which the labor of a country has ever been employed—a system which leads to idleness on the part of the laborer for a large part of the year, to indolence and indifference on the part of the farm owners—to decay and ruin in the farm, and a certain decline in the productive resources of the country. . . . It was not originally intended that the share contract should be other than a contract for the year, simply substituting a portion of the crop in lieu of money wages, and unless it can be carried back and kept to this original idea, it will impoverish any farmer who attempts to work under it.[48]

This report did not provide any details about how the "drift" from the share system to sharecropping occurred or who was responsible for initiating it, but the author clearly believed that the adoption of sharecropping was detrimental to southern agriculture and inconsistent with the best interests of planters. This judgment was shared by another correspondent to the *Southern Cultivator*, writing to assail the "utopian plan" of sharecropping. The singular flaw of sharecropping, according to this critic, was that it could work only on the completely erroneous assumption that "the negro is capable of farming without supervision."[49] Similarly, according to one of the respondents to Loring and Atkinson's survey, the drawback of sharecropping was that from "laborers great numbers of negroes have been transformed into tenantry, which takes the profit of production out of the hands of the planter."[50]

The evolution of labor relations on the Barrow plantation in Georgia also shows the importance of freedpeople's efforts to maximize their autonomy as a factor contributing to the rise of sharecropping. In the immediate postwar period the labor force on this plantation was divided into squads and worked under the direction of a "supertender." After a short time, however, "even the liberal control of the foreman grew irksome" to freedpeople, each desiring "to be his own 'boss,' and to farm to himself." A sharecropping system was subsequently established, with laborers working their own pieces of land; they then "began to 'want more elbow-room,' and so, one by one, they moved their houses on to their farms."[51]

Natchez planter William Mercer, whose story is told by historian Ronald Davis, responded in a much less accommodating manner to freedpeople's demand for greater independence. Like most other southern planters, Mercer was committed to the plantation system and strongly opposed to sharecropping; but unlike others Mercer adamantly refused to give in. He and his overseer were especially angered and frustrated by black laborers' refusal to accept supervision and by their hostility toward gang labor. In 1866, Mercer's employees insisted on the right "to work in family squads under their own supervision." Mercer regarded this as totally unacceptable, and accordingly he declined to accede to their demands. He was subsequently unable to retain a labor force and was compelled to lease portions of his land to whites, who in the end hired black workers as sharecroppers.[52]

Robert Brooks's research in Georgia also supports the contention that the primary impetus to sharecropping was blacks' insistence on independence. Planters' responses to Brooks's "inquiries" about postwar agricultural conditions and labor relations show how the unwillingness of blacks to "work in large bodies" and their desire "to get off to themselves" pressured landowners into breaking up the plantations into small farms. The following excerpts from replies by planters testify to the primacy of black demands in bringing about the decentralization of agricultural production in the South after the war:

> The negro became less willing to work in large bodies on the large plantations, they became harder to manage and many negroes began to desire to get off to themselves and run one and two horse farms. The large landowners finding that they could no longer get the negro low or cheap enough to allow a margin of profit, began to place their tenant houses all over their farms and rent to their tenants.
>
> In their effort to gain a still more independent position, they [freedpeople] began demanding rent privileges where they could enforce it.
>
> Can't control any system, but seek a good hand for wages, as cropper or tenant. The negro practically decides the system applied to farming. The negro naturally seeks the position as laborer affording the most absence of white supervision—the privilege of personal independence.[53]

Brooks's research documents the strength and persistence of blacks' opposition to supervision and their resistance to the gang-labor system. This was quite understandable, Brooks acknowledged, as "the plantation system of free hired labor meant almost as much restriction as did slavery."[54]

Planters resisted the initial adoption of sharecropping, and their subsequent experience with this system did not lead them to regard it any more favorably. It cannot be said, therefore, that planters finally settled on sharecropping because, contrary to their original expectations, they subsequently found it to be a beneficial arrangement. According to a South Carolina newspaper, for example, "No argument is needed to convince those who have tried cropping freemen for the past three years of the utter inefficiency and suicidal policy of that plan."[55] A Georgia planter in 1872 also expressed his continued dissatisfaction with the system of sharecropping, lamenting in particular its adverse affect on the black labor force:

> The cropping plant with the Fifteenth Amendment I consider the most hazardous undertaking that a planter ever embarked in. . . . I am fully satisfied the share system with the negro, has done more to demoralize him as a laborer, than all other influences that have ever been brought to bear upon him since his freedom.[56]

In the previous year, a South Carolina planter, echoing this sentiment, sounded a call to arms against sharecropping: "Let us stop the indiscriminate renting of land to destitute freedmen. . . . Let us abolish the imperfect system of 'cropping' with negroes."[57] Hope prevailed among some planters that blacks, if disabused of their "false pride," might be convinced of the evils of sharecropping and yield to the restoration of the plantation system:

> The principal objection to the colored man as a laborer I

think, is the false pride he is possessed of, which makes
him object to working for wages, and to insist on cropping.
... The scarcity of labor arises from this fact; I mean of
labor susceptible to control sufficient to work
improvement of lands in place of wearing them out. I
live in the hope that there will be an improvement in
this respect; and the sooner the negroes are *made* to
understand what every reflecting man sees and knows,
that 'cropping,' as he conducts it, will lead to ruin of all,
the sooner the improvement will begin.[58]

Planters persisted in their opposition to sharecropping and frequently put forward schemes intended to
reestablish some semblance of the plantation system.
One critic of sharecropping, for example, proposed an
alternative based on a time-sharing arrangement, where
laborers were allowed two days a week to work for
themselves on a piece of land provided by the landlord.
The advocate of this plan expected that it would go a long
way toward overcoming the defects of sharecropping and
restoring the system "of old":

This plan of dividing time also possesses advantages to the
land-holder or employer. In the first place, all the hands
can be worked together and at any kind of work desired.
Upon the share plan, each man wants his hand and team to
work his family or squad to himself; thus on a plantation
of any size there might be a half dozen squads; you can
have nothing done outside the cultivation of the crop, nor
even that as you might wish it. In your own time, you can
have absolute control over your business. ... In fact by
working diligently upon this plan, we can have our farms
and surroundings, appear more like they did of old than we
can under any other system, with our present form of
labor.[59]

Even when they agreed to sharecropping, as this recommendation shows, planters still looked forward to the possibility of establishing some alternative system through which they could reassert their "absolute control."

For most planters, sharecropping exhibited—though in extreme form—all the disadvantages of the share system, and more. Whereas under the share system, to the dismay of planters, blacks assumed the prerogatives of "co-partnership," under sharecropping, even worse, they looked upon themselves as independent proprietors. Planters' interests were not as well served by sharecropping as compared to gang labor, and their complaints about this system were perfectly understandable. From the perspective of planters, sharecropping meant too much independence for black laborers, and it rendered them less easily subject to control and supervision. The rise of sharecropping marked the end of a long-standing system of production in southern agriculture, a system that had worked well for planters in the past. They were strongly committed to this plantation system, and they struggled unsuccessfully to preserve it. But in the end, black resistance to gang labor forced planters to adopt sharecropping despite their recognition of the flaws and disadvantages of this system. The only benefit of share-cropping mentioned with any regularity by planters, and even this not without dire predictions for the future, was that by agreeing to it planters were able to procure a labor force and thus make a "bare support."

By adopting sharecropping, however, planters saved the plantations even as they sacrificed the plantation system. Of course, planters themselves rarely described the rise of sharecropping in such a positive light; they were inclined to emphasize less what they managed to retain with sharecropping than what they lost by abandoning gang labor. Yet, the rise of southern sharecropping, however much opposed by planters, did not fundamentally challenge ownership patterns or class relations or the system of racial domination in the South. Though enjoying more autonomy than in the past, blacks continued to serve as a subordinate agricultural labor force: for the vast majority of blacks, sharecropping did not serve as a stepping-stone to economic independence or land ownership.

The Rise of Southern Sharecropping: Freedpeople

Why did freedpeople agree to sharecropping, how did they evaluate it relative to other labor arrangements, and how well did sharecropping conform to their interests? In contrast to the case of planters, there is little evidence that clearly divulges the thinking and rationale of freedpeople as they entered into sharecropping agreements. Few written records exist showing blacks discussing the merits of different systems of labor or assessing their costs and benefits. Historical documents rarely describe what blacks thought about sharecropping, why they consented to this system, or how they viewed the prospect of becoming sharecroppers. Nevertheless, the material presented in previous chapters reveals much about the interests and preferences of the former slaves, what they fought for and what they fought against. On this basis, some conclusions can be drawn about how freedpeople regarded the rise of sharecropping and about how well this labor arrangement, the ultimate replacement for slavery, suited their interests.

The analysis presented thus far might leave the impression that sharecropping was adopted because freedpeople demanded it and had sufficient power to impose their wishes against those of planters. There is certainly something to this interpretation. Freedpeople did succeed in compelling planters to abandon the plantation system. Planters themselves often cited the insistence of the black labor force as the key factor explaining the emergence of sharecropping. In addition, freedpeople undoubtedly preferred sharecropping to the plantation system, with good reason. Sharecropping meant smaller production units, less supervision, and more autonomy; sharecropping also meant the end of gang labor. In contrast to the centralized plantation system, sharecropping allowed freedpeople greater independence and control in both their work lives and their family lives. Many freedpeople, moreover, may have initially imagined they would enjoy even greater gains than these with sharecropping, some envisioning an equal partnership with landowners, others supposing perhaps that sharecropping was a step up on the agricultural ladder, leading surely to independent farming.

The pressure exerted by the black labor force stands out as the decisive factor explaining the rise of southern sharecropping. Nevertheless, it would be misleading to say that sharecropping originated as an expression of the interests and demands of freedpeople. Although certainly a product of black resistance, sharecropping fell far short of what freedpeople hoped to achieve with emancipation. Sharecropping fulfilled some black demands, though most only partially so and many not at all. Only by focusing narrowly on what freedpeople gained from sharecropping is it possible to maintain that it arose as a reflection of their interests. While sharecropping certainly represented an improvement over gang labor, in many important respects it failed to meet the hopes and expectations of freedpeople as they struggled to give their own meaning to emancipation.

First, the transition from slavery to the postwar gang-labor system and from the latter to sharecropping did not presuppose or result in a fundamental change in the pattern of landholding; white southerners, the antebellum landed elite, more specifically, continued to own the plantation land after the war. In at least one important respect, therefore, the rise of sharecropping did not change the economic status of black laborers. Lacking land of their own and possessing their labor power only, freedpeople were still required to sign contracts with, and work for the profit of, white landowners. The adoption of share-cropping altered the nature of the contract system, abolishing collective agreements, but it did not transform property relations, nor did it liberate blacks from the agricultural labor market or from the need to hire themselves out to their former masters.

Second, while sharecropping permitted freedpeople more autonomy and independence than they had had under gang labor, particularly in their day-to-day activities, planters still retained ultimate managerial authority. The black labor force in the South, consequently, remained subject to the decision-making power and supervision of the planter. Although, as compared to the plantation system, blacks enjoyed more breathing room under sharecropping, it still did not allow them to work under their own authority, to be their own masters, or to free themselves altogether from the control of white landowners. Freedpeople, as sharecroppers, did not achieve the economic independence they hoped to gain with emancipation.

Third, as with slavery and the postwar gang-labor system, agricultural production under sharecropping remained oriented toward the market and governed by the profit-maximizing interests of planters and merchant suppliers. Black sharecroppers, consequently, who otherwise preferred subsistence farming because it allowed them to provide for themselves and to maintain their independence, continued to devote the bulk of their labor hours to the cultivation of the slave crops, especially cotton. Under sharecropping, therefore, blacks were forced to live with one of the most odious reminders of slavery.

Fourth, even with the transition from the gang-labor system to sharecropping, blacks remained a subordinate agricultural labor force, economically dependent on their former masters. Sharecropping, ultimately, failed to secure for freedpeople a strong enough economic base from which they could establish a political foothold. The economic and political vulnerability of black sharecroppers, which became particularly evident in the decades after Reconstruction, rendered them effectively powerless in the political arena, unable to promote their economic interests and protect their civil rights. Sharecropping, therefore, entailed political as well as economic costs for freedpeople.

Freedpeople agreed to sharecropping not only because they preferred it to gang labor, but also because southern whites managed to close off to them other possibilities, including employment opportunities outside of southern agriculture. Sharecropping, accordingly, was not an unequivocal victory for freedpeople; and planters were not nearly as powerless to influence the course of economic reconstruction as they sometimes proclaimed. The former slaves ended up as sharecroppers partly as a result of their own initiative, as they forced planters to abandon gang labor, but also as a result of the severe constraints and limited alternatives that they confronted. More specifically, to regard sharecropping as a victory for freedpeople fails to recognize the extent to which they were committed to the alternative possibility of landownership; and it fails to acknowledge the gap between the ideal of "forty acres and a mule" and the reality of southern sharecropping. According to one observer, writing in 1865:

> The sole ambition of the freedman at the present time
> appears to be to become the owner of a little piece of land,
> there to erect a humble home, and to dwell in peace and
> security at his own free will and pleasure. If he wishes, to
> cultivate the ground in cotton on his own account, to be able
> to do so without anyone to dictate to him hours or system of
> labor, if he wishes instead to plant corn or sweet potatoes—
> to be able to do *that* free from any outside control. . . . That
> is their idea, their desire and their hope."[60]

Needless to say, sharecropping, however much an improvement over gang labor, did not fulfill these ideas, desires, and hopes. Barbara Fields underscores this point in her analysis of labor relations in the postwar South: "In the end, sharecropping stood not as a symbol of the freedmen's triumph but as a measure of their defeat. Instead of a landowning peasantry, they became the next thing to wage hands."[61] Sharecropping did not free blacks from the influence of "outside control."

Finally, while black initiatives compelled planters to adopt sharecropping, freedpeople did not in fact expressly press for this particular labor arrangement. Sharecropping was not on the agenda of black people after the Civil War, and it was not something they set out to establish. Rather, freedpeople struggled to increase their independence and autonomy, ultimately hoping to fulfill the dream of "forty acres and a mule." Their struggles *resulted* in sharecropping but did not specifically *intend* it; their efforts produced sharecropping as a partial victory only, as a modest concession to their demand for independence. Ultimately, the success of freedpeople consisted less in compelling planters to adopt sharecropping than in forcing them to abandon the gang-labor system. Their victory consisted less in what they *got* than in what they *got out of*, less in what they achieved than in what they managed to avoid.

The situation for black sharecroppers and for the black population in the South as a whole deteriorated significantly in the years following the initial appearance of sharecropping. First, the development of the crop-lien system left many black sharecroppers in a state of permanent indebtedness, restricting their mobility, adding to their economic dependence, and culminating in a system of debt peonage that persisted for decades.[62] Second, the end of Reconstruction, the onset of Redemption, and the rise to dominance of the Democratic party in the South, gave planters in the mid-1870s the opportunity to enact a series of restrictive legal measures governing labor relations in southern agriculture. These laws, similar to the short-lived Black Codes passed by southern legislatures in 1865 and 1866, included measures that imposed severe penalties on laborers for breach of contract, limited the mobility of sharecroppers and the competition between planters, and ensured the priority of the landowner's lien on the crop. Designed "for the protection of the cotton planters," these legislative actions further tightened control over the black labor force in the South and further diminished the independence and bargaining power of sharecroppers.[63] Finally, in the 1890s, through the implementation of the poll tax, literacy requirements, property qualifications, and other restrictive registration laws, black people were effectively disenfranchised, deprived of civil rights and legitimate political means through which they might protect their economic interests. During the same decade, sanctioned by the 1896 Supreme Court decision in the case of *Plessy v. Ferguson*, southern whites established a rigid system of legal segregation, which further closed off to black people opportunities for economic advancement and for employment outside of southern agriculture.

Social Change and the Constriction of Possibilities

Southern sharecropping did not derive simply from the objective circumstances of the postwar South or from the operation of market mechanisms. Sharecropping, furthermore, cannot be attributed either to the preferences and designs of planters or to the desires and purposes of freedpeople. Neither embraced sharecropping eagerly. Rather, as suggested by the idea of constriction of possibilities, both planters and freedpeople were forced into sharecropping, as a result of the inability of each to achieve outcomes more beneficial to their respective interests. Planters and freedpeople, paradoxically, adopted sharecropping not because of its advantages, but despite its disadvantages. As a result of the capacity of each to obstruct the most preferred alternatives of the other, planters and freedpeople found themselves bound together in the unhappy compromise of southern sharecropping.

In conclusion, I will set aside the particular case of southern sharecropping and briefly describe, more generally, some of the characteristics of the idea of constriction of possibilities and some of the features of this idea that recommend it as a way of thinking about social change and conceptualizing the origins of new social institutions.[64]

First, the idea of constriction of possibilities suggests a framework for the study of social change that privileges the voices and behavior of historical actors themselves; it brings their interests, concerns, and reasoning back into the process of social change. From this perspective, which shares much with history "from the bottom up," the empirical point of departure consists of the considerations guiding the actions of people, their understandings of their interests and circumstances, and their experiences of the course of social change. What is particularly important from this perspective are the projects or "possibilities" promoted by different groups, the objectives they seek to implement, the goals they pursue. These constitute the basic data for studying the process of social change. This is not intended to downplay the causal significance of structural factors or objective conditions. In fact, the constraints on human action imposed by people's material surroundings are central to my argument. Nevertheless, it is people and not their circumstances that make history. Objective conditions need to be incorporated into the analysis of social change by showing their impact on the experiences and actions of the historical actors and by documenting how they shape group conflict and enter into the process of social change.

Second, this perspective also places the clash of wills and the struggle between contending groups at the center of the analysis of social change. Because people typically do not share a common vision of the future, because they have divergent interests, because they pursue incompatible "possibilities," social change is inevitably characterized by contention, conflicts of interest, and the exercise of power. This emphasis on the struggle between competing groups also serves to highlight the *process* of social change, the unpredictable and contingent course of events through which historical outcomes are generated.

Third, the idea of constriction of possibilities adopts a more encompassing historical perspective than often found in the study of social change. Rather than focusing narrowly on proximate struggles and developments, this perspective broadens the narrative by incorporating a wider range of factors, including especially the analysis of defeated possibilities. This conception of social change recognizes the empirical significance of failed human projects; the efforts of people to achieve their goals, even when unsuccessful, may have an important historical impact.

Fourth, the idea of constriction of possibilities implies that outcomes of social change are unlikely to reflect perfectly the interests or purposes of any particular group. What finally appears after a period of transition is often something that at the outset was not anticipated or actively promoted by any of the principal actors. Rarely do historical agents, whether individuals or groups, possess the capacity to control entirely the course of social change or the power to realize fully their primary objectives. Often, however, people do have the resources necessary to obstruct the goals of others. The origins of new social institutions, therefore, must be sought in the conflict between interests rather than in the purposes of particular historical agents. The outcome of social change, in other words, cannot be traced back simply to someone's designs. The idea of constriction of possibilities, rejecting both functionalist and teleological explanations, is especially sensitive to this characteristic of social change and to the indeterminancy and contingency of history more generally.

Finally, this conception of social change avoids the pitfalls of both structural and ideological determinism. Neither objective circumstances nor subjective will alone dictates the course of social change. Rather, this perspective recognizes the complex interplay between human will, conflicting interests, and constraining circumstances. The idea of constriction of possibilities gives priority to human agency without reducing social-change outcomes to the intentions of historical actors.

· Notes

Chapter 1

1. Robert Somers, *The Southern States Since the War, 1870–71* (Tuscaloosa: University of Alabama Press, 1965 [1871]), 128

2. Harold D. Woodman, "Sequel to Slavery: The New History Views the Postbellum South," *Journal of Southern History* 43 (November 1977): 523, 550. For other references to the uncertainty surrounding the transition from slavery to sharecropping, see August Meier and Elliott Rudwick, *From Plantation to Ghetto*, 3rd ed. (New York: Hill and Wang, 1976), 171–72; Jay R. Mandle, *The Roots of Black Poverty: The Southern Plantation Economy After the Civil War* (Durham, N.C.: Duke University Press, 1978), 25; Ralph Shlomowitz, "The Origins of Southern Sharecropping," *Agricultural History* 53 (July 1979): 557

3. Gerald David Jaynes, *Branches Without Roots: Genesis of the Black Working Class in the American South, 1862–1882* (New York: Oxford University Press, 1986), 30–32

4. The decline of the plantation system did not involve any fundamental transformation in ownership patterns, as the antebellum planter elite retained most of the plantation lands. On the continued presence in the postbellum South of concentrated landholdings and the antebellum planter elite, see Roger Wallace Shugg, "Survival of the Plantation System in Louisiana," *Journal of Southern History* 3 (August 1937): 311–25; William E. Highsmith, "Louisiana Landholding During War and Reconstruction," *Louisiana Historical Quarterly* 38 (January 1955): 39–54; Jonathan Wiener, "Planter Persistence and Social Change: Alabama, 1850–1870," *Journal of Interdisciplinary History* 7 (Fall 1976): 235–60; Wiener, *Social Origins of the New South: Alabama, 1860–1885*

(Baton Rouge: Louisiana State University Press, 1978), 3–34; Kenneth S. Greenberg, "The Civil War and the Redistribution of Land: Adams County, Mississippi, 1860–1870," *Agricultural History* 52 (April 1978): 292–307; A. Jane Townes, "The Effect of Emancipation on Large Landholdings, Nelson and Goochland Counties, Virginia," *Journal of Southern History* 45 (August 1979): 403–12; Michael Wayne, *The Reshaping of Plantation Society: The Natchez District, 1860–1880* (Baton Rouge: Louisiana State University Press, 1983), 75–109.

5. The term *constriction of possibilities* is drawn from E. L. Doctorow, *The Book of Daniel* (New York: New American Library, 1971), 163. The narrator of Doctorow's novel, recounting a Russian folk story, describes the process of dying as "a progressive deterioration of possibilities, a methodical constriction of options." I will explain more fully later in this chapter how the metaphor of "constriction of possibilities" suggests a perspective on the process of social change.

6. Parts of the following sections of this chapter have been reworked from a previously published article: Edward Royce, "The Origins of Southern Sharecropping: Explaining Social Change," *Current Perspectives in Social Theory* 6 (Greenwich, Conn.: JAI Press, 1985), 279–99.

7. Daniel Chirot, "The Growth of the Market and Servile Labor Systems in Agriculture," *Journal of Social History* 8 (Winter 1975): 67–80.

8. Robert Evans, Jr., "Some Notes on Coerced Labor," *Journal of Economic History* 30 (December 1970), 861–66.

9. Evsey D. Domar, "The Causes of Slavery or Serfdom: A Hypothesis," *Journal of Economic History* 30 (March 1970): 21.

10. For some critical observations on the applicability of Domar's hypothesis to the postwar South, see Stephen J. DeCanio, *Agriculture in the Postbellum South: The Economics of Production and Supply* (Cambridge, Mass.: MIT Press, 1974), 2–4; DeCanio, "Productivity and Income Distribution in the Post-Bellum South," *Journal of Economic History* 34 (June 1974): 422–23. For another critique of the explanatory power of the land/labor ratio from an explicitly "dialectical" perspective, see O. Nigel Bolland, "Systems of Domination after Slavery: The Control of Land and Labor in the British West Indies after 1838," *Comparative Studies in Society and History* 23 (1981): 591–619. See also Perry Anderson, *Passages from Antiquity to Feudalism* (London: New Left Books, 1974), 252–53. An additional factor bearing on the outcome of a high land/labor ratio, Anderson argues, is the presence of urban centers, which might serve as a haven for landless workers and provide nonagricultural employment opportunities. Planters in the postwar South clearly recognized that their ability to regain control over the black labor force required restrictions on the freedom of blacks to migrate into towns. They responded by pressing for the enactment of

various laws, including especially the Black Codes of 1865 and 1866, designed to prohibit the movement of blacks into towns and to limit the availability of alternative means of employment. I will discuss this in further detail in later chapters.

11. Enoch Marvin Banks, *The Economics of Land Tenure in Georgia* (New York: AMS Press, 1968 [1905]), 78–79.

12. Vernon Lane Wharton, *The Negro in Mississippi, 1865–1890* (New York: Harper & Row, 1965 [1947]), 68.

13. Jean-Paul Sartre, *Search for a Method,* trans. Hazel E. Barnes (New York: Vintage Books, 1963), 87. My analysis of this predisposing-conditions argument is informed by recent work in historical sociology that places emphasis on the study of social change and class conflict "from the bottom up." For an overview of some of this literature, see William G. Roy, "Class Conflict and Social Change in Historical Perspective," *Annual Review of Sociology* 10 (1984): 483–506. Of particular relevance is Roy's claim that this "new paradigm" has brought about a "shift from abstract textual and logical analysis toward historically rich, empirical studies of specific events, persons, relationships, and ideas." Roy contends, making exactly the same point as Sartre, that "in looking at Marx's dialectic between acting men (and women) and their contextual circumstances scholars are once again examining both elements. Earlier work focused almost entirely on the circumstances while neglecting the people" (484).

14. Indeed, a serious, more straightforwardly empirical problem with this explanation—as later chapters will make clear—is that planters did not in fact believe their interests would be well served by sharecropping and did not favor its adoption.

15. Barry Hindess, "Power, Interests and the Outcomes of Struggles," *Sociology* 16 (November 1982): 505.

16. There is something "whiggish" in how the predisposing-conditions argument reads backward from sharecropping in this manner and then traces forward. "The whig historian," according to Stocking, "reduces the mediating processes by which the totality of an historical past produces the totality of its consequent future to a search for the origins of certain present phenomena. He seeks out in the past phenomena which seem to resemble those of concern in the present, and then moves forward in time by tracing lineages up to the present in simple sequential movement." George W. Stocking, Jr., *Race, Culture, and Evolution: Essay in the History of Anthropology* (New York: Free Press, 1968), 3–4.

17. See Steven N. S. Cheung, *The Theory of Share Tenancy: With Special Application to Asian Agriculture and the First Phase of Taiwan Land Reform* (Chicago: University of Chicago Press, 1969). I have drawn upon two important critiques of the neoclassical approach, though both deal with a range of issues much broader than the origins of southern

sharecropping. See Woodman, "Sequel to Slavery," 523–54; Jonathan M. Wiener, "Class Structure and Economic Development in the American South, 1865–1955," *American Historical Review* 84 (October 1979): 970–92.

18. Joseph D. Reid, Jr., "Sharecropping as an Understandable Market Response: The Post-Bellum South," *Journal of Economic History* 33 (March 1973): 106–30.

19. Ralph Shlomowitz, " 'Bound' or 'Free'?: Black Labor in Cotton and Sugarcane Farming, 1865–1880," *Journal of Southern History* 50 (November 1984): 591.

20. Joseph D. Reid, Jr., "Sharecropping in History and Theory," *Agricultural History* 49 (April 1975): 438–39.

21. Robert Higgs, "Patterns of Farm Rental in the Georgia Cotton Belt, 1880–1900," *Journal of Economic History* 34 (June 1974): 468–82; Shlomowitz, "The Origins of Southern Sharecropping," 570–71, 574.

22. Reid, "Sharecropping as an Understandable Market Response," 126–27; Reid, "Sharecropping in History and Theory," 437; Reid, "The Evaluation and Implications of Southern Tenancy," *Agricultural History* 53 (January 1979): 158.

23. Reid, "Sharecropping as an Understandable Market Response," 125; Reid, "Sharecropping in History and Theory, pp. 433–39; Reid, "Sharecropping and Agricultural Uncertainty," *Economic Development and Cultural Change* 24 (April 1976): 570–71. Reid is the only proponent of the neoclassical perspective who makes this claim; both Cheung and Higgs argue that, because of the requirement of negotiating detailed contract stipulations, sharecropping entails higher transaction costs than alternative labor arrangements. See Cheung, *The Theory of Share Tenancy*, 67.

24. Cheung, *The Theory of Share Tenancy*, 68–71; Robert Higgs, *The Transformation of the American Economy, 1865–1914: An Essay in Interpretation* (New York: John Wiley, 1971), 93–96; Higgs, "Race, Tenure, and Resource Allocation in Southern Agriculture, 1910," *Journal of Economic History* 33 (March 1973): 149–69. Reid proposes a risk-reduction theory of sharecropping as an alternative to the risk-distribution model defended by Cheung and Higgs; see Reid, "Sharecropping as an Understandable Market Response," 120–27; Reid, "Sharecropping in History and Theory," 430–35; for criticisms of both Higgs and Reid, see Gavin Wright, "Comment on Papers by Reid, Ransom and Sutch, and Higgs," *Journal of Economic History* 33 (March 1973): 173–74.

25. See also Peter Kolchin, *First Freedom: The Responses of Alabama's Blacks to Emancipation and Reconstruction* (Westport, Conn.: Greenwood Press, 1972), 41–42. In a more strictly historical account of emancipation and reconstruction, Kolchin draws a similar

conclusion: "Sharecropping triumphed because both planters and freed-men favored the system."

26. Paul A. David et al., *Reckoning with Slavery: A Critical Study in the Quantitative History of American Negro Slavery* (New York: Oxford University Press, 1976), 340–41.

27. Whitelaw Reid, *After the War: A Tour of the Southern States, 1865–1866* (New York: Harper Torchbooks, 1965 [1866]), 59. I will consider blacks' opposition and resistance to the gang labor system in Chapter 2 and will examine the issue of black landownership in Chapter 3.

28. *Southern Cultivator* 27 (February 1869): 51.

29. I will discuss the efforts of planters to preserve the gang-labor system and their hostility toward sharecropping in Chapters 2 and 6 respectively.

30. See Mandle, *The Roots of Black Poverty*, 25. Mandle also criticizes those in the neoclassical tradition for failing "to deal with the wider context in which the market responsive behavior they are studying occurred."

31. Woodman, "Sequel to Slavery," 534.

32. Shlomowitz, "The Origins of Southern Sharecropping," 575.

33. I admit to being selective in my quotations from the studies discussed in this section; specifically, my analysis focuses on each author's summary characterizations and final descriptions of southern sharecropping, considered in isolation from their larger arguments and the details of their supporting research. To add insult to injury, I shamelessly exploit these sources for my own purposes in later substantive chapters. However, my objective here is not to provide a thoroughgoing critique of the historical research on southern sharecropping. Rather, I use these studies as a foil in order to show how a more comprehensive understanding of sharecropping can be achieved by restating the class-conflict argument in the terminology of "constriction of possibilities."

34. Ronald L. F. Davis, *Good and Faithful Labor: From Slavery to Sharecropping in the Natchez District, 1860–1890* (Westport, Conn.: Greenwood Press, 1982), 190. See also Davis, "Labor Dependency Among Freedmen, 1865–1880," in *From the Old South to the New: Essays on the Transitional South*, ed. Walter J. Fraser, Jr., and Winfred B. Moore, Jr. (Westport, Conn.: Greenwood Press, 1981), 155–65; Marjorie Stratford Mendenhall, "The Rise of Southern Tenancy," *Yale Review* 27 (September 1937): 125; Roger L. Ransom and Richard Sutch, "Sharecropping: Market Response or Mechanism of Race Control," in *What Was Freedom's Price?* ed. David G. Sansing (Jackson: University Press of Mississippi, 1978), 64–66.

35. Wiener, *Origins of the New South*, 66.

36. Charles L. Flynn, Jr., *White Land, Black Labor: Caste and*

Class in Late Nineteenth-Century Georgia (Baton Rouge: Louisiana State University Press, 1983), 67–72.

37. Mandle, *The Roots of Black Poverty*, 25–26.

38. See also Jay R. Mandle, "The Failed Revolution in the South," a review of *Reconstruction: America's Unfinished Revolution, 1863–1877*, by Eric Foner, *Socialist Review* 89 (July–September 1989), 153.

39. James Oakes, "The Present Becomes the Past: The Planter Class in the Postbellum South," in *New Perspectives on Race and Slavery in America: Essays in Honor of Kenneth M. Stampp*, ed. Robert H. Abzug and Stephen E. Maizlish (Lexington: University Press of Kentucky, 1986), 151.

40. Roger L. Ransom and Richard Sutch, *One Kind of Freedom: The Economic Consequences of Emancipation* (Cambridge: Cambridge University Press, 1977), 94.

41. James L. Roark, *Masters Without Slaves: Southern Planters in the Civil War and Reconstruction* (New York: W. W. Norton, 1977), 142–43. See also Gilbert Fite, *Cotton Fields No More: Southern Agriculture, 1865–1980* (Lexington: University Press of Kentucky, 1984), 3–4.

42. Gavin Wright, *Old South, New South: Revolutions in the Southern Economy Since the Civil War* (New York: Basic Books, 1986), 85–86.

43. In a brief comment on the origins of southern sharecropping, Michael Reich proposes a similar explanation: "Blacks preferred to own land while the planters preferred the gang-labor system. The power of the planters and their hostility to black landownership precluded one outcome—the resistance of the freed blacks precluded the other." Michael Reich, *Racial Inequality: A Political-Economic Analysis* (Princeton, N.J.: Princeton University Press, 1981), 228. See also Eric Foner, *Nothing But Freedom: Emancipation and Its Legacy* (Baton Rouge: Louisiana State University Press, 1983), 45.

44. Cited in Herbert G. Gutman, *Work, Culture and Society in Industrializing America* (New York: Vintage Books, 1977), 67.

45. See Karl Polanyi, *The Great Transformation: The Political and Economic Origins of Our Time* (Boston: Beacon Press, 1957 [1944]), 36. I have benefited from Polanyi's discussion of the unsuccessful resistance to the development of capitalism in England. Polanyi points out that the eventual victory of a trend cannot be taken as proof of the ineffectiveness of the efforts to block it: "That which is ineffectual in stopping a line of development altogether is not, on that account, altogether ineffectual." Though Polanyi is concerned with how ultimately unsuccessful efforts can affect the timing of social change and can slow down its progress—a point that is rather different from the one I am trying to make—he nevertheless draws attention to the empirical significance in history of defeated possibilities.

46. Theda Skocpol, *States and Social Revolutions: A Comparative Analysis of France, Russia, and China* (Cambridge: Cambridge University Press, 1979), 17–18.

47. Barrington Moore, Jr., *Injustice: The Social Bases of Obedience and Revolt* (White Plains, N.Y.: M. E. Sharpe, 1978), 376–81.

48. Moore, *Injustice,* 376.

49. Alan Dawley, *Class and Community: The Industrial Revolution in Lynn* (Cambridge, Mass.: Harvard University Press, 1976), 240, 196.

50. Reinhard Bendix, *Force, Fate, and Freedom: On Historical Sociology* (Berkeley: University of California Press, 1984), 55–56.

Chapter 2

1. On the organization of the labor force under slavery, see Kenneth M. Stampp, *The Peculiar Institution: Slavery in the Ante-Bellum South* (New York: Vintage Books, 1956), 34–85; Eugene Genovese, *Roll, Jordan, Roll: The World the Slaves Made* (New York: Vintage Books, 1976), 7–25, 285–324. On the postwar gang-labor system, see Roger L. Ransom and Richard Sutch, *One Kind of Freedom: The Economic Consequences of Emancipation* (Cambridge: Cambridge University Press, 1977), 56–61; Jonathan M. Wiener, *Social Origins of the New South: Alabama, 1860–1885* (Baton Rouge: Louisiana State University Press, 1978), 36–42.

2. Sidney Andrews, *The South Since the War* (Boston: Houghton Mifflin, 1971 [1866]), 101.

3. See, for example, Ira Berlin, Steven Hahn, Steven F. Miller, Joseph P. Reidy, and Leslie S. Rowland, "The Terrain of Freedom: The Struggle over the Meaning of Free Labor in the U.S. South," *History Workshop Journal* 22 (Autumn 1986): 108–30.

4. U.S. Congress, Senate, *Letter of the Secretary of War, Communicating . . . Reports of the Assistant Commissioners of Freedmen,* Executive Document Number 6, 39th Congress, 2nd Session (Washington, D.C.: Government Printing Office [GPO], 1867), 113 (hereafter cited as *Reports of the Assistant Commissioners of Freedmen*).

5. Andrews, *The South Since the War,* 398.

6. W.E.B. Du Bois, *Black Reconstruction in America, 1860–1880* (New York: Atheneum, 1977 [1935]), 55.

7. On the disintegration of slavery during the war, see Joe Gray Taylor, "Slavery in Louisiana During the Civil War," *Louisiana History* 8 (Winter 1967): 27–33; James L. Roark, *Masters Without Slaves: Southern Planters in the Civil War and Reconstruction* (New York: W. W. Norton, 1977), 68–108; Leon Litwack, *Been in the Storm So Long: The Aftermath of Slavery* (New York: Vintage Books, 1980), 3–166.

8. E. P. Thompson, *The Making of the English Working Class* (New York: Vintage Books, 1966), 194. Referring to England in the

nineteenth century, Thompson concludes that "the working class made itself as much as it was made."

9. On the origins of the contraband policy at Fortress Monroe, see Bell Irvin Wiley, *Southern Negroes, 1861–1865* (Baton Rouge: Louisiana State University Press, 1965 [1938]), 175–77; Louis S. Gerteis, *From Contraband to Freedman: Federal Policy Toward Southern Blacks, 1861–1865* (Westport, Conn.: Greenwood Press, 1973), 11–18.

10. On the self-emancipation of the slaves and on their contributions to northern victory, see James M. McPherson, *The Negro's Civil War* (New York: Vintage Books, 1965); Benjamin Quarles, *The Negro in the Civil War* (Boston: Little, Brown, 1969); Edward Magdol, *A Right to the Land: Essays on the Freedmen's Community* (Westport, Conn.: Greenwood Press, 1977), 3–15; Vincent Harding, *There is a River: The Black Struggle for Freedom in America* (New York: Vintage Books, 1983), 219–57; Ira Berlin, Barbara J. Fields, Thavolia Glymph, Joseph P. Reidy, and Leslie S. Rowland, *The Black Military Experience*, series 2 of *Freedom: A Documentary History of Emancipation 1861–1867* (Cambridge: Cambridge University Press, 1982); Berlin et al., *The Destruction of Slavery*, series 1, vol. 1 of *Freedom: A Documentary History of Emancipation, 1861–1867* (Cambridge: Cambridge University Press, 1985).

11. Cited in Edmund L. Drago, "How Sherman's March Through Georgia Affected the Slaves," *Georgia Historical Quarterly* 57 (Fall 1973), 363. See also Genovese, *Roll, Jordan, Roll*, 97–112.

12. See, for example, Eugene D. Genovese, *From Rebellion to Revolution: Afro-American Slave Revolts in the Making of the Modern World* (Baton Rouge: Louisiana State University Press, 1979).

13. Berlin et al., *The Destruction of Slavery*, 797.

14. James Oakes, "The Political Significance of Slave Resistance," *History Workshop Journal* 22 (Autumn 1986): 99, 97.

15. John G. Sproat, "Blueprint for Radical Reconstruction," *Journal of Southern History* 23 (February 1957): 25–44; James M. McPherson, *The Struggle for Equality: Abolitionists and the Negro in the Civil War and Reconstruction* (Princeton, N.J.: Princeton University Press, 1964), 182–88. For the order establishing the AFIC, see U.S. War Department, *The War of the Rebellion: A Compilation of the Official Records of the Union and Confederate Armies* (Washington, D.C.: GPO, 1880–1901), series 3, vol. 3, 73–74; for the preliminary report of the commission, see ibid., 430–54; and for the final report, see ibid., series 3, vol. 4, 289–383.

16. "Final Report of the American Freedmen's Inquiry Commission to the Secretary of War," 381–82.

17. Litwack, *Been in the Storm So Long*, 134.

18. On federal policy toward black labor during the war, see Gerteis, *From Contraband to Freedman*; Wiley, *Southern Negroes*;

Willie Lee Rose, *Rehearsal for Reconstruction: The Port Royal Experiment* (London: Oxford University Press, 1978 [1964]); J. Thomas May, "Continuity and Change in the Labor Program of the Union Army and the Freedmen's Bureau," *Civil War History* (September 1971): 245–54; C. Peter Ripley, *Slaves and Freedmen in Civil War Louisiana* (Baton Rouge: Louisiana State University Press, 1976); William F. Messner, *Freedmen and the Ideology of Free Labor: Louisiana, 1862–1865* (Lafayette: Center for Louisiana Studies, University of Southwestern Louisiana, 1978); Armstead L. Robinson, " 'Worser dan Jeff Davis': The Coming of Free Labor During the Civil War, 1861–1865," in *Essays on the Postbellum Southern Economy*, ed. Thavolia Glymph and John J. Kushma (College Station: Texas A & M University Press, 1985), 11–47.

19. Ronald L. F. Davis, *Good and Faithful Labor: From Slavery to Sharecropping in the Natchez District, 1860–1890* (Westport, Conn.: Greenwood Press, 1982), 62–63.

20. U.S. War Department, "Orders No. 9," *The War of the Rebellion: A Compilation of the Official Records of the Union and the Confederate Armies* (Washington, D.C.: GPO, 1880–1901), series 3, vol. 4, 168. On "Orders No. 9" and Thomas's role in the development of policy regarding the regulation of black labor in Mississippi, see Davis, *Good and Faithful Labor*, 63–73.

21. Davis, *Good and Faithful Labor*, 72.

22. On the free-labor experiment on the Sea Islands of South Carolina, see Rose, *Rehearsal for Reconstruction*, especially 37–38, 50, 65, 128, 173–74, 203–6, 217, 222–28; Gerteis, *From Contraband to Freedman*, 50–58. For a contemporary account of the Port Royal Experiment, see William Channing Gannett and Edward Everett Hale, "The Freedmen at Port Royal," *North American Review* 101 (July 1865): 1–28.

23. Rose, *Rehearsal for Reconstruction*, 65, 173–74, 222–26; Gerteis, *From Contraband to Freedmen*, 51–52.

24. Rose, *Rehearsal for Reconstruction*, 82, 224–25.

25. Gerteis, *From Contraband to Freedmen*, 57.

26. On federal policy toward black labor in the Gulf Department, see Ripley, *Slaves and Freedmen*; Wiley, *Southern Negroes*; Messner, *Freedmen and the Ideology of Free Labor*; Gerteis, *From Contraband to Freedmen*, 65–115.

27. May, "Continuity and Change"; Messner, *Freedmen and the Ideology of Free Labor*, 184–87; Gerteis, *From Contraband to Freedman*, 183–92.

28. Cited in William F. Messner, "Black Violence and White Response: Louisiana, 1862," *Journal of Southern History* 41 (February 1975): 24.

29. Messner, *Freedmen and the Ideology of Free Labor*, 4–5; Gerteis, *From Contraband to Freedman*, 66.

30. Messner, *Freedmen and the Ideology of Free Labor*, 5–9; Gerteis, *From Contraband to Freedman*, 65–68.

31. Ripley, *Slaves and Freedmen*, 27–35; Messner, *Freedmen and the Ideology of Free Labor*, 8–16; Gerteis, *From Contraband to Freedman*, 68–71.

32. Berlin et al., *The Destruction of Slavery*, 190–98; Messner, *Freedmen and the Ideology of Free Labor*, 7–8, 16–19, 32–34.

33. Messner, *Freedmen and the Ideology of Free Labor*, 32–43; Gerteis, *From Contraband to Freedman*, 72–73; Ripley, *Slaves and Freedmen*, 44–46; Wiley, *Southern Negroes*, 188–90; Roark, *Masters Without Slaves*, 114.

34. On the labor program of the military in the Gulf Department under Banks, see Ripley, *Slaves and Freedmen*, 46–68; Messner, *Freedmen and the Ideology of Free Labor*, 44–60; Gerteis, *From Contraband to Freedman*, 73–82; Wiley, *Southern Negroes*, 210–21; May, "Continuity and Change," 247–50.

35. Ripley, *Slaves and Freedmen*, 48–49. See also Messner, *Freedmen and the Ideology of Free Labor*, 54–55; May, "Continuity and Change," 247–48.

36. Messner, *Freedmen and the Ideology of Free Labor*, 58–59.

37. New Orleans *Tribune*, April 9, 1865. See also ibid., December 8, 1864; ibid., February 18, 1865; ibid., March 18, 1865; ibid., March 19, 1865. On the *Tribune's* attack on Banks's labor program, see also August Meier and Elliott Rudwick, *From Plantation to Ghetto*, 3rd ed. (New York: Hill and Wang, 1976), 168–69; Claude F. Oubre, *Forty Acres and a Mule: The Freedmen's Bureau and Black Landownership* (Baton Rouge: Louisiana State University Press, 1978), 12–16.

38. Litwack, *Been in the Storm So Long*, 184. See also Andrews, *The South Since the War*, 178, 188; U.S. Congress, House, *Report of the Joint Committee on Reconstruction*, Executive Document Number 30, 39th Congress, 1st Session (Washington, D.C.: GPO, 1866), part 2, 202; part 3, 122 (hereafter cited as *Report of the Joint Committee on Reconstruction*); U.S. Congress, Senate, *Report of Carl Schurz on the States of South Carolina, Georgia, Alabama, Mississippi, and Louisiana*, by Carl Schurz, Executive Document Number 2, 39th Congress, 1st Session (Washington, D.C.: GPO, 1866), 15, 17, 19, 21, 89 (hereafter cited as *Report of Carl Schurz*); U.S. Congress, House, *Freedmen's Bureau . . . a Report, by the Commissioner of the Freedmen's Bureau, of all Orders by him or any Assistant Commissioner*, Executive Document Number 70, 39th Congress, 1st Session (Washington, D.C.: GPO, 1866), 216, 365 (hereafter cited as *Freedmen's Bureau*); Henry E. Sterkx, "William C. Jordan and Reconstruction in Bullock County Alabama," *Alabama Review* 15 (January 1962): 64–65; Donald G. Nieman, *To Set the Law in Motion: The Freedmen's Bureau*

and the Legal Rights of Blacks, 1865–1868 (Millwood, N.Y.: KTO Press, 1979), 14.

39. Whitelaw Reid, *After the War: A Tour of the Southern States, 1865–1866* (New York: Harper & Row, 1965 [1866]), 45. See also George C. Benham, *A Year of Wreck* (New York: Harper and Brothers, 1880), 125–26, 130; U.S. Congress, Senate, *The Ku-Klux Conspiracy, Report of the Joint Select Committee to Inquire into the Conditions of Affairs in the Late Insurrectionary States,* Report No. 41, 42nd Congress, 2nd Session (Washington, D.C.: GPO, 1872), vol. 1, part 3, 352–53 (hereafter cited as *Ku-Klux Conspiracy*).

40. *Freedmen's Bureau,* Executive Document Number 70, 39th Congress, 1st Session, 167.

41. *Report of Carl Schurz,* 18.

42. *Report of Carl Schurz* (accompanying documents), 76. See also John Richard Dennett, *The South As It Is, 1865–1866* (New York: Viking Press, 1967 [1865–1866]), 91–92, 142.

43. *Report of the Joint Committee on Reconstruction,* part 2, 18, 42, 48, 50, 71, 83, 147, 154, 176, 182, 210, 214, 218–19, 243, 270; part 3, 10, 70, 122, 148; part 4, 40, 46, 62, 76.

44. Reid, *After the War,* 51, 145.

45. *Report of the Joint Committee on Reconstruction,* part 2, 185.

46. U.S. Congress, Senate, "A Report from Benjamin C. Truman," by Benjamin C. Truman, *Message of the President of the United States,* Executive Document Number 43, 39th Congress, 1st Session (Washington, D.C.: GPO, 1866), 12 (hereafter cited as "A Report from Benjamin C. Truman").

47. The term *contested terrain* is taken from Richard Edwards, *Contested Terrain: The Transformation of the Workplace in the Twentieth Century* (New York: Basic Books, 1979).

48. *Report of Carl Schurz* (accompanying documents), 81. See also *Report of Carl Schurz,* 24, 32, 45.

49. *Report of Carl Schurz,* 21.

50. *Report of Carl Schurz,* 35.

51 *Report of the Joint Committee on Reconstruction,* Part 3, 36.

52. *Report of the Joint Committee on Reconstruction,* Part 2, 67.

53. *Southern Cultivator* 24 (January 1866): 5.

54. *Report of Carl Schurz,* 16.

55. Andrews, *The South Since the War,* 398.

56. Reid, *After the War,* 34.

57. See, for example, Andrews, *The South Since the War,* 25, 97; Dennett, *The South As It Is,* 53, 65, 79, 212; Reid, *After the War,* 153, 217–18, 344, 405–6; *De Bow's Review* 1 (February 1866): 167; *Report of the Joint Committee on Reconstruction,* part 2, 29; *Reports of the*

Assistant Commissioners of Freedmen, Senate, Executive Document Number 6, 39th Congress, 2nd Session, 113.

58. On planters' commitment to a compulsory labor system and on their search for a functional alternative to slavery, see Reid, *After the War,* 151, 217–18, 337; Andrews, *The South Since the War,* 178; *Report of the Joint Committee on Reconstruction,* part 1, 107–8; part 2, 123; *Report of Carl Schurz* (accompanying documents), 51, 60; John T. Trowbridge, *The Desolate South, 1865–1866: A Picture of the Battlefields and of the Devastated Confederacy* (New York: Duell, Sloan and Pearce, 1956 [1866]), 155; U.S. Congress, House, *Freedmen's Bureau . . . Report of the Commissioner of the Bureau of Refugees, Freedmen, and Abandoned Lands,* Executive Document Number 11, 39th Congress, 1st Session (Washington, D.C.: GPO, 1865), 32 (hereafter cited as *Freedmen's Bureau*).

59. Andrews, *The South Since the War,* 101.

60. *The Nation* 1 (September 28, 1865): 393. See also Reid, *After the War,* 337; Dennett, *The South As It Is,* 48.

61. *Report of Carl Schurz,* 27. See also J. Carlyle Sitterson, "The Transition from Slave to Free Labor on the William J. Minor Plantation," *Agricultural History* 17 (October 1943): 218–21; Vernon Lane Wharton, *The Negro in Mississippi, 1865–1890* (New York: Harper and Row, 1965 [1947]), 68; Theodore Branter Wilson, *The Black Codes of the South* (Tuscaloosa: University of Alabama Press, 1965), 49–57; Dan T. Carter, "Fateful Legacy: White Southerners and the Dilemma of Emancipation," *Proceedings of the South Carolina Historical Association* (1977): 56–57.

62. Berlin et al., "The Terrain of Freedom," 111–12.

63. U.S. Congress, House, *Report of the Commissioner of Agriculture for the Year 1867,* Executive Documents, 40th Congress, 2nd Session (Washington, D.C.: GPO, 1868), 416–17. See also U.S. Congress, House, *Report of the Commissioner of Agriculture for the Year 1866,* Executive Document Number 107, 39th Congress, 2nd Session (Washington, D.C.: GPO, 1867), 574.

64. *Reports of the Assistant Commissioners of Freedmen,* Senate, Executive Document Number 6, 39th Congress, 2nd Session, 4. See also Nieman, *To Set the Law in Motion,* 40; Enoch Marvin Banks, *The Economics of Land Tenure in Georgia* (New York: AMS Press, 1968 [1905]), 79; James H. Street, *The New Revolution in the Cotton Economy* (Chapel Hill: University of North Carolina Press, 1957), 19.

65. Berlin et al., "The Terrain of Freedom," 112.

66. Reid, *After the War,* 211, 291, 346–47, 372–74; Ripley, *Slaves and Freedmen,* 69; *Southern Cultivator* 25 (April 1867): 112; ibid. 27 (March 1869): 90; F. W. Loring and C. F. Atkinson, *Cotton Culture and the South Considered With Reference to Emigration* (Boston: A. Williams and Co., 1869), 68.

67. *Report of Carl Schurz* (accompanying documents), 69, 91.

68. *Report of Carl Schurz* (accompanying documents), 83. See also *De Bow's Review* 7 (February 1869): 153.

69. Reid, *After the War*, 344. See also ibid., 362–63.

70. Loring and Atkinson, *Cotton Culture and the South*, 4.

71. Loring and Atkinson, *Cotton Culture and the South*, 9.

72. Cf. Charles L. Flynn, Jr., *White Land, Black Labor: Caste and Class in Late Nineteenth-Century Georgia* (Baton Rouge: Louisiana State University Press, 1983), 6–28.

73. Charles Nordhoff, *The Cotton States in the Spring and Summer of 1875* (New York: Burt Franklin, 1876), 72.

74. Cited in Eric Foner, *Reconstruction: America's Unfinished Revolution, 1863–1877* (New York: Harper & Row, 1988), 103.

75. Eric Foner, *Politics and Ideology in the Age of the Civil War* (Oxford: Oxford University Press, 1980), 106. See also Joel Williamson, *After Slavery: The Negro in South Carolina During Reconstruction, 1861–1877* (New York: W. W. Norton, 1975 [1965]), 44–46.

76. Frances B. Leigh, *Ten Years on a Georgia Plantation* (London: Richard Bentley and Sons, 1883), 25–26, 58–59.

77. For planters' complaints about labor scarcity, see, for example, *De Bow's Review* 1 (January 1866): 7, 93; ibid. 1 (June 1866), 607; *Southern Cultivator* 27 (March 1869), 85; Loring and Atkinson, *Cotton Culture and the South*, 3–20; Williamson, *After Slavery*, 110–11; Wiener, *Social Origins of the New South*, 42–47; Ransom and Sutch, *One Kind of Freedom*, 44–47, 55.

78. *Report of Carl Schurz* (accompanying documents), 49; Williamson, *After Slavery*, 34–39; Litwack, *Been in the Storm So Long*, 292–301; Nieman, *To Set the Law in Motion*, 38; Carter, "Fateful Legacy," 57–58; Foner, *Reconstruction*, 80–84; John Preston McConnell, *Negroes and Their Treatment in Virginia from 1865 to 1867* (New York: Negro Universities Press, 1969 [1910]), 18–19; Peter Kolchin, *First Freedom: The Responses of Alabama's Blacks to Emancipation and Reconstruction* (Westport, Conn.: Greenwood Press, 1972), 4–8.

79. Trowbridge, *The Desolate South*, 38.

80. In Chapter 3 I will discuss in greater detail the possibility of black landownership and the issues raised in the following two paragraphs.

81. *Southern Cultivator* 27 (March 1869): 90.

82. Loring and Atkinson, *Cotton Culture and the South*, 6, 13, 15, 18, 20; Benham, *A Year of Wreck*, 124; Nieman, *To Set the Law in Motion*, 161; Howard A. White, *The Freedmen's Bureau in Louisiana* (Baton Rouge: Louisiana State University Press, 1970), 115.

83. Reid, *After the War*, 335–36.

84. U.S. Congress, House, *Report of the Commissioner of Agriculture for the Year 1867*, x.

85. *Freedmen's Bureau*, Executive Document Number 70, 39th

Congress, 1st Session, 351–52; *Freedmen's Bureau*, Executive Document Number 11, 39th Congress, 1st Session, 7–8; *Report of the Joint Committee on Reconstruction*, Part 3, 41; Robert P. Brooks, *The Agrarian Revolution in Georgia, 1865–1912* (Westport, Conn.: Negro Universities Press, 1970 [1914]), 26, 46.

86. *The Nation* 1 (October 5, 1865): 426. See also ibid. 1 (September 28, 1865): 393; U.S. Congress, House, *Report of the Commissioner of Agriculture for the Year 1867*, 421; Rose, *Rehearsal for Reconstruction*, 79; Williamson, *After Slavery*, 44.

87. Cited in Gerald David Jaynes, *Branches Without Roots: Genesis of the Black Working Class in the American South, 1862–1882* (New York: Oxford University Press, 1986), 73.

88. *The Nation* 1 (September 28, 1865): 393. See also *Freedmen's Bureau*, Executive Document Number 70, 39th Congress, 1st Session, 252, 263–64.

89. Trowbridge, *The Desolate South*, 293.

90. Andrews, *The South Since the War*, 221–22.

91. Dorothy Sterling, ed., *The Trouble They Seen: Black People Tell the Story of Reconstruction* (Garden City, N.Y.: Doubleday, 1976), 43. See also *Report of the Joint Committee on Reconstruction*, Part 2, 206; *The Nation* 4 (January 17, 1867): 43; Williamson, *After Slavery*, 88–90; Charles H. Wesley, *Negro Labor in the United States, 1850–1925: A Study in American Economic History* (New York: Vanguard Press, 1927), 133–34.

92. U.S. Congress, House, *Report of the Commissioner of Agriculture for the Year 1866*, 573. See also Brooks, *The Agrarian Revolution*, 27.

93. U.S. Congress, House, *Report of Major General O. O. Howard, Commissioner of Bureau of Refugees, Freedmen, and Abandoned Lands, to the Secretary of War*, Executive Document Number 1, 40th Congress, 3rd Session (Washington, D.C.: GPO, 1868), 1042, 1046 (hereafter cited as *Report of Major General O. O. Howard*); *Report of Carl Schurz*, 29; *Report of the Joint Committee on Reconstruction*, part 3, 189; *De Bow's Review* 7 (February 1869): 153; Wiley, *Southern Negroes*, 236–37.

94. *Reports of the Assistant Commissioners of Freedmen*, Executive Document Number 6, 39th Congress, 2nd Session, 51, 104, 116; *Freedmen's Bureau*, Executive Document Number 70, 39th Congress, 1st Session, 225, 311, 351; *Freedmen's Bureau*, Executive Document Number 11, 39th Congress, 1st Session, 25; *Report of General O. O. Howard*, Executive Document Number 1, 40th Congress, 3rd Session, 1038, 1040, 1043; *Report of the Joint Committee on Reconstruction*, part 2, 52; part 3, 142; part 4, 64; *Report of Carl Schurz* (accompanying documents), 82; Sterling, *The Trouble They Seen*, 43, 51; Trowbridge, *The Desolate South*, 176, 194; Magdol, *A Right to the Land*, 150–52.

95. Ransom and Sutch, *One Kind of Freedom*, 44–46. On the withdrawal of women and children from the labor market, see Loring and Atkinson, *Cotton Culture and the South*, 4, 14, 15, 18, 20; Messner, *Freedom and the Ideology of Free Labor*, 74; Litwack, *Been in the Storm So Long*, 244–46; Foner, *Reconstruction*, 85–87; Herbert G. Gutman, *The Black Family in Slavery and Freedom, 1750–1925* (New York: Vintage Books, 1977), 166–68; Jacquelyn Jones, *Labor of Love, Labor of Sorrow: Black Women, Work, and the Family from Slavery to the Present* (New York: Basic Books, 1985), 58–60.

96. Loring and Atkinson, *Cotton Culture and the South*, 7.

97. Cited in Brooks, *The Agrarian Revolution*, 21–22.

98. Cited in Thavolia Glymph, "Freedpeople and Ex-Masters: Shaping a New Order in the Postbellum South, 1865–1868," in *Essays on the Postbellum Southern Economy*, ed. Glymph and Kushma, 60.

99. Reid, *After the War*, 323.

100. Williamson, *After Slavery*, 46; Reid, *After the War*, 546–50; Claude H. Nolen, *The Negro's Image in the South: The Anatomy of White Supremacy* (Lexington: University Press of Kentucky, 1967), 164–65; Michael Schwartz, *Radical Protest and Social Structure: The Southern Farmers' Alliance and Cotton Tenancy, 1880–1890* (New York: Academic Press, 1976), 58.

101. Berlin et al., *The Black Military Experience*, 733–823; Kolchin, *First Freedom*, 33; White, *The Freedmen's Bureau in Louisiana*, 110–12; Marvin Fletcher, "The Negro Volunteer in Reconstruction, 1865–1866," *Military Affairs* 32 (December 1968): 128–29.

102. Berlin et al., *The Black Military Experience*, 747–48.

103. Berlin et al., *The Black Military Experience*, 755–56.

104. *Southern Cultivator* 27 (February 1869): 50. See also *De Bow's Review* 1 (June 1866): 578; *The Ku-Klux Conspiracy*, vol. 3, part 10, 1410, 1955; Loring and Atkinson, *Cotton Culture and the South*, 15–16.

105. *Southern Cultivator* 26 (September 1868): 260.

106. *The Ku-Klux Conspiracy*, vol. 3, part 10, 1490.

107. *Reports of the Assistant Commissioners of Freedmen*, Senate, Executive Document Number 6, 39th Congress, 2nd Session, 50. See also *Report of Carl Schurz*, 17–19; Litwack, *Been in the Storm So Long*, 303–4.

108. Sterling, *The Trouble They Seen*, 8.

109. *Report of the Joint Committee on Reconstruction*, part 2, 222; part 3, 5; part 4, 83; Wyn Craig Wade, *The Fiery Cross: The Ku Klux Klan in America* (New York: Simon & Schuster, 1987), 18, 26.

110. *Reports of the Assistant Commissioners of Freedmen*, Senate, Executive Document Number 6, 39th Congress, 2nd Session, 113. See also ibid., 63, 86.

111. On the formation of combinations and cartels among

planters, see *Report of the Joint Committee on Reconstruction*, part 2, 5, 243; part 3, 9, 30, 149; Reid, *After the War*, 373; Andrews, *The South Since the War*, 206; *De Bow's Review* 5 (February 1868): 213, 224; *Report of Carl Schurz* (accompanying documents), 84–86; Wiener, *Social Origins of the New South*, 40–41; McConnell, *Negroes and Their Treatment in Virginia*, 33; Sylvia H. Krebs, "Will the Freedmen Work?: White Alabamians Adjust to Free Labor," *Alabama Historical Quarterly* 36 (Summer 1974): 157–58.

112. *Southern Cultivator* 26 (January 1868): 13.

113. Trowbridge, *The Desolate South*, 427.

114. For doubts about the effectiveness of planter combinations, see Roark, *Masters Without Slaves*, 135–36; Wharton, *The Negro in Mississippi*, 94; Robert Higgs, *Competition and Coercion: Blacks in the American Economy, 1865–1914* (Cambridge: Cambridge University Press, 1977), 47–49.

115. Dennett, *The South As It Is*, 16. See also *De Bow's Review* 1 (June 1866): 579; ibid. 4 (October 1867): 364.

116. *Southern Cultivator* 25 (January 1867): 11.

117. Berlin et al., "The Terrain of Freedom," 116.

118. Dennett, *The South As It Is*, 133.

119. Dennett, *The South As It Is*, 131.

120. On the Black Codes, see Wilson, *The Black Codes*; Du Bois, *Black Reconstruction*, 166–80; Nieman, *To Set the Law in Motion*, 72–102; William Cohen, "Negro Involuntary Servitude in the South, 1865–1940: A Preliminary Analysis," *The Journal of Southern History* 42 (February 1976): 31–60; Daniel A. Novak, *The Wheel of Servitude: Black Forced Labor After Slavery* (Lexington: University Press of Kentucky, 1978), 1–8.

121. Cited in Novak, *The Wheel of Servitude*, 5.

122. Du Bois, *Black Reconstruction*, 179.

123. W. Kloosterboer, *Involuntary Labour Since the Abolition of Slavery: A Survey of Compulsory Labour Throughout the World* (Leiden: E. J. Brill, 1960), 191.

124. Nieman, *To Set the Law in Motion*, 72–73; Wilson, *The Black Codes*, 57–60; Novak, *The Wheel of Servitude*, 4, 9.

125. Du Bois, *Black Reconstruction*, 167.

126. *Report of Carl Schurz*, 21.

127. Truman, "A Report from Benjamin C. Truman," 8–9.

128. *Reports of the Assistant Commissioners of Freedmen*, Senate, Executive Document Number 6, 39th Congress, 2nd Session, 141; *Freedmen's Bureau*, Executive Document Number 70, 39th Congress, 1st Session, 213, 217, 219, 226, 278; *The Ku-Klux Conspiracy*, vol. 3, part 10, 1738; Lewis C. Chartock, *A History and Analysis of Labor Contracts Administered by the Bureau of Refugees, Freedmen, and Abandoned Lands in Edgefield, Abbeville and Anderson Counties in*

South Carolina, 1865–1868 (Ph.D. diss., Bryn Mawr College, 1973),
101–2.

129. Cohen, "Negro Involuntary Servitude," 35, 37–38, 42.

130. Cited in Wilson, *The Black Codes*, 99.

131. Cited in Litwack, *Been in the Storm So Long*, 367.

132. *Reports of the Assistant Commissioners of Freedmen,*
Senate, Executive Document Number 6, 39th Congress, 2nd Session,
102. See also ibid., 34; McConnell, *Negroes and Their Treatment in
Virginia*, 97–102.

133. Krebs, "Will the Freedmen Work?" 159–60.

134. Sterling, *The Trouble They Seen*, 68.

135. See Litwack, *Been in the Storm So Long*, 191; Gutman, *The
Black Family*, 402–12.

136. Wilson, *The Black Codes*, 75; Novak, *The Wheel of Servitude*, 4. See also *Report of the Joint Committee on Reconstruction*, part
2, 21; Wesley, *Negro Labor in the United States*, 121.

137. Nieman, *To Set the Law in Motion*, 72–155; Litwack, *Been
in the Storm So Long*, 370; Wharton, *The Negro in Mississippi*, 91–93.

138. Novak, *The Wheel of Servitude*, 18–28.

139. Cohen, "Negro Involuntary Servitude," 31. See also Pete
Daniel, *The Shadow of Slavery: Peonage in the South, 1901–1969*
(Urbana: University of Illinois Press, 1972); Daniel, "The Metamorpho-
sis of Slavery, 1865–1900," *Journal of American History* 60 (June 1979):
88–99.

140. John Hope Franklin, "Whither Reconstruction Historiogra-
phy?" *Journal of Negro Education* (Fall 1948): 458. See also Litwack,
Been in the Storm So Long, 370; Ransom and Sutch, *One Kind of
Freedom*, 36.

141. Ransom and Sutch, *One Kind of Freedom*, 67; Nieman, *To
Set the Law in Motion*, 161; Michael Wayne, *The Reshaping of
Plantation Society: The Natchez District, 1860–1880* (Baton Rouge:
Louisiana State University Press, 1983), 47–49.

142. For general studies of the Ku Klux Klan in the postwar years,
see Wade, *The Fiery Cross*; Stanley F. Horn, *Invisible Empire: The Story
of the Ku Klux Klan, 1866–1871* (Boston: Houghton Mifflin, 1939);
Thomas B. Alexander, "Ku Kluxism in Tennessee, 1865–1869," *Tennes-
see Historical Quarterly* 8 (September 1949): 195–219; Otto H. Olsen,
"The Ku Klux Klan: A Study in Reconstruction Politics and Propa-
ganda," *North Carolina Historical Review* 39 (July 1962): 340–62; David
M. Chalmers, *Hooded Americanism: The History of the Ku Klux Klan*
(Chicago: Quadrangle, 1968), 8–21; Allen W. Trelease, *White Terror:
The Ku Klux Klan Conspiracy and Southern Reconstruction* (New York:
Harper Torchbooks, 1971); Edward Magdol, "Local Black Leaders in the
South, 1867–75: An Essay Toward the Reconstruction of Reconstruction
History," *Societas—A Review of Social History* 4 (Spring 1974): 81–110.

143. For evidence on the role of the Klan as an instrument of labor control, see Foner, *Reconstruction*, 428–29; Chalmers, *Hooded Americanism*, 18; Trelease, *White Terror*, xvii, xlvi–xlvii, 288, 320–21; Wade, *The Fiery Cross*, 76; Manual Gottlieb, "The Land Question in Georgia During Reconstruction," *Science and Society* 3 (Summer 1939): 383–84; Vernon Burton, "Race and Reconstruction: Edgefield County, South Carolina," *Journal of Social History* 12 (Fall 1978): 37.

144. Wiener, *Social Origins of the New South*, 61–66; J.C.A. Stagg, "The Problem of Klan Violence: The South Carolina Up-Country, 1868–1871," *Journal of American Studies* 8 (No. 3, 1974): 303–18.

145. Wiener, *Social Origins of the New South*, 61.

146. Wiener, *Social Origins of the New South*, 64.

147. Cited in Foner, *Reconstruction*, 428–29.

148. See also Trelease, *White Terror*, xix–xx, 51–52, 296, 332.

149. Stagg, "The Problem of Klan Violence," 315.

150. Stagg, "The Problem of Klan Violence," 312–13.

151. See, for example, Trelease, *White Terror*, xlvi–xlvii; Wiener, *Social Origins of the New South*, 64.

152. Cited in McConnell, *Negroes and Their Treatment in Virginia*, 15.

153. Cf. Wayne, *The Reshaping of Plantation Society*, 41–42; Jaynes, *Branches Without Roots*, 111–12; William S. McFeely, *Yankee Stepfather: General O. O. Howard and the Freedmen* (New Haven, Conn.: Yale University Press, 1968), 151–53.

154. John William De Forest, *A Union Officer in the Reconstruction* (New Haven, Conn.: Yale University Press, 1948 [1868–1869]), 28.

155. See, for example, *Freedmen's Bureau*, Executive Document Number 70, 39th Congress, 1st Session, 250; U.S. Congress, Senate, *Message From the President of the United States, Communicating . . . the Reports of the Assistant Commissioners of the Freedmen's Bureau*, Executive Document Number 27, 39th Congress, 1st Session (Washington, D.C.: GPO, 1866), 21.

156. Sterling, *The Trouble They Seen*, 51–52.

157. For examples and discussions of contracts under the postwar gang-labor system, see Ransom and Sutch, *One Kind of Freedom*, 56–61; Higgs, *Competition and Coercion*, 43–45; Wiener, *Social Origins of the New South*, 36–39; McFeely, *Yankee Stepfather*, 149–53; Litwack, *Been in the Storm So Long*, 409–12; Chartock, *A History and Analysis of Labor Contracts*, 121–81; Joseph D. Reid, Jr., "Sharecropping as an Understandable Market Response: The Post-Bellum South," *Journal of Economic History* 33 (March 1973): 107–9; Robert A. Calvert, "The Freedmen and Agricultural Prosperity," *Southwestern Historical Quarterly* 76 (April 1973): 461–71.

158. The Mial contract is reproduced in Ransom and Sutch, *One Kind of Freedom*, 58–59. For another analysis of the same contract,

see Reid, "Sharecropping as an Understandable Market Response," 107–8.

159. Reid, "Sharecropping as an Understandable Market Response," 108–9.

160. Higgs, *Competition and Coercion*, 43–44.

161. Litwack, *Been in the Storm So Long*, 409.

162. Wiener, *Social Origins of the New South*, 38–39.

163. Higgs, *Competition and Coercion*, 45.

164. Chartock, *A History and Analysis of Labor Contracts*, 137–62.

165. Chartock, *A History and Analysis of Labor Contracts*, 191.

166. Chartock, *A History and Analysis of Labor Contracts*, 188.

167. Williamson, *After Slavery*, 97.

168. On the Freedmen's Bureau and its role in the regulation of labor relations in the postwar South, see especially Nieman, *To Set the Law in Motion*; McFeely, *Yankee Stepfather*, 149–65; Wiener, *The Social Origins of the New South*, 47–58; White, *The Freedmen's Bureau in Louisiana*, 101–33; George R. Bentley, *A History of the Freedmen's Bureau* (New York: Octagon Books, 1970 [1955]), 76–88; Martin Abbott, *The Freedmen's Bureau in South Carolina* (Chapel Hill: University of North Carolina Press, 1967), 66–81; Robert Francis Engs, *Freedom's First Generation: Black Hampton, Virginia, 1861–1890* (Philadelphia: University of Pennsylvania Press, 1979), 99–136.

169. In Chapter 3 I will discuss in greater detail the role of the Freedmen's Bureau with respect to the possibility of black landownership.

170. Bentley, *A History of the Freedmen's Bureau*, 77–79, 84; Jerry Thornbery, "Northerners and the Atlanta Freedmen, 1865–1869," *Prologue* (1976): 241–43; William Cohen, "Black Immobility and Free Labor: The Freedmen's Bureau and the Relocation of Black Labor, 1865–1868," *Civil War History* 30 (September 1984): 228.

171. Cohen, "Black Immobility and Free Labor," 221–34; Jaynes, *Branches Without Roots*, 67–68.

172. Nieman, *To Set the Law in Motion*, 61–65, 162–90; Wiener, *Social Origins of the New South*, 47–58.

173. Andrews, *The South Since the War*, 179.

174. Cited in Abbott, *The Freedmen's Bureau in South Carolina*, 120. See also ibid., 114–29; Loring and Atkinson, *Cotton Culture and the South*, 15; Nieman, *To Set the Law in Motion*, 41–42; Bentley, *A History of the Freedmen's Bureau*, 104–6; White, *The Freedmen's Bureau in Louisiana*, 38–40; Roark, *Masters Without Slaves*, 139.

175. Reid, *After the War*, 550, 577; *Report of Carl Schurz*, 40; Litwack, *Been in the Storm So Long*, 381.

176. Charles Stearns, *The Black Man of the South and the Rebels; or, The Characteristics of the Former, and the Recent Outrages of the Latter* (New York: Kraus Reprint Co., 1969 [1872]), 108–9.

177. Dennett, *The South As It Is*, 291–92. See also ibid., 70–74, 220.

178. Wiener, *Social Origins of the New South*, 55–57; McFeely, *Yankee Stepfather*, 157–58; Litwack, *Been in the Storm So Long*, 382–86; Nieman, *To Set the Law in Motion*, 16.

179. Andrews, *The South Since the War*, 24, 203. See also Nieman, *To Set the Law in Motion*, 15–16; White, *The Freedmen's Bureau in Louisiana*, 32–38; Bentley, *A History of the Freedmen's Bureau*, 138–39; Litwack, *Been in the Storm So Long*, 382; Abbott, *The Freedmen's Bureau in South Carolina*, 23, 28–29.

180. Engs, *Freedom's First Generation*, 105–11; McFeely, *Yankee Stepfather*, 69.

181. Dennett, *The South As It Is*, 54–55, 109–10, 124–26, 221–23, 270–71; Nieman, *To Set the Law in Motion*, 11–15; Abbott, *The Freedmen's Bureau in South Carolina*, 19–22; Litwack, *Been in the Storm So Long*, 383.

182. Litwack, *Been in the Storm So Long*, 385.

183. *Reports of the Assistant Commissioners of Freedmen*, Senate, Executive Document Number 6, 39th Congress, 2nd Session, 141.

184. Nieman, *To Set the Law in Motion*, 156–60.

185. Nieman, *To Set the Law in Motion*, 158.

186. Cited in Litwack, *Been in the Storm So Long*, 380.

187. *Freedmen's Bureau*, Executive Document Number 70, 39th Congress, 1st Session, 139. See also *Reports of the Assistant Commissioners of Freedmen*, Senate, Executive Document Number 6, 39th Congress, 2nd Session, 2.

188. Foner, *Politics and Ideology*, 101. See also Cohen, "Black Immobility and Free Labor," 221–34.

189. See, for example, Wiener, *Social Origins and the New South*, 57; Litwack, *Been in the Storm So Long*, 519; Engs, *Freedom's First Generation*, 104.

190. Cited in Litwack, *Been in the Storm So Long*, 386.

Chapter 3

1. Ira Berlin, Steven Hahn, Steven F. Miller, Joseph P. Reidy, and Leslie S. Rowland, "The Terrain of Freedom: The Struggle over the Meaning of Free Labor in the U.S. South," *History Workshop Journal* 22 (Autumn 1986), 129.

2. U.S. Congress, Senate, *Report of Carl Schurz on the States of South Carolina, Georgia, Alabama, Mississippi, and Louisiana*, by Carl Schurz, Executive Document Number 2, 39th Congress, 1st Session (Washington, D.C.: Government Printing Office [GPO], 1866), (accompanying documents), 82 (hereafter cited as *Report of Carl Schurz*).

3. Claude Oubre argues that historians, preoccupied with the

development of sharecropping in the postbellum South, have not given enough study to the failure of freedpeople to become landowners. Yet blacks' struggle for land, however much a neglected theme, is not just another interesting tale to tell alongside that of the rise of sharecropping, for the story of the defeat of the possibility of black landownership and the story of the origins of southern sharecropping are inseparably tied to one another. See Claude Oubre, *Forty Acres and a Mule: The Freedmen's Bureau and Black Landownership* (Baton Rouge: Louisiana State University Press, 1978), xi.

4. On the confiscation acts of 1861 and 1862, see James G. Randall, "Some Legal Aspects of the Confiscation Acts of the Civil War," *American Historical Review* 18 (October 1912): 79–96; Randall, *Constitutional Problems Under Lincoln,* rev. ed. (Urbana: University of Illinois Press, 1951), 275–15; Louis S. Gerteis, *From Contraband to Freedman: Federal Policy Toward Southern Blacks, 1861–1865* (Westport, Conn.: Greenwood Press, 1973), 136–37.

5. On the confiscation of southern property for nonpayment of taxes, see Randall, *Constitutional Problems Under Lincoln,* 317–23; Oubre, *Forty Acres and a Mule,* 8–11; James M. McPherson, *The Struggle for Equality: Abolitionists and the Negro in the Civil War and Reconstruction* (Princeton, N.J.: Princeton University Press, 1964), 249–55; Willie Lee Rose, *Rehearsal for Reconstruction: The Port Royal Experiment* (London: Oxford University Press, 1978 [1964], 199–217, 272–96; Carol K. Rothrock Bleser, *The Promised Land: The History of the South Carolina Land Commission, 1868–1890* (Columbia: University of South Carolina Press, 1969), 4–7.

6. Randall, *Constitutional Problems Under Lincoln,* 323–341; Randall, "Captured and Abandoned Property During the Civil War," *American Historical Review* 19 (October 1913): 65–79.

7. On the policy of the Freedmen's Bureau with respect to the disposition of captured and abandoned lands, see Oubre, *Forty Acres and a Mule,* 22–45; George R. Bentley, *A History of the Freedmen's Bureau* (New York: Octagon Books, 1970 [1955]), 89–102; LaWanda Cox, "The Promise of Land for the Freedmen," *Mississippi Valley Historical Review* 45 (December 1958): 413–40; Martin Abbott, *The Freedmen's Bureau in South Carolina, 1865–1872* (Chapel Hill: University of North Carolina Press, 1967), 52–65; Howard A. White, *The Freedmen's Bureau in Louisiana* (Baton Rouge: Louisiana State University Press, 1970), 41–63; Donald Nieman, *To Set the Law in Motion: The Freedmen's Bureau and the Legal Rights of Blacks, 1865–1868* (Millwood, N.Y.: KTO Press, 1979), 46–53.

8. Cited in Oubre, *Forty Acres and a Mule,* 21.

9. Nieman, *To Set the Law in Motion,* 46.

10. Oubre, *Forty Acres and a Mule,* 37, 44–45.

11. On Sherman's land program, see Oubre, *Forty Acres and a*

Mule, 46–71; Rose, *Rehearsal for Reconstruction*, 320–31; Abbott, *The Freedmen's Bureau in South Carolina*, 57–63; Joel Williamson, *After Slavery: The Negro in South Carolina During Reconstruction, 1861–1877* (New York: W. W. Norton, 1975 [1965]), 59–63; Vincent Harding, *There Is a River: The Black Struggle for Freedom in America* (New York: Random House, 1981), 267–70.

12. Cox, "The Promise of Land for the Freedmen," 429.

13. U.S. War Department, "Special Field Orders, No. 15," *The War of the Rebellion: A Compilation of the Official Records of the Union and the Confederate Armies* (Washington, D.C.: GPO, 1880–1901), Series 1, vol. 47, part 2, 60–62.

14. On the restoration of lands possessed by freedpeople under the authority of Special Field Order No. 15, see Rose, *Rehearsal for Reconstruction*, 346–77; Oubre, *Forty Acres and a Mule*, 49–71; William S. McFeely, *Yankee Stepfather: General O. O. Howard and the Freedmen* (New Haven, Conn.: Yale University Press, 1968), 84–148.

15. Cited in Rose, *Rehearsal for Reconstruction*, 348.

16. Abbott, *The Freedmen's Bureau in South Carolina*, 60; Edward Magdol, *A Right to the Land: Essays on the Freedmen's Community* (Westport, Conn.: Greenwood Press, 1977), 167; Robert Francis Engs, *Freedom's First Generation: Black Hampton, Virginia, 1861–1890* (Philadelphia: University of Pennsylvania Press, 1979), 104; Lawrence N. Powell, *New Masters: Northern Planters During the Civil War and Reconstruction* (New Haven, Conn.: Yale University Press, 1980), 99–100.

17. On the Southern Homestead Act, see Oubre, *Forty Acres and a Mule*, 72–157; Paul Wallace Gates, "Federal Land Policy in the South, 1866–1888," *Journal of Southern History* 6 (August 1940): 303–30; Patrick W. Riddleberger, "George W. Julian: Abolitionist Land Reformer," *Agricultural History* 29 (July 1955): 108–15; Christie Farnham Pope, "Southern Homesteads for Negroes," *Agricultural History* 44 (April 1970): 201–17; Warren Hoffnagle, "The Southern Homestead Act: Its Origins and Operation," *Historian* 22 (August 1970): 615–29.

18. Oubre, *Forty Acres and a Mule*, 188.

19. Cited in Eric Foner, *Politics and Ideology in the Age of the Civil War* (Oxford: Oxford University Press, 1980), 134.

20. On the proponents of confiscation and redistribution and their unsuccessful efforts to achieve southern land reform, see Foner, *Politics and Ideology*, 128–49; McPherson, *The Struggle for Equality*, 246–59; Kenneth M. Stampp, *The Era of Reconstruction, 1865–1877* (New York: Vintage Books, 1965), 126–31.

21. *Commerical and Financial Chronicle* 1 (July 1, 1865): 5; ibid. 1 (August 26, 1865): 260; ibid. 1 (September 23, 1865): 388; ibid. 1 (December 9, 1865): 740; ibid. 2 (February 17, 1866): 197–98; ibid. 6 (January 18, 1868): 70–71. See also the *Merchants Magazine and*

Commercial Review 58 (February 1868): 121–24. The *New York Times*, owned and edited by Henry J. Raymond, maintained a similar position; see Thomas Wagstaff, "Call Your Old Master—'Master': Southern Political Leaders and Negro Labor During Presidential Reconstruction," *Labor History* 10 (Summer 1969): 329–31.

22. *Commercial and Financial Chronicle* 1 (September 23, 1865): 388. See also Foner, *Politics and Ideology*, 136–37, 143–44.

23. *Commercial and Financial Chronicle* 1 (August 26, 1865): 260.

24. *Commercial and Financial Chronicle* 1 (September 23, 1865): 387–88.

25. Peter Kolchin, "The Business Press and Reconstruction, 1865–1868," *Journal of Southern History* 33 (May 1967): 183–96.

26. Kolchin, "The Business Press and Reconstruction," 183–96; Earle D. Ross, "Horace Greeley and the South," *South Atlantic Quarterly* 16 (October 1917): 324–38; William B. Hesseltine, "Economic Factors in the Abandonment of Reconstruction," *Mississippi Valley Historical Review* 22 (September 1935): 191–92; Richard W. Griffin, "Problems of the Southern Cotton Planters after the Civil War," *Georgia Historical Quarterly* 39 (June 1955): 106; Stanley Coben, "Northeastern Business and Radical Reconstruction: A Re-examination," *Mississippi Valley Historical Review* 46 (June 1959): 85.

27. Foner, *Politics and Ideology*, 109; Rose, *Rehearsal for Reconstruction*, 164; Cox, "The Promise of Land for the Freedmen," 435–37; Henry L. Swint, "Northern Interest in the Shoeless Southerner," *Journal of Southern History* 16 (November 1950): 457–71.

28. Gerald David Jaynes, *Branches Without Roots: Genesis of the Black Working Class in the American South, 1862–1882* (New York: Oxford University Press, 1986), 8–15. Jaynes argues that northern opposition to the confiscation of the southern estates grew more from these financial considerations than from concern for the sanctity of the private property rights of the southern landowner.

29. On how the free-labor ideology informed opposition to the program of confiscation and redistribution, see Stampp, *The Era of Reconstruction*, 129–30; Rose, *Rehearsal for Reconstruction*, 223; Foner, *Politics and Ideology*, 131–32, 136; Powell, *New Masters*, 76–77; W.E.B. Du Bois, *Black Reconstruction in America, 1860–1880* (New York: Atheneum, 1969 [1935]), 601–2.

30. *The Nation* 4 (May 9, 1867): 375–76; cf. Stampp, *The Era of Reconstruction*, 130.

31. Cited in Foner, *Politics and Ideology*, 144. See also White, *The Freedmen's Bureau in Louisiana*, 44–45; Vernon Lane Wharton, *The Negro in Mississippi, 1865–1890* (New York: Harper & Row, 1965 [1947]), 60; John G. Sproat, "Blueprint for Radical Reconstruction," *Journal of Southern History* 23 (February 1957): 43; Eric Foner, *Recon-*

struction: America's Unfinished Revolution, 1863–1877 (New York: Harper & Row, 1988), 309–10.

32. Du Bois, *Black Reconstruction*, 368.

33. *De Bow's Review* 4 (December 1867): 586–88. See also Roger Wallace Shugg, "Survival of the Plantation System in Louisiana," *Journal of Southern History* 3 (August 1937): 316.

34. Powell, *New Masters*, xii–xiii.

35. Powell, *New Masters*, 54. See also Stampp, *The Era of Reconstruction*, 131.

36. Cited in Wagstaff, "Call Your Old Master—'Master,' " 340.

37. Wharton, *The Negro in Mississippi*, 17; Oubre, *Forty Acres and a Mule*, 182; Foner, *Reconstruction*, 51, 71–72, 105–6; James S. Allen, *Reconstruction: The Battle for Democracy, 1865–1876* (New York: International Publishers, 1937), 43–44; Michael Wayne, *The Reshaping of Plantation Society: The Natchez District, 1860–1880* (Baton Rouge: Louisiana State University Press, 1983), 34.

38. Cited in Manual Gottlieb, "The Land Question in Georgia During Reconstruction," *Science and Society* 3 (Summer 1939): 359.

39. Litwack, *Been in the Storm So Long: The Aftermath of Slavery* (New York: Random House, 1979), 400. See also Sidney Andrews, *The South Since the War* (Boston: Houghton Mifflin, 1971 [1866]), 233.

40. Cited in Foner, *Reconstruction*, 105.

41. Cited in Leon F. Litwack, *Been in the Storm So Long*, 402.

42. Cited in Allen, *Reconstruction*, 33.

43. Cited in Oscar Zeichner, "The Transition from Slave to Free Agricultural Labor in the Southern States," *Agricultural History* 13 (January 1939): 23. See also Wharton, *The Negro in Mississippi*, 59; Nieman, *To Set the Law in Motion*, 160; Walter L. Fleming, " 'Forty Acres and a Mule,' " *North American Review* 182 (1906): 722–23.

44. Gerteis, *From Contraband to Freedman*, 175–81; Oubre, *Forty Acres and a Mule*, 17–18; Wharton, *The Negro in Mississippi*, 39–42.

45. See, for example, Jonathan M. Wiener, *Social Origins of the New South: Alabama, 1860–1885* (Baton Rouge: Louisiana State University Press, 1978), 47–48.

46. Abbott, *The Freedmen's Bureau in South Carolina*, 53; Abbott, "Free Land, Free Labor, and the Freedmen's Bureau," *Agricultural History* 30 (October 1956): 151–52; Wharton, *The Negro in Mississippi*, 59; Zeichner, "The Transition from Slave to Free Agricultural Labor," 23; *The Nation* 1 (September 28, 1865): 393.

47. Litwack, *Been in the Storm So Long*, 402.

48. Ira Berlin, Barbara J. Fields, Thavolia Glymph, Joseph P. Reidy, and Leslie S. Rowland, *The Black Military Experience*, series 2 of *Freedom: A Documentary History of Emancipation, 1861–1867* (Cam-

bridge: Cambridge University Press, 1982), 737–39; Allen, *Reconstruction*, 53–55; Magdol, *A Right to the Land*, 143–44; Wagstaff, "Call Your Old Master—'Master,'" 341; White, *The Freedmen's Bureau in Louisiana*, 110.

49. U.S. Congress, House, *Freedmen's Bureau . . . a Report by the Commissioner of the Freedmen's Bureau, of all Orders by him or any Assistant Commissioner*, Executive Document Number 70, 39th Congress, 1st Session (Washington, D.C.: GPO, 1866), 367 (hereafter cited as *Freedmen's Bureau*). See also Andrews, *The South Since the War*, 24–25; *Report of Carl Schurz*, 31; Fleming, "'Forty Acres and a Mule,'" 731–32; Zeichner, "The Transition from Slave to Free Agricultural Labor," 25; John T. Trowbridge, *The Desolate South, 1865–1866: A Picture of the Battlefields and of the Devastated Confederacy* (New York: Duell, Sloan and Pearce, 1956 [1866]), 194; Whitelaw Reid, *After the War: A Tour of the Southern States, 1865–1866* (New York: Harper Torchbooks, 1965 [1866]), 335–36, 344.

50. Andrews, *The South Since the War* 97.

51. U.S. Congress, House, *Freedmen's Bureau . . . Report of the Commissioner of the Bureau of Refugees, Freedmen, and Abandoned Lands*, Executive Document Number 11, 39th Congress, 1st Session (Washington, D.C.: GPO, 1865), 12–13 (hereafter cited as *Freedmen's Bureau*); *Freedmen's Bureau*, Executive Document Number 70, 39th Congress, 1st Session, 1866, 4–5, 25–26, 34, 58, 95, 135, 147, 162–63, 250, 252, 309, 311, 367–68, 391, 394; Magdol, *A Right to the Land*, 141–42; Bleser, *The Promised Land*, 11–12; Engs, *Freedom's First Generation*, 102–4; Jerry Thornbery, "Northerners and the Atlanta Freedmen, 1865–1869," *Prologue* 6 (1976): 241.

52. Cited in Gottlieb, "The Land Question in Georgia," 364.

53. *The Nation* 1 (September 28, 1865): 393. See also Gottlieb, "The Land Question in Georgia," 362–64; Magdol, *A Right to the Land*, 141–42; Wharton, *The Negro in Mississippi*, 59; White, *The Freedmen's Bureau in Louisiana*, 57.

54. Fleming, "Forty Acres and a Mule," 732–35; Gottlieb, "The Land Question in Georgia," 370–72, 375–78; Litwack, *Been in the Storm So Long*, 552–53; Magdol, *A Right to the Land*, 142; Oubre, *Forty Acres and a Mule*, 184; Foner, *Reconstruction*, 290; Roger Ransom and Richard Sutch, *One Kind of Freedom: The Economic Consequences of Emancipation* (Cambridge: Cambridge University Press, 1977), 82.

55. Edward Magdol, "Local Black Leaders in the South, 1867–75: An Essay Toward the Reconstruction of Reconstruction History," *Societas—A Review of Social History* 4 (Spring 1974): 103.

56. Charles Nordhoff, *The Cotton States in the Spring and Summer of 1875* (New York: Burt Franklin, 1876), 49.

57. Andrews, *The South Since the War*, 97.

58. Reid, *After the War*, 344.

59. Cited in Wagstaff, "Call Your Old Master—Master,' " 340.

60. Cited in Foner, *Reconstruction*, 291–92.

61. Andrews, *The South Since the War*, 36.

62. Magdol, *A Right to the Land*, 140; Wagstaff, "Call Your Old Master—'Master,' " 340–42; Allen, *Reconstruction*, 53; Litwack, *Been in the Storm So Long*, 425–30; Dan T. Carter, "The Anatomy of Fear: The Christmas Day Insurrection Scare of 1865," *Journal of Southern History* 42 (August 1976): 345–64; Willie Lee Rose, *Slavery and Freedom*, ed. William W. Freehling (New York: Oxford University Press, 1982), 79.

63. Cited in Charles L. Flynn, Jr., *White Land, Black Labor: Caste and Class in Late Nineteenth-Century Georgia* (Baton Rouge: Louisiana State University Press, 1983), 93.

64. Trowbridge, *The Desolate South*, 123. See ibid., 293.

65. See, for example, Foner, *Reconstruction*, 103–10; Williamson, *After Slavery*, 54; Abbott, *The Freedmen's Bureau in South Carolina*, 52–53; Thomas F. Armstrong, "From Task Labor to Free Labor: The Transition Along Georgia's Rice Coast, 1820–1880," *Georgia Historical Quarterly* 64 (Winter 1980): 440–42.

66. *The Nation* 1 (September 28, 1865): 393.

67. Reid, *After the War*, 564.

68. Reid, *After the War*, 59.

69. Cited in Dorothy Sterling, ed., *The Trouble They Seen: Black People Tell the Story of Reconstruction* (Garden City, N.Y.: Doubleday, 1976), 30; Harding, *There Is a River*, 262–63.

70. Cited in Armstead L. Robinson, " 'Worser dan Jeff Davis': The Coming of Free Labor during the Civil War, 1861–1865," in *Essays on the Postbellum Southern Economy*, ed. Thavolia Glymph and John J. Kushma (Arlington: Texas A & M University Press, 1985), 41.

71. *Southern Cultivator* 25 (March 1867): 69. See also ibid. 27 (March 1869): 90.

72. F. W. Loring and C. F. Atkinson, *Cotton Culture and the South Considered with Reference to Emigration* (Boston: A. Williams and Co., 1869), 4.

73. John Richard Dennett, *The South As It Is: 1865–1866* (New York: Viking Press, 1967 [1865–1866]), 341–42.

74. Cited in Vernon Burton, "Race and Reconstruction: Edgefield County, South Carolina," *Journal of Social History* 12 (Fall 1978): 35.

75. Walter L. Fleming, ed., *Documentary History of Reconstruction* (Gloucester, Mass.: Peter Smith, 1960 [1906–1907]), 450–51.

76. Foner, *Politics and Ideology*, 109.

77. U.S. Congress, Senate, *The Ku-Klux Conspiracy, Report of the Joint Select Committee to Inquire into the Conditions of Affairs in the Late Insurrectionary States*, Report No. 41, 42nd Congress, 2nd Session (Washington, D.C.: GPO, 1872), vol. 1, part 2, 574 (hereafter cited as *Ku-Klux Conspiracy*).

78. Foner, *Reconstruction*, 134.

79. *De Bow's Review* 1 (January 1866): 72–73.

80. U.S. Congress, House, *Report of the Joint Committee on Reconstruction*, Executive Document Number 30, 39th Congress, 1st Session (Washington, D.C.: GPO, 1866), part 4, 9 (hereafter cited as *Report of the Joint Committee on Reconstruction*).

81. *Report of the Joint Committee on Reconstruction*, part 3, 101. See also ibid, part 2, 176, 269, 243, 245; part 3, 4, 6, 25, 27, 30, 36, 62, 71, 122, 145, 148, 151; part 4, 56, 69, 117.

82. Cited in Foner, *Politics and Ideology*, 111.

83. Reid, *After the War*, 151.

84. See, for example, Nieman, *To Set the Law in Motion*, 42–43; Wharton, *The Negro in Mississippi*, 64; Williamson, *After Slavery*, 99.

85. *Southern Cultivator* 26 (May 1868): 133.

86. *Southern Cultivator* 27 (February 1869): 57.

87. Philip Bruce, *The Plantation Negro as Freedman: Observations on his Character, Condition, and Prospects in Virginia* (New York: G. P. Putnam's Sons, 1889), 214–15.

88. *Southern Cultivator* 26 (May 1868): 133. See also ibid. 27 (February 1869): 57; ibid. 29 (February 1871): 45–46.

89. Bruce, *The Plantation Negro*, 214–15.

90. New Orleans *Tribune*, January 20, 1869. See ibid., January 8, 1869; ibid., January 15, 1869; ibid., February 7, 1869; ibid., February 26, 1869.

91. Williamson, *After Slavery*, 99.

92. *Southern Cultivator* 29 (February 1871): 45.

93. *Southern Cultivator* 27 (February 1869): 57.

94. Williamson, *After Slavery*, 99; Magdol, *A Right to the Land*, 149.

95. John Preston McConnell, *Negroes and Their Treatment in Virginia from 1865 to 1867* (New York: Negro Universities Press, 1969 [1910]), 35, 40. See also Nieman, *To Set the Law in Motion*, 41.

96. Reid, *After the War*, 565.

97. Dennett, *The South As It Is*, 108.

98. Nordhoff, *The Cotton States*, 70–71.

99. Andrews, *The South Since the War*, 206. See also Sterling, *The Trouble They Seen*, 262–64; *Report of the Joint Committee on Reconstruction*, part 2, 21, 54; part 3, 6, 36, 101; Gottlieb, "The Land Question in Georgia," 387–88; Litwack, *Been in the Storm So Long*, 407; White, *The Freedmen's Bureau*, 61; Burton, "Race and Reconstruction," 36–38; Magdol, *A Right to the Land*, 149.

100. New Orleans *Tribune*, February 7, 1869. See also *Ku-Klux Conspiracy*, vol. 2, part 4, 605–11.

101. Dennett, *The South As It Is*, 344.

102. Reid, *After the War*, 564–65.

103. *Report of the Joint Committee on Reconstruction*, part 2, 21.

104. George C. Benham, *A Year of Wreck* (New York: Harper and Brothers, 1880), 126.

105. *Southern Cultivator* 28 (January 1970): 15. See also Ronald L. F. Davis, *Good and Faithful Labor: From Slavery to Sharecropping in the Natchez District, 1860–1890* (Westport, Conn.: Greenwood Press, 1982), 78.

106. Steven Hahn, "Hunting, Fishing, and Foraging: Common Rights and Class Relations in the Postbellum South," *Radical History Review* 26 (1982): 44–45. See also Flynn, *White Land, Black Labor*, 115–22; J. Crawford King, Jr., "The Closing of the Southern Range: An Exploratory Study" *Journal of Southern History* 48 (1982): 56–57.

107. Ransom and Sutch, *One Kind of Freedom*, 83.

108. Magdol, *A Right to the Land*, 145–46. See also Williamson, *After Slavery*, 25–26; Ransom and Sutch, *One Kind of Freedom*, 82.

109. Ransom and Sutch, *One Kind of Freedom*, 83–86.

110. On black property holdings in the postbellum South, see Oubre, *Forty Acres and a Mule*, 158–80; Armstrong, "From Task Labor to Free Labor," 441–43; Edward H. Bonekemper, III, "Negro Ownership of Real Property in Hampton and Elizabeth City County, Virginia, 1860–1870," *Journal of Negro History* 55 (July 1970): 165–81; Peter C. Ripley, *Slaves and Freedmen in Civil War Louisiana* (Baton Rouge: Louisiana State University Press, 1976), 76–82.

111. Oubre, *Forty Acres and a Mule*, 195.

112. Thavolia Glymph, "Introduction," in *Essays on the Postbellum Southern Economy*, ed. Glymph and Kushma, 6.

Chapter 4

1. Walter L. Fleming, "Immigration to the Southern States," *Political Science Quarterly* 20 (June 1905): 276. Fleming's assertion that, prior to the early 1880s, "the southern people desired no immigration either from the North or from foreign countries" is certainly incorrect. R. H. Woody, "The Labor and Immigration Problems of South Carolina During Reconstruction," *Mississippi Valley Historical Review* 18 (September 1931): 195–212; and Bert James Loewenberg, "Efforts to Encourage Immigration, 1865–1900," *South Atlantic Quarterly* 33 (October 1934): 363–85, both specifically criticize Fleming on this point. On the possibility of southern immigration, see also Vernon Lane Wharton, *The Negro in Mississippi, 1865–1890* (New York: Harper & Row, 1965 [1947]), 97–105; Rowland T. Berthoff, "Southern Attitudes Toward Immigration, 1865–1914," *Journal of Southern History* 17 (August 1951): 328–60; Joel Williamson, *After Slavery: The Negro in South Carolina During Reconstruction* (New York: W. W. Norton, 1975 [1965]): 118–20; Claude H. Nolen, *The Negro's Image in the South: The*

Anatomy of White Supremacy (Lexington: University Press of Kentucky, 1967), 171–88; William Warren Rogers, *The One-Gallused Rebellion: Agrarianism in Alabama, 1865–1896* (Baton Rouge: Louisiana State University Press, 1970), 80–86; James L. Roark, *Masters Without Slaves: Southern Planters in the Civil War and Reconstruction* (New York: W. W. Norton, 1977), 165–68; Leon F. Litwack, *Been in the Storm So Long: The Aftermath of Slavery* (New York: Random House, 1979), 351–53; Stephen Steinberg, *The Ethnic Myth: Race, Ethnicity, and Class in America* (Boston: Beacon Press, 1981), 182–85; Charles L. Flynn, Jr., *White Land, Black Labor: Caste and Class in Nineteenth-Century Georgia* (Baton Rouge: Louisiana State University Press, 1983), 152–54.

2. Woody, "The Labor and Immigration Problem of South Carolina," 195. Woody observes, with respect to South Carolina, that "excluding accounts of the political, financial, and perhaps agricultural conditions of the state, one finds more editorials, letters, and news items on immigration than on any other single subject discussed in the public press."

3. J.D.B. De Bow, "Future of the South," *De Bow's Review* 1 (January 1866): 6–16; C. L. Fleishman, "Opening New Fields to Immigration," *De Bow's Review* 1 (January 1866): 87–91; E. C. Cahell, "White Immigrants to the South," *De Bow's Review* 1 (January 1866): 91–94.

4. *Commercial and Financial Chronicle* 1 (August 12, 1865): 199–200; ibid. 1 (September 2, 1865): 293–95; 1 (October 14, 1865): 486. See also Earle D. Ross, "Horace Greeley and the South, 1865–1872," *South Atlantic Quarterly* 16 (October 1917): 333; William B. Hesseltine, "Economic Factors in the Abandonment of Reconstruction," *Mississippi Valley Historical Review* 22 (September 1935): 191–210.

5. Loewenberg, "Efforts to Encourage Immigration," 375.

6. U.S. Department of Agriculture, Theodore C. Peters, "Report of an Agricultural Survey of the South," *Monthly Reports* (June 1, 1867): 193.

7. The figures in this paragraph are taken from Thomas Walker Page, "The Distribution of Immigrants in the United States Before 1870," *Journal of Political Economy* 20 (June, 1912): 676–94.

8. On the connection between slavery and the lack of immigration to the South, see William L. Miller, "Slavery and the Population of the South," *Southern Economic Journal* 28 (July 1961): 46–54. Miller argues than an overabundance of labor, not slavery per se, was the main hindrance to southern immigration. Gavin Wright, *The Political Economy of the Cotton South: Households, Markets, and Wealth in the Nineteenth Century* (New York: W. W. Norton, 1978), 121–25, defends the traditional view that slavery itself discouraged southern immigration.

9. Cited in Eugene D. Genovese, *The Political Economy of Slavery* (New York: Vintage, 1967), 231.

10. *De Bow's Review* 1 (January 1866): 88.

11. Reported in *De Bow's Review* 1 (January 1866): 15–16.

12. *De Bow's Review* 1 (March 1866): 254.

13. Kenneth Stampp, *The Peculiar Institution: Slavery in the Ante-Bellum South* (New York: Vintage, 1956), 7–8. Stampp points out that even before the war some southern whites rejected the argument that white laborers were ill-suited for southern agriculture. The important distinction, Stampp observes, was that "negro slaves, unlike free whites, could be forced to toil in the rice swamps regardless of the effect upon their health."

14. J. C. Nott, "Climates of the South in Their Relation to White Labor," *De Bow's Review* 1 (February 1866): 166–73.

15. *De Bow's Review* 1 (February 1866): 168, 172. See also ibid. 1 (March 1866): 255; ibid. 3 (March 1867): 306–7; *Commercial and Financial Chronicle* 1 (September 2, 1865): 294; ibid. 1 (August 12, 1865): 200; F. W. Loring and C. F. Atkinson, *Cotton Culture and the South Considered With Reference to Emigration* (Boston: A. Williams and Co., 1869), 11, 88, 92, 93, 95.

16. *Southern Cultivator* 25 (December 1867): 374.

17. *Southern Cultivator* 27 (November 1869): 338.

18. See, for example, Loring and Atkinson, *Cotton Culture and the South*, 8, 71, 87, 90–91.

19. See Paul M. Gaston, *The New South Creed: A Study in Southern Mythmaking* (New York: Alfred A. Knopf, 1970), 1–42; Dan T. Carter, "Fateful Legacy: White Southerners and the Dilemma of Emancipation," *Proceedings of the South Carolina Historical Association* (1977), 52–53, 60.

20. Cited in *De Bow's Review* 4 (July 1867): 150–51. On the conflict between plantation owners and agrarian reformers over the issue of immigration, see also Wharton, *The Negro in Mississippi*, 103–4; Eric Foner, *Nothing But Freedom: Emancipation and Its Legacy* (Baton Rouge: Louisiana State University Press, 1983), 47.

21. Cited in Carter, "Fateful Legacy," 52.

22. Loring and Atkinson, *Cotton Culture and the South*, 89. See also ibid., 130–40; Theodore Saloutos, "Southern Agriculture and the Problem of Readjustment: 1865–1877," *Agriculture History* 30 (April 1956): 59.

23. *De Bow's Review* 3 (April/May 1867): 489. Their dependence on unreliable free black labor also led some planters to express doubts about the viability of the large plantations. See, for example, *Southern Cultivator* 25 (April 1867): 112; Charles Stearns, *The Black Man of the South* (New York: Kraus Reprint Co., 1969 [1872]), 99.

24. *De Bow's Review* 4 (July 1867): 150–51.

25. *De Bow's Review* 1 (January 1866): 93.

26. *Southern Cultivator* 25 (February 1867): 41. See also U.S. Congress, House, *The Report of the Commissioner of Agriculture for the Year 1866*, Executive Document Number 107, 39th Congress, 2nd Session (Washington, D.C.: Government Printing Office [GPO], 1867), 6.

27. William E. Highsmith, "Louisiana Landholding During War and Reconstruction," *Louisiana Historical Quarterly* 38 (January 1955): 44–45. See also Roger W. Shugg, "Survival of the Plantation System in Louisiana," *Journal of Southern History* 3 (August 1937): 370–73; Shugg, *Origins of Class Struggle in Louisiana* (Baton Rouge: Louisiana State University Press, 1968 [1939]), 253–56; William Ivy Hair, *Bourbonism and Agrarian Protest: Louisiana Politics, 1877–1900* (Baton Rouge: Louisiana State University Press, 1969), 37–38.

28. *De Bow's Review* 4 (July 1867): 100. See also ibid., 148–50.

29. *De Bow's Review* 3 (June 1867): 525.

30. Cited in Nolen, *The Negro's Image in the South*, 177.

31. *De Bow's Review* 3 (April/May 1867): 479.

32. *Southern Cultivator* 25 (January 1867): 10.

33. *De Bow's Review* 1 (January 1866): 93.

34. Lawrence N. Powell, *New Masters: Northern Planters during the Civil War and Reconstruction* (New Haven, Conn.: Yale University Press, 1980); Michael Wayne, *The Reshaping of Plantation Society: The Natchez District, 1860–1880* (Baton Rouge: Louisiana State University Press, 1983): 61–62.

35. John T. Trowbridge, *The Desolate South, 1865–1866: A Picture of the Battlefields and of the Devastated Confederacy* (New York: Duell, Sloan and Pierce, 1956 [1866]), 40. See also ibid., 208; U.S. Congress, House, *Report of the Joint Committee on Reconstruction*, Executive Document Number 30, 30th Congress, 1st Session (Washington, D.C.: GPO, 1866), part 2, 128; part 3, 180 (hereafter cited as *Report of the Joint Committee on Reconstruction*).

36. Whitelaw Reid, *After the War: A Tour of the Southern States, 1865–1866* (New York: Harper and Row, 1965 [1866]), 211. See also ibid., 53.

37. Reid, *After the War*, 374, 564. See also Wharton, *The Negro in Mississippi*, 103–4.

38. Shugg, "The Survival of the Plantation System," 322–23.

39. John Richard Dennett, *The South As It Is, 1865–1866* (New York: Viking Press, 1967 [1865–1866]), 366.

40. Highsmith, "Louisiana Landholding During the War and Reconstruction," 45.

41. Nolen, *The Negro's Image in the South*, 180–81; Eric Foner, *Reconstruction: America's Unfinished Revolution, 1863–1877* (New York: Harper & Row, 1988), 420.

42. *Southern Cultivator* 27 (August 1869): 238. See also ibid. 27 (November 1869): 334–35.

43. *Southern Cultivator* 27 (August 1869): 238.

44. *Southern Cultivator* 27 (August 1869): 238.

45. *Southern Cultivator* 27 (August 1869): 238.

46. *Southern Cultivator* 27 (October 1869): 302.

47. *Southern Cultivator* 27 (December 1869): 372.

48. *Southern Cultivator* 28 (May 1870): 132.

49. *Southern Cultivator* 28 (May 1870): 132. For additional contributions to this debate, see ibid. 27 (September 1869): 281; ibid. 28 (January 1870): 15; ibid. 28 (October 1870): 332–34; ibid. 28 (November 1870): 376–77; *Commercial and Financial Chronicle* 9 (October 23, 1869): 519.

50. *Southern Cultivator* 28 (May 1870): 141.

51. *Southern Cultivator* 27 (November 1869): 338.

52. On the possibility of Chinese immigration, see Loring and Atkinson, *Cotton Culture and the South*, 9, 54, 84, 87, 93, 94, 97, 98, 114; Wharton, *The Negro in Mississippi*, 96–99; Gunther P. Barth, *Bitter Strength: A History of the Chinese in the United States, 1850–1870* (Cambridge, Mass.: Harvard University Press, 1964), 188–97; James W. Loewen, *The Mississippi Chinese: Between Black and White* (Cambridge, Mass.: Harvard University Press, 1971); Lucy M. Cohen, "Entry of Chinese to the Lower South from 1865 to 1870: Policy Dilemmas," *Southern Studies* 17 (Spring 1978): 5–38.

53. Reid, *After the War*, 417.

54. Cited in Foner, *Nothing But Freedom*, 48. See also Nolen, *The Negro's Image in the South*, 171–75.

55. Cohen, "Entry of Chinese to the Lower South," 8–16; Foner, *Nothing But Freedom*, 47–48.

56. *Southern Cultivator*, 25 (December 1867): 374.

57. Reid, *After the War*, 397.

58. *Southern Cultivator* 28 (January 1870): 15.

59. Cited in Loewenberg, "Efforts to Encourage Immigration," 368.

60. *Southern Cultivator* 25 (December 1867): 374–75; ibid. 28 (May 1870): 141; Loewenberg, "Efforts to Encourage Immigration," 368; Loewen, *The Mississippi Chinese*, 4.

61. *Southern Cultivator* 27 (November 1869): 338. See also Loring and Atkinson, *Cotton Culture and the South*, 94; Wharton, *The Negro in Mississippi*, 98.

62. Foner, *Reconstruction*, 282–86. On planters' complaints about blacks' political involvement and its adverse effect on their performance as laborers, see also Robert Somers, *The Southern States Since the War, 1870–1871* (Tuscaloosa: University of Alabama Press, 1965 [1871]), 65, 76; J. Carlyle Sitterson, "The Transition from Slave to

Free Labor on the William J. Minor Plantation," *Agricultural History* 17 (October 1943): 222.

63. *Southern Cultivator* 28 (July 1870): 193.

64. *Southern Cultivator* 27 (September 1869): 281.

65. Nolen, *The Negro's Image in the South*, 171; *De Bow's Review* 4 (July 1867): 96.

66. For planters' descriptions of the qualities presumably possessed by Chinese laborers, in addition to references cited below, see *Southern Cultivator* 24 (November 1866): 252–53; ibid. 28 (January 1870): 12–13, 15; Nolen, *The Negro's Image in the South*, 174–75; Wharton, *The Negro in Mississippi*, 97; Wayne, *The Reshaping of Plantation Society*, 61.

67. *Southern Cultivator* 27 (November 1869): 338.

68. *Southern Cultivator* 25 (December 1867): 375.

69. *Southern Cultivator* 27 (November 1869): 338.

70. *De Bow's Review* 7 (July 1869): 589–90; Loring and Atkinson, *Cotton Culture and the South*, 87, 114.

71. *Southern Cultivator* 27 (September 1869): 281.

72. Loring and Atkinson, *Cotton Culture and the South*, 97–98. See ibid., 54.

73. Loewen, *The Mississippi Chinese*, 23–24; *De Bow's Review* 4 (October 1867): 364.

74. *De Bow's Review* 7 (July 1869): 560–62. For fears that Chinese immigration might contribute to race problems, see ibid. 9 (July 1870): 579–82; ibid. 7 (August 1869): 709–24; ibid. 4 (July 1867): 102; *Southern Cultivator* 29 (May 1871): 221; Loewenberg, "Efforts to Encourage Immigration," 368.

75. *Southern Cultivator* 27 (November 1869): 334; Loring and Atkinson, *Cotton Culture and the South*, 97; Nolen, *The Negro's Image in the South*, 176.

76. *Southern Cultivator* 27 (December 1869): 374.

77. Loring and Atkinson, *Cotton Culture and the South*, 93; Wharton, *The Negro in Mississippi*, 96–98.

78. *Southern Cultivator* 29 (June 1871): 221; U.S. Congress, House, *The Report of the Commissioner of Agriculture for the Year 1870*, 41st Congress, 3rd Session (Washington, D.C.: GPO, 1871), 573. The character of the Chinese as "soujourners" is discussed in detail in Loewen, *The Mississippi Chinese*, 26–31.

79. *Commercial and Financial Chronicle* 3 (October 6, 1866): 419.

80. *Southern Cultivator* 29 (June 1871): 221.

81. *Southern Cultivator* 26 (May 1868): 133. See also Nolen, *The Negro's Image in the South*, 176.

82. Rogers, *The One-Gallused Rebellion*, 82. See also Foner, *Nothing But Freedom*, 48.

83. *Commercial and Financial Chronicle* 3 (October 6, 1866), 418–19.

84. U.S. Congress, House, *The Report of the Commissioner of Agriculture for the Year 1867*, 40th Congress, 2nd Session (Washington, D.C.: GPO, 1868), xiii.

85. Cohen, "Entry of Chinese to the Lower South," 14–15; E. P. Hutchinson, *Legislative History of American Immigration Policy: 1798 to 1965* (Philadelphia: University of Pennsylvania Press, 1981), 52.

86. Richard W. Griffin, "Problems of the Southern Cotton Planters After the Civil War," *Georgia Historical Quarterly* 39 (June 1955): 117.

87. *De Bow's Review* 4 (July 1867): 151–52; ibid. 4 (October 1867): 362–64.

88. *De Bow's Review* 7 (August 1869): 714.

89. *Southern Cultivator* 28 (June 1870): 173.

90. Wharton, *The Negro in Mississippi*, 99.

91. U.S. Census Office, *Twelfth Census of the United States, 1900*, vol. 1, *Population*, part 1 (Washington: GPO, 1901), 487, table 13; 565, table 20.

92. Somers, *The Southern States Since the War*, 163–64; Nolen, *The Negro's Image in the South*, 176; Loewen, *The Mississippi Chinese*, 1–2; Barth, *Bitter Strength*, 196–97.

93. Nolen, *The Negro's Image in the South*, 177; George Ruble Woolfolk, *The Cotton Regency: The Northern Merchants and Reconstruction, 1865–1880* (New York: Bookman Associates, 1958), 103.

94. *Report of the Joint Committee on Reconstruction*, part 3, 180.

95. *De Bow's Review* 3 (June 1867): 584. On the possibility of white immigration, see also Loring and Atkinson, *Cotton Culture and the South*, 4–5, 8, 9, 11, 17, 21, 68, 84–91; Dennett, *The South As It Is*, 16, 130, 194; *Report of the Joint Committee on Reconstruction*, part 2, 29, 48, 244; Part 4, 2; Berthoff, "Southern Attitudes Toward Immigration," 328–29; Loewenberg, "Efforts to Encourage Immigration," 365–67; Roark, *Masters Without Slaves*, 164–65; Wharton, *The Negro in Mississippi*, 101; John Preston McConnell, *Negroes and Their Treatment in Virginia from 1865 to 1867* (New York: Negro Universities Press, 1969 [1910]), 32–33.

96. Sidney Andrews, *The South Since the War: As Shown by Fourteen Weeks of Travel and Observation in Georgia and the Carolinas* (Boston: Houghton Mifflin, 1971 [1866]), 363.

97. Cited in *De Bow's Review* 3 (June 1867): 585–86.

98. Andrews, *The South Since the War*, 360. See also Nolen, *The Negro's Image in the South*, 171; Litwack, *Been in the Storm So Long*, 351–52; Williamson, *After Slavery*, 118; Foner, *Nothing But Freedom*, 47.

99. Berthoff, "Southern Attitudes Toward Immigration," 330.
100. *Report of the Joint Committee on Reconstruction,* part 3, 170.
101. Cited in Robert Calvert, "The Freedmen and Agricultural Prosperity," *Southwestern Historical Quarterly* 76 (April 1973): 462.
102. *De Bow's Review* 4 (November 1867): 421.
103. Reid, *After the War,* 373.
104. Page, "The Distribution of Immigrants," 678. See also U.S. Congress, House, R. S. Chilton, commissioner of immigration, *Immigration,* Executive Document Number 39, 39th Congress, 2nd Session (Washington, D.C.: GPO, 1867), 71–73; U.S. Congress, House, J. R. Dodge, "Report of the Statistician," *Report of the Commissioner of Agriculture for the Year 1869,* Executive Documents, 41st Congress, 2nd Session (Washington, D.C.: GPO, 1870), 59; Sylvia Krebs, "'Will the Freedmen Work?' White Alabamians Adjust to Free Labor," *Alabama Historical Quarterly* 36 (Summer 1974): 155.
105. On planters' experiments with white immigrant labor and complaints about their performance, see Frances B. Leigh, *Ten Years on a Georgia Plantation Since the War* (London: Richard Bentley and Sons, 1883): 202–6; *Southern Cultivator* 27 (December 1869): 374; *Southern Planter and Farmer* (July 1869): 406–7; Williamson, *After Slavery,* 119–20; Sitterson, "The Transition from Slave to Free Labor," 223; Roark, *Masters Without Slaves,* 167; Litwack, *Been in the Storm So Long,* 352–53; Wharton, *The Negro in Mississippi,* 101; Flynn, *White Land, Black Labor,* 153–54; McConnell, *The Negroes and Their Treatment in Virginia,* 33; Nolen, *The Negro's Image in the South,* 177; Wayne, *The Reshaping of Plantation Society,* 60, 69–70; Powell, *New Masters,* 73–74.
106. Reid, *After the War,* 563–64; *De Bow's Review* 1 (February 1866): 224; ibid. 4 (December 1867): 576–77; ibid. 5 (February 1868): 213; Dennett, *The South As It Is,* 2.
107. *De Bow's Review* 1 (January 1866): 88.
108. *Southern Cultivator* 27 (June 1869): 180.
109. Andrews, *The South Since the War,* 207–8.
110. *Southern Cultivator* 25 (February 1867): 41.
111. *Southern Cultivator* 29 (June 1871): 211.
112. *De Bow's Review* 7 (July 1869): 239.
113. *Southern Cultivator* 27 (August 1869): 239.
114. Berthoff, "Southern Attitudes Toward Immigration," 331.
115. Cited in Litwack, *Been in the Storm So Long,* 353.
116. *Southern Cultivator* 27 (February 1869): 57. See also Somers, *The Southern States Since the War,* 76; Reid, *After the War,* 276, 564; Nolen, *The Negro's Image in the South,* 11–12.
117. *Southern Planter and Farmer* (July 1869): 407. See also *De Bow's Review* 7 (November 1869): 489.

118. Cited in Woody, "The Labor and Immigration Problem of South Carolina," 204. For other references to black attitudes toward southern immigration, see New Orleans *Tribune*, February 25, 1869; Litwack, *Been in the Storm So Long*, 547; Wharton, *The Negro in Mississippi*, 100; Nolen, *The Negro's Image in the South*, 176; Saloutos, "Southern Agriculture and the Problems of Readjustment," 68; Charles H. Wesley, *Negro Labor in the United States, 1850–1925: A Study in American Economic History* (New York: Vanguard Press, 1927), 197; David J. Hellwig, "Black Attitudes Toward Immigrant Labor in the South, 1865–1910," *The Filson Club Historical Quarterly* 54 (April 1980): 151–68.

Chapter 5

1. *The Nation* 1 (October 26, 1865): 523.

2. John Richard Dennett, *The South As It Is, 1865–1866* (New York: Viking Press, 1967 [1865–1866]), 76.

3. Whitelaw Reid, *After the War: A Tour of the Southern States, 1865–1866* (New York: Harper & Row, 1965 [1866]), 361.

4. Walter L. Fleming, "Deportation and Colonization: An Attempted Solution of the Race Problem," in *Studies in Southern History and Politics* (New York: Columbia University Press, 1914), 30.

5. Henry N. Sherwood, "Early Negro Deportation Projects," *Mississippi Valley Historical Review* 2 (March 1916): 484–85. On the colonization movement prior to the rise of the American Colonization Society, see also Benjamin Brawley, *A Social History of the American Negro* (New York: Collier, 1971 [1921]), 116–27; Don B. Kates, Jr., "Abolition, Deportation, Integration: Attitudes Toward Slavery in the Early Republic," *Journal of Negro History* 53 (January 1968): 33–47; Winthrop D. Jordan, *White Over Black: American Attitudes Toward the Negro, 1550–1812* (Baltimore: Penguin, 1969), 542–69.

6. Jordan, *White Over Black*, 551.

7. Jordan, *White Over Black*, 561. See also Brawley, *A Social History of the American Negro*, 121–22; Frederic Bancroft, "The Early Antislavery Movement and African Colonization," in *Frederic Bancroft: Historian*, ed. Jacob E. Cooke (Norman: University of Oklahoma Press, 1957), 156.

8. Jordan, *White Over Black*, 565.

9. On the American Colonization Society, see Bancroft, "The Early Antislavery Movement," 156–91; Henry N. Sherwood, "The Formation of the American Colonization Society," *Journal of Negro History* 2 (July 1917): 209–28; Early Lee Fox, *The American Colonization Society, 1817–1840* (Baltimore: Johns Hopkins University Press, series 37, number 3, Johns Hopkins University Studies in Historical and Political Science, 1919); Brainard Dyer, "The Persistence of the Idea of Negro Colonization," *Pacific Historical Review* 12 (March 1943): 53–65;

Charles I. Foster, "The Colonization of Free Negroes in Liberia, 1816–35," *Journal of Negro History* 38 (January 1953): 41–66; Willis Dolmond Boyd, *Negro Colonization in The National Crisis, 1860–1870* (Ph.D. diss., University of California at Los Angeles, 1953), especially chapters 1–3; P. J. Staudenraus, *The African Colonization Movement, 1816–1865* (New York: Columbia University Press, 1961).

10. Staudenraus, *The African Colonization Movement*, 15, 19–20, 120–21; Leon Litwack, *North of Slavery: The Negro in the Free States, 1790–1860* (Chicago: University of Chicago Press, 1961), 20–22; George M. Fredrickson, *The Black Image in the White Mind: The Debate on Afro-American Character and Destiny, 1818–1914* (New York: Harper & Row, 1971), 12–24.

11. Jordan, *White Over Black*, 566; Litwack, *North of Slavery*, 254; Bancroft, "The Early Antislavery Movement," 159–62; Ira Berlin, *Slaves Without Masters: The Free Negro in the Antebellum South* (New York: Random House, 1974): 201–2.

12. Fox, *The American Colonization Society*; Staudenraus, *The African Colonization Movement*, 104–06, 120–21.

13. Staudenraus, *The African Colonization Movement*, 251; Fleming, "Deportation and Colonization," 5.

14. Louis Mehlinger, "The Attitude of the Free Negro Toward African Colonization," *Journal of Negro History* 1 (July 1916): 301. On the hostility of free blacks toward African colonization in the prewar period, see also Litwack, *North of Slavery*, 24–26; Berlin, *Slaves Without Masters*, 204–7; Brawley, *A Social History of the American Negro*, 159–64. See especially William Lloyd Garrison, *Thoughts on African Colonization* (New York: Arno Press, 1968 [1832]), part 2, which consists of numerous statements and resolutions by free blacks expressing opposition to colonization schemes generally and to the American Colonization Society specifically.

15. Litwack, *North of Slavery*, 28–29, 252–53; Bancroft, "The Early Antislavery Movement," 187–88; Staudenraus, *The African Colonization Movement*, chapters 17 and 18.

16. On increased support among blacks for colonization during the 1850s, see Litwack, *North of Slavery*, 257–62; Berlin, *Slaves Without Masters*, 356–59; Howard H. Bell, "The Negro Emigration Movement, 1849–1854: A Phase of Negro Nationalism, *Phylon* 20 (1959): 132–42; Eric Foner, *Free Soil, Free Labor, Free Men: The Ideology of the Republican Party Before the Civil War* (New York: Oxford University Press, 1970), 274–75; Richard Blackett, "Martin R. Delany and Robert Campbell: Black Americans in Search of an African Colony," *Journal of Negro History* 62 (January 1977): 217–34. Blackett makes a useful distinction between "nationalist emigrationists," "guided primarily by the desire to develop a black nation," and "antislavery emigrationists," "directed more by their displeasure with the United States as a bastion

of slavery." The decade of the 1850s was characterized by a relative increase in sentiment favorable to the "nationalist emigrationists."

17. John G. Nicolay and John Jay, eds., *Complete Works of Abraham Lincoln*, new and enlarged ed. (New York: Lamb Publishing Company, 1905), vol. 8, 1–9. For typical selections from Lincoln on emancipation and colonization, see also ibid., vol. 2, 337–39; vol. 7, 270–74; vol. 8, 117–31. For useful discussions of Lincoln's position on emancipation and colonization, see Kenneth Stampp, *The Era of Reconstruction, 1865–1877* (New York: Random House, 1965), 32–35; Gary R. Planck, "Abraham Lincoln and Black Colonization: Theory and Practice," *Lincoln Herald* 72 (Summer 1970): 61–77; George M. Fredrickson, "A Man but Not a Brother: Abraham Lincoln and Racial Equality," *Journal of Southern History* 41 (February 1975): 30–58. On black reaction, mostly unfavorable, to Lincoln's colonization proposals, see Benjamin Quarles, *Lincoln and the Negro* (New York: Oxford University Press, 1962), 116–19; James M. McPherson, *The Negro's Civil War: How American Negroes Felt and Acted During the War for the Union* (New York: Random House, 1965), 77–97; McPherson, "Abolitionist and Negro Opposition to Colonization During the Civil War," *Phylon* 26 (1965): 391–99.

18. For Mitchell's views, see Warren A. Beck, "Lincoln and Negro Colonization in Central America," *Abraham Lincoln Quarterly* 6 (September 1950): 172–76.

19. U.S. Congress, House, *Emancipation and Colonization*, Report Number 148, 37th Congress, 2nd Session (Washington, D.C.: Government Printing Office [GPO], 1862), 13–14 (hereafter cited as *Emancipation and Colonization*). See also Robert H. Zoellner, "Negro Colonization: The Cimate of Opinion Surrounding Lincoln, 1860–1865," *Mid-America* 42 (July 1960): 137–41.

20. *Emancipation and Colonization*, 14–18. See also Zoellner, "Negro Colonization," 142–43; Fleming, "Deportation and Colonization," 14.

21. *Emancipation and Colonization*, 19. See also Foner, *Free Soil, Free Labor, Free Men*, 272–74.

22. *Emancipation and Colonization*, 23–24.

23. Zoellner, "Negro Colonization," 139.

24. For the contract between Ambrose Thompson and the U.S. government, see U.S. Congress, House, *Acounts of the Colonization Agent*, Executive Document Number 227, 41st Congress, 2nd Session (Washington, D.C.: GPO, 1870), 2–4. For official documents pertaining to the Chiriqui project, see U.S. Congress, Senate, *Message from the President of the United States . . . Respecting the Transportation, Settlement, and Colonization of Persons of the African Race*, Executive Document Number 55, 39th Congress, 1st Session (Washington, D.C.: GPO, 1866), 4–11, 13–18 (hereafter cited as *Message from the President*,

Colonization). See also Fleming, "Deportation and Colonization, 18–22; Planck, "Abraham Lincoln and Black Colonization," 65–71; Beck, "Lincoln and Negro Colonization," 166–83; Boyd, *Negro Colonization in the National Crisis*, 170–79; Frederic Bancroft, "Schemes to Colonize Negroes in Central America," in *Frederic Bancroft*, ed. Cooke, 203–27; Charles H. Wesley, "Lincoln's Plan for Colonizing the Emancipated Negroes," *Journal of Negro History* 4 (January 1919): 16–17; N. Andrew N. Cleven, "Some Plans for Colonizing Liberated Negro Slaves in Hispanic America," *Journal of Negro History* 11 (January 1926): 35–49; Paul J. Schieps, "Lincoln and the Chiriqui Colonization Project," *Journal of Negro History* 37 (October 1952): 418–53.

25. *Message from the President, Colonization*, 51.
26. For official documents pertaining to the island of à Vache project, see *Message from the President, Colonization*, 11–12, 24–30, 35–37, 40–42, 45–46, 50–52. See also Frederic Bancroft, "The Ile à Vache Experiment in Colonization," in *Frederic Bancroft*, ed. Cooke, 228–58; Boyd, *Negro Colonization in The National Crisis*, 180–208; Fleming, "Deportation and Colonization," 21–26; Planck, "Abraham Lincoln," 72–75; Wesley, "Lincoln's Plan for Colonizing the Emancipated Negroes," 17–19.
27. See especially Schieps, "Lincoln and the Chiriqui Colonization Project," 448–50; G. S. Boritt, "The Voyage to the Colony Linconia: The Sixteenth President, Black Colonization, and the Defense Mechanism of Avoidance," *The Historian* 37 (August 1975): 619–32; Mark E. Neely, Jr., "Abraham Lincoln and Black Colonization: Benjamin Butler's Spurious Testimony," *Civil War History* 25 (March 1979): 77–83.
28. Fleming, "Deportation and Colonization," 11; Zoellner, "Negro Colonization," 137–41; Bancroft, "Schemes to Colonize Negroes," 198–202.
29. U.S. Congress, Senate, *The Congressional Globe*, 37th Congress, 2nd Session (April 11, 1862), vol. 32, part 2, 1633.
30. *Emancipation and Colonization*, 15.
31. Zoellner, "Negro Colonization," 140.
32. Litwack, *North of Slavery*, 275–79; Robert F. Durden, "Ambiguities in the Antislavery Crusade of the Republican Party," in *The Antislavery Vanguard: New Essays on the Abolitionists*, ed. Martin Duberman (Princeton, N.J.: Princeton University Press, 1965), 362–94; Martin Duberman, "The Northern Response to Slavery," in ibid., 395–413; William H. Pease and Jane H. Pease, "Antislavery Ambivalence: Immediatism, Expediency, Race," *American Quarterly* 17 (Winter 1965): 682–95; Larry Gara, "Slavery and the Slave Power: A Crucial Distinction," *Civil War History* 15 (March 1969): 5–18.
33. V. Jacque Voegeli, *Free But Not Equal: The Midwest and the Negro During the Civil War* (Chicago: University of Chicago Press, 1967), 4–9.

34. Voegeli, *Free But Not Equal*, 7, 20, 58; Durden, "Ambiguities in the Antislavery Crusade," 386–88, 393.

35. Voegeli, *Free But Not Equal*, 110–11. See also Fredrickson, *The Black Image in the White Mind*, 166–67; Lawrence N. Powell, *New Masters: Northern Planters During the Civil War and Reconstruction* (New Haven, Conn.: Yale University Press, 1980), 2–3.

36. Voegeli, *Free But Not Equal*, 118–23.

37. Willis Dolmond Boyd, *Negro Colonization in The National Crisis*, chapters 8 and 9; Boyd, "Negro Colonization in the Reconstruction Era, 1865–1870," *Georgia Historical Quarterly* 40 (December 1965): 360–82.

38. Lawrence J. Friedman, *The White Savage: Racial Fantasies in the Postbellum South* (Englewood Cliffs, N.J.: Prentice-Hall, 1970), 26.

39. John T. Trowbridge, *The Desolate South, 1865–1866: A Picture of the Battlefields and of the Devastated Confederacy* (New York: Duell, Sloan and Pierce, 1956 [1866]): 68.

40. *Southern Cultivator* 25 (January 1867): 11.

41. *Southern Cultivator* 27 (February 1869): 50–51.

42. Sidney Andrews, *The South Since the War: As Shown by Fourteen Weeks of Travel and Observation in Georgia and the Carolinas* (Boston: Houghton Mifflin, 1971 [1866]): 157.

43. *De Bow's Review* 1 (January 1866): 73. See also ibid. 1 (January 1866): 59–67; Friedman, *The White Savage*, 23–26.

44. U.S. Congress, House, *Report of the Joint Committee on Reconstruction*, Executive Document Number 30, 39th Congress, 1st Session (Washington, D.C.: GPO, 1866), part 2, 34 (hereafter cited as *Report of the Joint Committee on Reconstruction*).

45. Reid, *After the War*, 417.

46. *Report of the Joint Committee on Reconstruction*, part 2, 128. See also ibid., part 2, 176; U.S. Congress, Senate, *Report of Carl Schurz on the States of South Carolina, Georgia, Alabama, Mississippi, and Louisiana*, by Carl Schurz, Executive Document Number 2, 39th Congress, 1st Session (Washington, D.C.: GPO, 1866), 21 (hereafter cited as *Report of Carl Schurz*); *Southern Cultivator* 26 (November 1868): 328–29; Vernon Lane Wharton, *The Negro in Mississippi, 1865–1890* (New York: Harper & Row, 1965 [1947]), 49–50.

47. Dennett, *The South As It Is*, 171–72.

48. James L. Roark, *Masters Without Slaves: Southern Planters in Civil War and Reconstruction* (New York: W. W. Norton, 1977), 169.

49. *Report of the Joint Committee on Reconstruction*, part 2, 128.

50. Andrews, *The South Since the War*, 28. See also *Report of the Joint Committee on Reconstruction*, part 2, 34; part 3, 16.

51. Herbert Aptheker, ed., *A Documentary History of the Negro People in the United States* (New York: Citadel Press, 1951), 468–69.

52. Andrews, *The South Since the War*, 157.

53. Cited in Thomas Wagstaff, "Call Your Old Master—'Master': Southern Political Leaders and Negro Labor During Presidential Reconstruction," *Labor History* 10 (Summer 1969): 336.

54. *Report of the Joint Committee on Reconstruction*, part 2, 76–77. See also ibid., part 2, 29, 32, 207, 244; Dennett, *The South As It Is*, 169.

55. Andrews, *The South Since the War*, 177.

56. Cited in Dorothy Sterling, ed., *The Trouble They Seen: Black People Tell the Story of Reconstruction* (New York: Doubleday, 1976), 43.

57. Andrews, *The South Since the War*, 27, 36, 321; Dennett, *The South As It Is*, 190; Trowbridge, *The Desolate South*, 190; *Report of Carl Schurz*, 32; *The Nation* 1 (July 27, 1865): 107; John Preston McConnell, *Negroes and Their Treatment in Virginia from 1865 to 1867* (New York: Negro Universities Press, 1969 [1910]), 16; Joel Williamson, *After Slavery: The Negro in South Carolina During Reconstruction, 1861–1877* (New York: W. W. Norton, 1975 [1965]), 248–52; Claude H. Nolen, *The Negro's Image in the South: The Anatomy of White Supremacy* (Lexington: University Press of Kentucky, 1967), 40–50, 181–82.

58. Kenneth Stampp, *The Peculiar Institution: Slavery in the Ante-Bellum South* (New York: Vintage, 1956), 11; Stampp, *The Imperiled Union: Essays on the Background of the Civil War* (Oxford: Oxford University Press, 1980), 241–43.

59. *Report of Carl Schurz* (accompanying documents), 65. See also Manual Gottlieb, "The Land Question in Georgia During Reconstruction," *Science and Society* 3 (Summer 1939): 376. The threat of another St. Domingue, even more than a half a century later, was a source of constant worry to southern whites. According to Gottlieb, "The Negro revolution in San Domingo was to the ruling class of the South what the Bolshevik Revolution is to the present-day bourgeoisie: the sum of all possible horrors.

60. Cited in Boyd, "Negro Colonization in the Reconstruction Era," 363.

61. Trowbridge, *The Desolate South*, 198. Italics added.

62. *Report of the Joint Committee on Reconstruction*, part 2, 93–94.

63. *De Bow's Review* 4 (July 1867): 15–16.

64. *De Bow's Review* 1 (February 1866) 166–67. See also ibid. 1 (March 1866): 269–70; ibid. 2 (September 1866): 285; Dennett, *The South As It Is*, 102–3.

65. *The Nation* 1 (July 27, 1865): 107. In subsequent issues the editors of the *Nation* took issue with the prediction that free blacks were doomed to extinction. See ibid. 1 (September 14, 1865): 325–27; ibid. 1 (September 21, 1865): 362.

66. F. W. Loring and C. F. Atkinson, *Cotton Culture and the South Considered With Reference to Emigration* (Boston: A. Williams and Co., 1869), 20. See also ibid., 5–11; *De Bow's Review* 6 (October 1867): 363; Trowbridge, *The Desolate South*, 47–48, 174, 176–77, 243, 263; Dennett, *The South As It Is*, 290, 351; *Report of the Joint Committee on Reconstruction*, part 3, 136; part 4, 131; McConnell, *Negroes and Their Treatment in Virginia*, 47.

67. Dennett, *The South As It Is*, 6. See also *De Bow's Review* 2 (September 1866): 285.

68. Aptheker, ed., *A Documentary History of the Negro People*, 467.

69. Friedman, *The White Savage*, 32, 36.

70. Reid, *After the War*, 44–45. See also Dennett, *The South As It Is*, 163–64.

71. Dennett, *The South As It Is*, 15.

72. Cited in Dennett, *The South As It Is*, 133. On the idea that careful legislation might prevent the extinction of the black race, see also Loring and Atkinson, *Cotton Culture and the South*, 6–7; Reid, *After the War*, 410.

73. Cf. Charles L. Flynn, Jr., *White Land, Black Labor: Caste and Class in Late Nineteenth-Century Georgia* (Baton Rouge: Louisiana State University Press, 1983), 14.

74. Reid, *After the War*, 146–47.

75. *The Nation* 1 (September 28, 1865): 393.

76. Reid, *After the War*, 146–47. See also *Report of the Joint Committee on Reconstruction*, part 2, 248; part 3, 28.

77. Cited in Leon Litwack, *Been in the Storm So Long: The Aftermath of Slavery* (New York: Random House, 1979), 516.

78. Cited in Claude F. Oubre, *Forty Acres and a Mule: The Freedmen's Bureau and Black Land Ownership* (Baton Rouge: Louisiana State University Press, 1978), 6. On black opposition to colonization, see also ibid., 7–8; Andrews, *The South Since the War*, 98; Litwack, *Been in the Storm So Long*, 308, 504, 515–16.

79. *Report of the Joint Committee on Reconstruction*, part 2, 56.

80. Litwack, *North of Slavery*, 262; Boyd, "Negro Colonization in the Reconstruction Era," 378–79.

81. On the growing interest in emigration among blacks in the late and post-Reconstruction period, see Nolen, *The Negro's Image in the South*, 182–88; Walter L. Fleming, "'Pap' Singleton, The Moses of the Colored Exodus," *American Journal of Sociology* 15 (July 1909): 61–82; Fred J. Rippy, "A Negro Colonization Project in Mexico, 1895," *Journal of Negro History* 6 (January 1921): 66–73; John G. Van Deusen, "The Exodus of 1879," *Journal of Negro History* 21 (April 1936): 111–29; Leo Alilunas, "Statutory Means of Impeding Emigration of the Negro," *Journal of Negro History* 22 (April 1937): 148–62; Joseph H. Taylor, "The

Great Migration From North Carolina in 1879," *North Carolina Historical Review* 31 (January 1954): 18–33; Frenise A. Logan, "The Movement of Negroes From North Carolina, 1876–1894," *North Carolina Historical Review* 33 (January 1956): 45–65; Nell Irvin Painter, *Exodusters: Black Migration to Kansas After Reconstruction* (New York: Alfred A. Knopf, 1977).

82. Cited in Williamson, *After Slavery,* 252.

83. On the possibility of white emigration from the South after the war, see Roark, *Masters Without Slaves,* 120–31; J. Fred Rippy, "Mexican Projects of the Confederates," *Southwestern Historical Quarterly* 22 (April 1919): 291–317; Lawrence F. Hill, "Confederate Exiles to Brazil," *Hispanic American Historical Review* 7 (May 1927): 192–210; Hill, "The Confederate Exodus to Latin America I," *Southwestern Historical Quarterly* 39 (October 1935): 100–134; Hill, "The Confederate Exodus to Latin America II," *Southwestern Historical Quarterly* 39 (January 1936): 161–99; Hill, "The Confederate Exodus to Latin American III," *Southwestern Historical Quarterly* 39 (April 1936): 309–26; George D. Harmon, "Confederate Migration to Mexico," *Hispanic American Historical Review* 17 (November 1937): 458–87; Blanche Henry Clark Weaver, "Confederate Emigration to Brazil," *Journal of Southern History* 27 (February 1961): 33–53; Andrew F. Rolle, *The Lost Cause: The Confederate Exodus to Mexico* (Norman: University of Oklahoma Press, 1965); Robert E. Shalhope, "Race, Class, Slavery, and the Antebellum Southern Mind," *Journal of Southern History* 37 (November 1971): 556–74; Michael Wayne, *The Reshaping of Plantation Society: The Natchez District, 1860–1880* (Baton Rouge: Louisiana State University Press, 1983), 53–58; Daniel E. Sutherland, "Exiles, Emigrants, and Sojourners: The Post-Civil War Confederate Exodus in Perspective," *Civil War History* 31 (September 1985): 237–56.

84. New Orleans *Tribune,* August 17, 1865.

85. Hill, "The Confederate Exodus to Latin America I," 116–17.

86. Weaver, "Confederate Emigration to Brazil," 33–53; Hill, "Confederate Exiles to Brazil," 193–94; Hill, "The Confederate Exodus to Latin America I," 114–17; Harmon, "Confederate Migration to Mexico," 458–59. See also Trowbridge, *The Desolate South,* 231; *Report of the Joint Committee on Reconstruction,* part 4, 114, 145.

87. Hill, "Confederate Exiles to Brazil," 192–96; Hill, "The Confederate Exodus to Latin America I," 114; Weaver, "Confederate Emigration to Brazil," 33–53; Harmon, "Confederate Migration to Mexico," 461–65.

88. Hill, "Confederate Exiles to Brazil," 192; Hill, "The Confederate Exodus to Latin American I," 121–22; Dennett, *The South As It Is,* 64; Reid, *After the War,* 211, 374.

89. Sutherland, "Exiles, Emigrants, and Sojourners," 238. Suther-

land estimates that approximately 5,000 southerners emigrated to Brazil; 2,500 to Mexico; 1,000 to Honduras; and 500 to Venezuela.

90. Trowbridge, *The Desolate South*, 222.

91. Cited in Hill, "The Confederate Exodus to Latin America I," 110–11.

92. Wayne, *The Reshaping of Plantation Society*, 54–55; Hill, "The Confederate Exodus to Latin America III," 317–18.

93. Cited in Shalhope, "Race, Class, Slavery," 562–64. On the issue of motivation, see Roark, *Masters Without Slaves*, 122–24; Sutherland, "Exiles, Emigrants, and Sojourners," 237–56; Hill, "The Confederate Exodus to Latin America I," 110–13; Powell, *New Masters*, 41–42.

94. Weaver, "Confederate Emigration to Brazil," 37, 45–46; Hill, "Confederate Exiles to Brazil," 193; Harmon, "Confederate Migration to Mexico," 459, 477–79.

95. *De Bow's Review* 1 (January 1866): 108; ibid. 1 (June 1866): 623; ibid., 2 (July 1866): 30–38; ibid. 4 (December 1867): 537–45.

96. Harmon, "Confederate Migration to Mexico," 476–77, 485–86; Roark, *Masters Without Slaves*, 122.

97. Wayne, *The Reshaping of Plantation Society*, 56; Sutherland, "Exiles, Emigrants, and Sojourners," 239, 242–43; Hill, "The Confederate Exodus to Latin America II," 161–99; Hill, "The Confederate Exodus to Latin America III," 309–26; Harmon, "Confederate Migration to Mexico," 473–87; Weaver, "Confederate Emigration to Brazil," 47–53.

Chapter 6

1. For some attempts to sort through the variety of labor arrangements in postbellum southern agriculture, see Enoch Marvin Banks, *The Economics of Land Tenure in Georgia* (New York: AMS Press, 1968 [1905]), 80–93; Rosser H. Taylor, "Post-Bellum Southern Rental Contracts," *Agricultural History* 17 (April 1943): 122; Vernon Lane Wharton, *The Negro in Mississippi, 1865–1890* (New York: Harper & Row, 1965 [1947]), 62–64; Joel Williamson, *After Slavery: The Negro in South Carolina During Reconstruction, 1861–1877* (New York: W. W. Norton, 1975 [1965]), 128–29; Ralph Shlomowitz, "The Origins of Southern Sharecropping," *Agricultural History* 53 (July 1979): 561–62; John David Smith, "More Than Slaves, Less Than Freedmen: The 'Share Wages' Labor System During Reconstruction," *Civil War History* 26 (September 1980): 256–57; Charles L. Flynn, Jr., *White Land and Black Labor: Caste and Class in Late Nineteenth-Century Georgia* (Baton Rouge: Louisiana State University Press, 1983): 57–83.

2. On the idea of the "agricultural ladder" as it applied to postbellum southern agriculture, see Charles S. Mangum, Jr., *The Legal Status of the Tenant Farmer in the Southeast* (Chapel Hill: University of North Carolina Press, 1952), 12; LaWanda F. Cox, "Tenancy in the

United States, 1865–1900: A Consideration of the Validity of the Agricultural Ladder Hypothesis," *Agricultural History* 18 (July 1944): 97–103.

3. Cited in Harold D. Woodman, "Post–Civil War Southern Agriculture and Law," *Agricultural History* 53 (January 1979) 324–25. On the legal distinction between sharecropping and tenancy, see also Mangum, *The Legal Status of the Tenant Farmer*, 17; A. B. Book, "A Note on the Legal Status of Share-Tenants and Share-Croppers in the South," *Law and Contemporary Problems* 4 (October 1937): 539–45; Oscar Zeichner, "The Legal Status of the Agricultural Laborer in the South," *Political Science Quarterly* 55 (September 1940): 412–28; Marjorie Mendenhall Applewhite, "Sharecropper and Tenant in the Courts of North Carolina," *North Carolina Historical Review* 31 (April 1954): 134–49.

4. A. F. Robertson, "On Sharecropping," *Man: The Journal of the Royal Anthropology Institute* 15 (September 1980): 411–12.

5. Woodman, "Post–Civil War Southern Agriculture and the Law," 327n.13

6. Mangum, *The Legal Status of the Tenant Farmer*, 12. See also Book, "A Note on the Legal Status of Share-Tenants and Share-Croppers," 540; Zeichner, "The Legal Status of the Agricultural Laborer," 414.

7. M. B. Hammond, *The Cotton Industry: An Essay in American Economic History* (New York: Macmillan, 1897): 190n1.

8. On merchandising arrangements and the crop-lien system in postwar southern agriculture, see Thomas D. Clark, "The Furnishing and Supply System in Southern Agricultural Since 1865," *Journal of Southern History* 12 (February 1946): 24–44; Jacqueline P. Bull, "The General Merchant in the Economic History of the New South," *Journal of Southern History* 18 (February 1952): 36–59; Glen N. Sisk, "Rural Merchandising in the Alabama Black Belt, 1875–1917," *Journal of Farm Economics* 37 (November 1955): 705–15; Harold D. Woodman, *King Cotton and His Retainers: Financing and Marketing the Cotton Crop of the South, 1800–1925* (Lexington: University Press of Kentucky, 1968): 295–314; Michael Schwartz, *Radical Protest and Social Structure: The Southern Farmers' Alliance and Cotton Tenancy, 1880–1890* (New York: Academic Press, 1976): 19–56; Roger L. Ransom and Richard Sutch, *One Kind of Freedom: The Economic Consequences of Emancipation* (Cambridge: Cambridge University Press, 1977): 117–148; Jonathan M. Wiener, *Social Origins of the New South, Alabama, 1860–1885* (Baton Rouge: Lousiana State University Press, 1978), 77–133.

9. *De Bow's Review* 2 (July 1866): 211.

10. On the distinction between the gang-labor system or the "share wages" system and sharecropping, see Wiener, *Social Origins of the New South*, 70; Ransom and Sutch, *One Kind of Freedom*, 60–61,

90–94; Smith, "More Than Slaves, Less Than Freedmen," 256–57; Robert Preston Brooks, *The Agrarian Revolution in Georgia, 1865–1912* (Westport, Conn.: Negro Universities Press, 1970 [1914]), 66; James L. Roark, *Masters Without Slaves: Southern Planters in the Civil War and Reconstruction* (New York: W. W. Norton, 1977), 142.

11. F. W. Loring and C. F. Atkinson, *Cotton Culture and the South Considered with Reference to Emigration* (Boston: A. Williams & Co., 1869), 26.

12. *Southern Cultivator* 27 (February 1869): 54–55; Loring and Atkinson, *Cotton Culture and the South,* 28–34. All of the quotations in the text that follows, unless noted, are taken from these two sources. In discussing Evans's analysis, I do not strictly follow his order of presentation.

13. *De Bow's Review* 6 (February 1869): 152.

14. *Southern Planter* (March 1867): 125–26. See also ibid., (September 1867): 511.

15. *Southern Cultivator* 26 (May 1868): 201. See also U.S. Congress, House, *The Report of the Commissioner of Agriculture for the Year 1867,* Executive Documents, 40th Congress, 2nd Session (Washington, D.C.: Government Printing Office [GPO], 1868): 417, 422.

16. U.S. Congress, Senate, *Letter of the Secretary of War, Communicating . . . Reports of the Assistant Commissioners of Freedmen,* Executive Document Number 6, 39th Congress, 2nd Session (Washington, D.C.: GPO, 1867), p. 104 (hereafter cited as *Reports of the Assistant Commissioners of Freedmen*).

17. See, for example, *Reports of the Assistant Commissioners of Freedmen,* Executive Document Number 6, 39th Congress, 2nd Session, 44, 118, 119, 123; U.S. Congress, House, *Freedmen's Bureau. . . Report of the Commissioner of the Bureau of Refugees, Freedmen, and Abandoned Lands,* Executive Document Number 11, 39th Congress, 1st Session (Washington, D.C.: GPO, 1865), 25 (hereafter cited as *Freedmen's Bureau*); U.S. Congress, House, *Report of Major General O. O. Howard, Commissioner of the Bureau of Refugees, Freedmen, and Abandoned Lands, to the Secretary of War,* Executive Document Number 1, 40th Congress, 3rd Session (Washington, D.C.: GPO, 1868), 1039; U.S. Congress, House, *Report of the Joint Committee on Reconstruction,* Executive Document Number 30, 39th Congress, 1st Session (Washington, D.C.: GPO, 1866), part 2, 189 (hereafter cited as *Report of the Joint Committee on Reconstruction*).

18. *Southern Cultivator* (September 1867): 511. See also ibid. (October 1867): 573–74.

19. *Southern Cultivator* 27 (July 1869): 208.

20. *Southern Cultivator* 26 (September 1868): 267.

21. Loring and Atkinson, *Cotton Culture and the South,* 32.

22. *Southern Cultivator* 27 (July 1869): 208.

23. *Southern Cultivator* 26 (May 1868): 133.

24. See, for example, the *Commercial and Financial Chronicle* 9 (September 4, 1869): 294–95; John T. Trowbridge, *The Desolate South, 1865–1866: A Picture of the Battlefields and of the Devastated Confederacy* (New York: Duell, Sloan and Pearce, 1956 [1866]), 204; Robert Somers, *The Southern States Since the War, 1870–71* (Tuscaloosa: University of Alabama Press, 1965 [1871]), 146; Charles Nordhoff, *The Cotton States in the Spring and Summer of 1875* (New York: Burt Franklin, 1876): 21.

25. "Southerner," "Agricultural Labor at the South," *Galaxy Magazine* 12 (September 1871): 331.

26. *Southern Cultivator* 30 (April 1872): 127–28.

27. *Southern Cultivator* 30 (February 1872): 59.

28. *Southern Cultivator* 29 (October 1871): 370–71.

29. *Southern Cultivator* 26 (January 1868): 14.

30. Frances B. Leigh, *Ten Years on a Georgia Plantation* (London: Richard Bentley & Sons, 1883), 25–26, 39, 55.

31. "Southerner," "Agricultural Labor at the South," 331.

32. "Southerner," "Agricultural Labor at the South," 332. See also Somers, *The Southern States Since the War*, 60, 128.

33. Loring and Atkinson, *Cotton Culture and the South*, 32.

34. Loring and Atkinson, *Cotton Culture and the South*, 32.

35. See, for example, *Southern Cultivator* 26 (May 1868): 133; ibid. 27 (July 1869): 208; ibid. 30 (February 1872): 57–58; "Southerner," "Agricultural Labor at the South," 331; Somers, *The Southern States Since the War*, 66, 147; *Commercial and Financial Chronicle* 9 (September 4, 1869): 294–95.

36. See, for example, Somers, *The Southern States Since the War*, 31; *Report of the Joint Committee on Reconstruction*, part 2, 5, 189; Leigh, *Ten Years on a Georgia Plantation*, 51–52; Freedmen's Bureau, Executive Document Number 11, 39th Congress, 1st Session, 25.

37. *The Nation* 1 (September 7, 1865): 295.

38. Flynn, *White Land, Black Labor*, 71–72.

39. Taylor, "Post-Bellum Southern Rental Contracts," 121–22; Theodore Saloutos, "Southern Agriculture and the Problems of Readjustment, 1865–1877," *Agricultural History* 30 (April 1956): 70.

40. Wharton, *The Negro in Mississippi*, 69. See also Joseph D. Reid, Jr., "Sharecropping As an Understandable Market Response," *Journal of Economic History* 33 (March 1973): 110.

41. Ransom and Sutch, *One Kind of Freedom*, 65.

42. Ransom and Sutch, *One Kind of Freedom*, 70.

43. Ransom and Sutch, *One Kind of Freedom*, 73–77.

44. See Stanley L. Engerman, "The Legacy of Slavery" (unpublished paper, presented at the Duke University Symposium on *One Kind of Freedom*, February 11, 1978), 13–14. For another brief discussion of

Engerman's argument, see Jonathan M. Wiener, "Class Structure and Economic Development in the American South, 1865–1955," *American Historical Review* 84 (October 1979): 973.

45. See, for example, David C. Barrow, Jr., "A Georgia Plantation," *Scribner's Monthly* 21 (April 1881): 830–36; *The Report of the Commissioner of Agriculture for the Year 1867*, 416–18; Zeichner, "The Legal Status of the Agricultural Labor in the South," 412–13; Wiener, *Social Origins of the New South*, 35–42, 66–69; Brooks, *The Agrarian Revolution in Georgia*, 18–27; Hammond, *The Cotton Industry*, 120–33; James H. Street, *The New Revolution in the Cotton Economy: Mechanization and Its Consequences* (Chapel Hill: University of North Carolina Press, 1957): 19–20; Peter Kolchin, *First Freedom: The Responses of Alabama's Blacks to Emancipation and Reconstruction* (Westport, Conn.: Greenwood Press, 1972): 30–48; Robert Higgs, *Competition and Coercion: Blacks in the American Economy, 1865–1914* (Cambridge: Cambridge University Press, 1977): 43–45; Ronald L. F. Davis, *Good and Faithful Labor: From Slavery to Sharecropping in the Natchez District, 1860–1890* (Westport, Conn.: Greenwood Press, 1982): 90.

46. *De Bow's Review* 6 (February 1869): 152.

47. Cited in Wiener, *Social Origins of the New South*, 66. See also ibid., 68.

48. *Southern Cultivator* 27 (February 1866): 211.

49. *Southern Cultivator* 26 (February 1868): 61–62.

50. Loring and Atkinson, *Cotton Culture and the South*, 5.

51. Barrow, "A Georgia Plantation," 831–32.

52. The case of William Mercer is recounted in Davis, *Good and Faithful Labor*, 90–92.

53. Brooks, *The Agrarian Revolution in Georgia*, 53–54.

54. Brooks, *The Agrarian Revolution in Georgia*, 27. See also ibid., 25–26, 46, 52–54.

55. Cited in J.C.A. Stagg, "The Problem of Klan Violence: The South Carolina Up-Country, 1868–1871," *Journal of American Studies* 8 (1974): 311.

56. *Southern Cultivator* 30 (May 1872): 168. On the persistence of criticisms of sharecropping throughout the nineteenth and into the twentieth century, see, for example, Banks, *The Economics of Land Tenure in Georgia*, 100–109; Hammond, *The Cotton Industry*, 190–91; Ransom and Sutch, *One Kind of Freedom*, 99–103; Street, *The New Revolution in the Cotton Economy*, 20–24.

57. *Southern Cultivator* 29 (January 1871): 10.

58. *Southern Cultivator* 28 (February 1870): 44.

59. *Southern Cultivator* 29 (December 1871): 461–62.

60. Cited in Eric Foner, *Reconstruction: America's Unfinished Revolution, 1863–1877* (New York: Harper & Row, 1988), 109.

61. Barbara Jeanne Fields, "The Advent of Capitalist Agriculture: The New South in a Bourgeois World," in *Essays on the Postbellum Southern Economy*, ed. Thavolia Glymph and John J. Kushma (Arlington: Texas A & M University Press, 1985): 85.

62. Ransom and Sutch, *One Kind of Freedom*, 149–70; Pete Daniel, *The Shadow of Slavery: Peonage in the South, 1901–1969* (New York: Oxford University Press, 1973); William Cohen, "Negro Involuntary Servitude in the South, 1865–1940," *Journal of Southern History* 42 (February 1976): 31–60.

63. Cited in Eric Foner, *Politics and Ideology in the Age of the Civil War* (Oxford: Oxford University Press, 1980), 123. See also Michael Perman, *Emancipation and Reconstruction, 1862–1879* (Arlington Heights, Ill.: Harlan Davidson, 1987), 104–7.

64. The theoretical and methodological implications derived from the idea of constriction of possibilities, as discussed below, incorporate many of the diverse concerns of what William Roy has called the "new paradigm" in historical sociology. See William G. Roy, "Class Conflict and Social Change in Historical Perspective," *Annual Review of Sociology* 10 (1984): 483–506.

· Index

Abolition of slavery: and colonization, 24, 150–51, 154–55, 161,
162, 163; and immigration, 120,
122, 145; planters' resistance to,
26, 41–42, 66–67, 84, 110; planters' view of, 43–44, 63, 106, 164;
and survival of plantation system, 1, 25, 125–26; and white
emigration, 175–76. *See also*
Slaves
African Repository, 154
Agricultural ladder, 185, 215
American Colonization Society,
154–56, 163
American Freedmen's Inquiry
Commission, 31–32
Amnesty proclamation, 75, 91
Anderson, Perry, 224n.10
Andrews, Sidney, 26, 45, 53, 103,
168
Apprenticeship laws, 62–63, 66–67

Banks, Enoch, 4–5
Banks, Nathaniel P., 39–40
Bascott, Peter, 73
Bendix, Reinhard, 19
Black Codes, 27, 63–68, 69, 70, 71,
113, 219, 224–25n.10
Black soldiers, 30, 58–59, 102–3,
116, 162–63

Blackett, Richard, 259–60n.16
Blair, Francis P., 161
Braudel, Fernand, 17
Breach-of-contract laws, 65–66
Brooks, Robert, 210
Brown, Orlando, 81–82
Brownlow, William Gannaway,
171–72
Bureau of Refugees, Freedmen,
and Abandoned Lands. *See*
Freedmen's Bureau
Butler, Benjamin F., 28–29, 36–39,
40

Cahill, E. C., 126
Captured and abandoned property,
75, 89–92. *See also* Confiscation
of land
Cardoza, F. L., 108–9
Chartock, Lewis, 74–75
Chase, Salmon P., 89
Chinese immigrants: and black
labor, 135, 137–38; compared to
black labor, 136, 139–40, 141;
compared to white labor, 137,
139–40, 143; northern opposition to, 141–42; numbers of,
136, 143; problems with, 140–
42; qualities of, 139–42. *See also*
Immigration

274 · Index

Freedmen's Bureau; Northern opinion; Union army
Northern presence in South: complaints about, 59–60, 77–79, 95, 131, 165, 166; and protection of freedpeople, 41, 42, 77, 84. See also Freedmen's Bureau
Nott, J. C., 123–24

Oakes, James, 14–15
"Orders No. 9," 34, 36
Oubre, Claude, 242–43n.3

Paternalism, 112, 164, 171. See also Integrationists
Peters, Theodore, 120
Philbrick, Edward S., 34–35, 89
Plantation system: black opposition to, 11, 14, 23, 50, 52, 54–55, 99–100, 106, 108–9, 110–12, 119, 132, 206, 210, 213, 214–18; characteristics of, 1, 25, 181; compared to slavery, 1, 25–26; decentralization of, 2–3, 181–82, 184, 186, 188, 189, 190, 204, 206, 207–8, 210, 213, 215; instability of, 25–26, 50–57, 86–87, 104, 109, 110, 112, 118, 119, 149; as obstacle to economic progress, 125–27. See also "Forty acres and a mule"; Freedmen's Bureau; Freedpeople; Immigration; Labor mobility; Labor scarcity; Planters; Share system; Sharecropping; Wage system
Planters: debate over immigration, 130–35; and legislative control over black labor, 3, 47, 62, 63–68, 70, 84, 172–73; opposition to black landownership, 67, 86–87, 94, 109–18; opposition to black renters, 111–15; organization of cartels, 26, 61–62, 84; reluctance to sell land,

129; use of violence, 26, 60, 69–71, 72, 84, 114–15; view of free black labor, 26, 44–50, 56–57, 63, 84, 111–12, 150, 164–65, 166–67, 173, 178–79, 183, 191, 200, 201, 202. See also Abolition of slavery; Chinese immigrants; Colonization; Freedpeople; Immigration; Labor mobility; Labor scarcity; Plantation system; Share system; Sharecropping; Wage system; White immigration
Planters' Banner, 126
Polanyi, Karl, 228n.45
Pomeroy, Samuel Clark, 159
Powell, Lawrence, 98
Predisposing-conditions argument, 3–7, 20, 21, 225nn. 13, 16
Property rights, enforcement of, 115–16

Radical Reconstruction, 96
Radical Republicans, 31, 32, 92, 95, 96
Ransom, Roger L., and Richard Sutch, 15–16, 54, 116–17, 205–7
Reconstruction Act, 104
Reich, Michael, 228n.43
Reid, Joseph D., Jr., 7–8, 226n.24
Reid, Whitelaw, 9–10, 45, 47, 129, 174
Ripley, C. Peter, 39–40
Roark, James, 16
Roberts, Percy, 189
Robertson, A. F., 186
Rock, John, 171
Roy, William G., 225n.13, 271n.64
Ruffin, Edmund, 28, 122

Sartre, Jean-Paul, 5
Saxton, Rufus, 89, 91, 110
Scott, R. K., 26
Share system: compared to sharecropping, 189–90, 204–5, 213;